Homes of the American Presidents

Books by Cranston Jones

HOMES OF THE AMERICAN PRESIDENTS
ARCHITECTURE TODAY AND TOMORROW
MARCEL BREUER: WORK AND PROJECTS *1921–1961*

HOMES

of the

AMERICAN

PRESIDENTS

❧

Cranston Jones

photographer and picture editor WILLIAM H. SCHLEISNER

McGRAW-HILL BOOK COMPANY, INC.

New York Toronto London

LIBRARY OF CONGRESS CATALOG CARD NUMBER: 62-19158

32710

CONTENTS

INTRODUCTION

After all, history is people, and particularly in great periods of history, Presidents.

JOHN FITZGERALD KENNEDY

Mount Vernon (opposite) has from first to last stood pre-eminent in the hearts of Americans. While it is neither the oldest, most sumptuous, nor even the most elegant of these homes that give color and high light to our national heritage, Mount Vernon at every turn testifies to the taste, planning, and dignity of General Washington himself, a Virginia gentleman who would brook no slur on his honor and could not tolerate mediocrity. No house in America so compellingly evokes the manners, concerns and delights of a great age now past. Moving through the spacious rooms that knew Washington's own measured tread, we are in an ambience of Washington's own creating, aware that for him Mount Vernon was more precious than worldly honors.

The curving colonnades on either side of Mount Vernon's entrance link the main house to the kitchen and, on the far side, to the plantation office.

Mount Vernon's rooms were furnished with rare taste and elegance. The Music Room (far left) contains the harpsichord General Washington imported from London in 1793 for his step-daughter Nelly Custis. The Banquet-Hall mantel (left) was a gift of an English admirer. Above it is a portrait of Washington by Gilbert Stuart. The small brass firedogs in the fireplace are original. The Dining Room (right) has a mirrored plateau bought by Gouverneur Morris for Washington and its original Waterford cut-glass candelabra. The ornate mantel was carved for Washington in 1775 at Mount Vernon, by an unnamed French craftsman.

The great houses of Virginia set, at the establishment of the Republic, a standard of excellence rarely equaled and never surpassed. At Mount Vernon, Washington relied heavily on furnishings from England; at Monticello, Jefferson favored French workmanship. Jefferson's original designs, executed by local craftsman, were no less tasteful.

Jefferson's Monticello had a brick-lined pool stocked with fresh carp for the dinner table. The blue dining room, lit by skylight above, opens into the tea room beyond the arch. Jefferson's alcove bed was set between bedroom and study and still has a pillow he used. Jefferson's inventiveness is suggested by his revolving chair, adjustable table, and foot rest as well as by dumbwaiters (at either end of the dining-room mantel) which brought up wine from the cellar.

The Adams House at Quincy (above), which housed four generations, began with the small stone section at right. The garden in the foreground was planted by Abigail Adams, wife of John Adams and mother of John Quincy Adams. In Virginia (left), Berkeley Plantation (top), built in 1726, was the birthplace of William Henry Harrison; Montpelier (bottom), with its monumental portico designed by Jefferson, was Madison's favorite home. The original Hermitage built by Andrew Jackson (opposite, top) was a humble log cabin. One of the slave cabins (below) still stands.

In Virginia the Georgian brick of Harrison's Berkeley and the classical portico of Madison's Montpelier flourished. In New England, the Adamses added on to their Quincy house each generation. On the Tennessee frontier, log cabins at The Hermitage housed both master and slave.

Andrew Jackson, inspired by a
visit to Mount Vernon, built
The Hermitage with a classic
portico and surrounded it with
lush gardens that evoke an
arcadian vision of the ante-
bellum South.

*The present Hermitage is the third built by Andrew
Jackson, the second to occupy this site. The columns,
topped by cast-iron capitals, support a two-story
portico. The gardens, trampled by Union cavalry
during the Civil War, have been restored to their
original state, in which they were tenderly cared for
by Rachel Jackson, who was buried here shortly
before President-elect Jackson left for the White
House.*

Wheatland, near Lancaster, was James Buchanan's bachelor home. Built in 1828, it gives the appearance of being three houses joined to make one. The rear view (above) and front view (right) show the imposing presence of the residence built by local craftsmen. Buchanan accepted his presidential nomination on the colonnaded front porch. Inside can still be seen the ornate writing table, campaign flag, and bucolic view to be had from the windows.

James Buchanan's 17-room Wheatland, set in the fertile Pennsylvania grain fields outside Lancaster, was far more commodious than his simple bachelor needs required. But its imposing brick façade proved an invaluable background betokening prosperity, success, and respectability for his campaign for the Presidency.

Lincoln's Springfield house, valued at $3,000 in 1861, includes many of the original furnishings. From left to right are Lincoln's bedroom with his shaving mirror and washstand; the hallway with Lincoln's gloves on the chair and cane, wallet, and hat on the original hatrack; the dining room with dessert service on the table; the living room with Brussels carpet, mohair sofa, and shawl; children's bedroom with toy wagon, hoops, and straw couch.

Lincoln's Springfield, Illinois, home symbolizes the remarkable rise in the world made by this frontier rail-splitter and circuit lawyer up to the time he was elected President. But its furnishings owed more to the social ambitions of Mary Todd Lincoln, who used her small inheritance to add a second story and saw to it that the walls were papered and floor carpeted with bright Victorian designs, that a mohair sofa was in the parlor and a Gothic hat rack, on which Abe's stovepipe hat is still perched, adorned the hall.

Grant's home in Galena, Illinois, was maintained as his residence from 1865 to 1881. The 1857 house with its prominently bracketed eaves was furnished with a mixture of elegance and period practicality (left). The bedroom (below, left) has Mrs. Grant's furniture. Slippers were Mrs. Grant's; leather hatbox was used by Grant on his round-the-world tour. The parlor (bottom), where Grant received news of his election, has rosewood, marble-topped table, pampas grass in vase. Kerosene lamp at left is original, as are twin vases on mantel, given Grant by the King of Bohemia. Steel engraving over fireplace depicts Generals Sherman, Grant, and Sheridan. The bedroom of Grant's daughter, Nellie, has her parasol and other girlish souvenirs of the period.

*General Ulysses S. Grant's hillside house in Galena,
Illinois, was an outright gift from his fellow citizens at the
end of the Civil War. Grant himself was moved to tears
by this act of generosity. The rich interiors, with velvet-
covered chairs and Oriental-designed rugs, make a superb
period ensemble that unself-consciously combines burgundy
drapery with burnished spittoon.*

Sagamore Hill within is a monument to Teddy Roosevelt's robust taste for hunting trophies and souvenirs of material glory. The North Room (left), framed by elephant tusks presented by Emperor Menelik of Abyssinia, has on distant wall the Presidential flag designed personally by T.R. Buffalo heads and elk were all shot by Roosevelt's hunting rifle, and his Rough Rider hat and binoculars used in Cuba hang from horns of the nearest elkhead at left. The Philippine mahogany table in the center is embellished with miniature suit of Japanese armor presented by Admiral Togo. The massive mahogany-railed bathtub on raised platform was installed in 1887.

Theodore Roosevelt's Sagamore Hill at Oyster Bay, Long Island, is the Queen Anne bungalow with all sails set. From massive central chimney and shingled gables to its flaring porte-cochère and broad piazza it testifies to the leisurely pace of the turn of the century.

*The tastes and something of the personality of two great
Americans is revealed by F.D.R.'s ancestral home at Hyde
Park (above) and General Eisenhower's retirement home
by the battlefield of Gettysburg (below).*

*Hyde Park (above) contains many of Franklin
Delano Roosevelt's ancestral furnishings. The dining
room table, now permanently set for two, could be extended to seat twenty. The walnut sideboard was purchased by James Roosevelt, Sr., in Italy in 1869. The
river side of the mansion retains the appearance of the
original 1826 house purchased by James Roosevelt,
Sr., in 1867. At right is the new library wing added
in 1915. Dwight D. Eisenhower's Gettysburg farm
(left) is built around a hundred-year-old Pennsylvania Dutch farmhouse. This rear view shows the
glassed-in porch—General Eisenhower's favorite room
—and small informal garden.*

WRITING LONG AFTER the War for Independence, Thomas Jefferson and John Adams both agreed that future generations would, in all likelihood, know little of the stirring events surrounding the formation of the Republic. In fact they were wrong. Perhaps because the Founding Fathers were so largely drawn from the legal profession, early documents, letters and diaries were safeguarded in quantity. But succeeding generations took less care of the actual physical structures which served as background to this history, including the Presidents' own homes, which were often allowed to go to ruin.

Today, when more than a million visitors each year visit Washington's Mount Vernon, it seems hard to realize that this historic mansion was preserved only through the heroic efforts of the Mount Vernon Ladies' Association which purchased the house in 1858. Jefferson's incomparable Monticello was for a time actually left abandoned. Andrew Jackson's Hermitage also stood empty, water pouring through its roof, turning wallpaper to sodden pulp, until patriotic women, modeling themselves on the Mount Vernon Association, came to the rescue. In the case of many less-revered Presidents, conservation efforts came too late or not at all. Of the ninety-one structures known to have existed with important historical associations with the thirty-four Presidents, nineteen have by now totally disappeared, forty-seven are still in private hands, and thirty-nine are open to the public.

What determines the selection of Presidents' homes? Birthplaces, first of all. These have always exerted a curious fascination for Americans, and a remarkable number of the log cabins in which so many American Presidents down to Garfield were born have been piously preserved, if not always made of their original logs or placed on their first sites. While such pioneering structures have their own special romance and remain graphic demonstration of the rigorous, primitive surroundings which nurtured some of our greatest men, the later houses these same men built often provide a far more accurate portrait of their particular aspirations and tastes. However, it must be borne in mind that houses in America have a way of growing with the years, changing in fashion and form beyond all recognition. Madison's Montpelier, for instance, still retains its elegant portico, but the wings added to bring its rooms to forty-four, plus the complete modernization and redecoration of the interior, present an appearance that would assuredly baffle Madison himself, were he to revisit his old home today.

Of most value are those Presidential homes that have come down to us in something very close to their original state, homes such as that of Andrew Johnson in Greeneville, Tennessee, or the Adams House in Quincy, Massachusetts. It was with this fact in mind that Franklin Delano Roosevelt before his death deeded his Hyde Park estate to the nation as a National Historic Site, an intention respected by the Roosevelt family who relinquished their lifetime interest so that it could be opened to the public.

In most cases, however, a degree of restoration has been necessary. Even at Mount Vernon, America's most popular President's Home, individual pieces are still being returned and the abandoned outer buildings and greenhouse have had to be rebuilt. Where the original furnishings have been dispersed, local historical societies have shown considerable ingenuity in refurnishing the spaces with pieces that are at least authentic to the period. This has been done with skill at Grant's house in Galena, where original items and authentic pieces of the time have been carefully blended. Buchanan's house in Lancaster, Pennsylvania, is still largely furnished with original pieces. Here the custodians went to great trouble to replace the carpet. Ultimately they chose a rug from Saratoga's old Grand Union Hotel, which proved to be an almost perfect match for the floor covering shown in early drawings and photographs of "Old Buck's" Wheatland.

As curatorial staffs are increasingly attempting to measure up to the high standards set by Mount Vernon, Monticello, The Hermitage, and Sagamore Hill, we are approaching the ideal—a house representative of each President which can recapture the complete ambiance of the period and, at the same time, cast new light and shadow on the personality of the President himself. For many, a visit to these historic houses can unlock the whole pageantry of history, summoning up the past with an immediacy and intimacy of detail that both illuminates the nature of the men who inhabited them and evokes a whole era with a vividness that printed documents often fail to communicate.

No one, for instance, can visit the ample Pierce Homestead in New Hampshire, with its second-floor ballroom, without sensing the pre-eminent position staked out in what was then the wilderness by Pierce's Revolutionary War father. Combine this with the lonely ex-President's bedroom in the mansarded mansion in Concord, where the widowed Pierce (who left his high office remarking, "After the White House, what is there to do but drink?") died, and one gains a surprisingly fresh insight into this Yankee-born Southern sympathizer who has come to be known as "The Forgotten President."

The gardens beside The Hermitage where Andrew Jackson's beloved Rachel lies buried still seem to retain some memory of the gaunt frontier fighter who nightly came to stand by her grave. At Hyde Park we see Franklin D. Roosevelt's heroic battle for health recorded in the unobtrusive reinforced bannisters and wheelchair ramps. At Plymouth Notch, we find the neatly trimmed lamp on the parlor table where in the early morning hours a dour Vermont farmer administered to his son, Cal Coolidge, the President's oath of office. In Abilene, Kansas, the light frame house with its family Bible conveys its message of a strict religious family in the small town where the six scrapping Eisenhower brothers grew up. In Springfield, Lincoln's house with its Victorian wallpaper seems, at first sight, at odds with our image of Honest Abe; we are somehow reassured to learn that Mary Todd Lincoln never could cure her husband of his habit of stretching out on the floor to read!

These historic houses owe their status as national shrines to the historical happenstance that they belonged to men who were chosen for the nation's highest office. Judged purely as architecture, perhaps only a single structure, Jefferson's Monticello, would rank as one of the great houses of the New World. Yet, taken as a whole, these dwellings show the whole evolution of domestic architecture in America. Doubly valuable when they have been maintained in anything like their original state, they are both within and without a remarkable panorama of changing taste, an invaluable documentation of the organization and development of the American home.

These Presidents' houses reach back in time to the birthplace of John Adams, a saltbox with a lean-to, built in 1682. This is one of our earliest prototypes derived from English cottage architecture; the style moved westward over the years and is still to be found as the core of Garfield's rambling house at Mentor, Ohio. Equally fascinating is the extension westward of the Southern plantation Big House, derived from the English Palladian manor house, with its classic, symmetrical composition, its portico, front-to-back corridor hallway (acting as a breezeway), high ceilings, detached kitchen and slave quarters. It was an image of grandeur that faded slowly; Andrew Jackson, we discover, was inspired to forsake his log cabin and build The Hermitage after a visit to Mount Vernon. General William Henry Harrison, who had the good fortune to be born and raised in Berkeley, one of the greatest of the Virginia plantation houses, repeated Berkeley's general organization in logs and clapboard in his "Big House" at North Bend, and again in brick with "Grouseland," the so-called "White House of the West," still standing in Vincennes, Indiana.

In the tides of shifting fashion that swept, wave after wave, across the decades of the nineteenth century, there was hardly a style in houses that was not a favorite of one or another President. Jefferson was himself a prime instigator of the classic revival; Millard Fillmore's Gothic manse on Buffalo's Niagara Square was an outstanding example of the romantic style that produced West Point, Wall Street's Trinity Church, and the Smithsonian Institution in Washington. Martin Van Buren at Kinderhook hired one of the leading architects of his day to convert his staid Hudson River house into the "Italianate" grotesquery of "Lindenwald," complete with a campanile and gingerbread trim hanging from the eaves; this wild confection seems to have reached its ultimate when the present owner tacked on a portico modeled on Mount Vernon!

Pierce's mansarded mansion in Concord records the vogue accorded France's Second Empire; Roosevelt's "Sagamore Hill" is only one of the many Victorian houses with multiple dormers and gables that architectural historians lump together under the heading of "Queen Anne." Cleveland's "Westland" in Princeton—a building actually modeled on the colonial governor's mansion in the same college town —is highly representative of the Georgian revival, which derived much impetus from the sense of history engendered by the 1876 Philadelphia Centennial. The excesses to which this movement lead are grandiloquently summarized by the hotel-sized New Jersey Governor's seaside mansion, a souvenir of Chicago's 1893 Fair, in which Woodrow Wilson patiently awaited his nomination to the Presidency.

But perhaps the strongest trend in housing was the one forced by the inescapable facts of family life, the need to expand. Americans, it would seem, have a native genius for adding on. John Adams' four-room birthplace had already been enlarged to eight rooms by a lean-to by the time he was born. Washington built throughout the Revolution, successively adding upper stories and wings. And, in later times, we find Mary Todd Lincoln using all of her small inheritance to gain the added dignity that an extra story would give in early Springfield. The art of assemblage often produced curious results: Rutherford B. Hayes doubled "Spiegel

Grove" by the simple expedient of building a duplicate structure alongside, and in the process created an eighty-foot-long veranda for his rainy-weather promenades. John Tyler assembled "Sherwood Forest" by linking together five separate structures until the façade grew to three-hundred-feet in length. James Buchanan's "Wheatland" was assembled all of a piece in much the same pattern, and is perhaps the first split-level house.

It is notable that the majority of our Presidents were capable of building their own houses and many did. Nor was a vigorous interest in domestic architecture lacking. Washington, Jefferson, Jackson, William Henry Harrison all drew their own plans and personally instructed their servants how to make and lay bricks. So successful was Jefferson, in fact, that he went on to design houses for two other Virginia Presidents, Madison and Monroe, in addition to the Virginia Capitol and the University of Virginia.

If later generations were less skilled as carpenters, they certainly did not lack decisiveness in planning their own homes. Theodore Roosevelt detailed precisely the interior spaces he wanted at Sagamore Hill, reluctantly hired an architect only because, as he confessed, "I did not know enough to be sure what I wished in outside matters." Woodrow Wilson drew the plans for his half-timbered Princeton house after making a clay study-model. Franklin D. Roosevelt, in his woodworking shop, built a small-scale model to guide the conversion of Hyde Park from a Victorian summer house to a Georgian mansion, and also drew up the plans for his summer hideaway near Hyde Park called "Top House," with fieldstone walls and sloping eaves.

F.D.R. was decidedly a conservative when it came to architecture, lauding "the charm of line, the judgment of location, the spirit of simplicity of the homes of our ancestors." And so, it would seem, have been most of our Presidents. It is significant that no President in the twentieth century has lived in a house that could remotely be called "modern": John F. Kennedy, wealthiest President since George Washington, owns only one house, the Cape Cod cottage at Hyannis Port, built around 1905; Sagamore Hill dates from 1886, Hyde Park from 1867, and Harry Truman's house in Independence was built in 1865.

The interiors of these Presidents' houses all bear the stamp of their era. When they have been maintained as unities, we can find the whole complex mixture of practical and sentimental, utilitarian and ceremonial fixtures and furnishings that give the life of the family its particular identity in time. Here—in terms of living rooms, sleeping quarters, parlors, and kitchens—is to be seen the whole evolution of family life in America. The walls show us the shift from hand-hewn logs, calked with mud and wattle, to plaster, ornamented with stencils, then early imported French wallpaper, giving way by the 1850s to the bright patterned paper of the Victorians.

The floors change from the two-foot-wide planks cut from trees standing on the site to ornate parquets, floor coverings from sand and rush to oilcloth (in back areas) and brilliantly dyed Brussels carpeting (in halls and living rooms). In these houses can be traced the history of American plumbing, from hip baths, tubs, the first tub-with-shower (Buchanan), to such monuments as the oversized bathtubs of Taft and Theodore Roosevelt. Porches go back as far as Mount Vernon (a columned veranda of such scale was apparently original with Washington), but their sudden resurgence immediately following the Civil War points to a new appreciation of outdoor living which coincides with the boom in mountain and seaside resorts and watering places.

It is an American trait to prefer the practical, the convenient, the inexpensive. This is nowhere better documented than in the kitchens, ranging down through the years from open hearths and hand spits to the modern kitchenettes. Here are to be found the changing fashions in cooking, ironing, washing, that have so revolutionized the American home and the role of the woman who runs it. From the attic, where the first gravity water tanks were installed, to the old root cellar and milk-cooler which was enlarged to accommodate the furnace (Van Buren at "Lindenwald" appears the first to install central heating), we can see the modern home coming into being. Andrew Johnson, for instance, returned home to Tennessee to install his first icebox. When Benjamin Harrison left the White House he replaced the gas fixtures in his home with new-fangled electricity (and found the experience terrifying).

In Canton, Ohio, McKinley was the first to have a direct telephone line to convention headquarters, and in an idle moment picked up the receiver, to his astonishment found the circuit open and heard the Republican convention in St. Louis cheering his name "like a storm at sea with wild fitful shrieks." Barns gave way to garages, porte-cocheres to carports as Theodore Roosevelt became the first motorized President (T.R. also was first to fly in a plane, first to go down in a submarine). Grace Coolidge is unquestionably the first First Lady to become a baseball fan by listening to games broadcast over the radio.

So rapid has been the change in modes of living between the day when Jefferson rode up the winding road to Monticello on horseback to our own time, when Kennedy helicopters to his jet "Caroline," that we can well benefit by pausing to mark time in these historic houses of the

24

past. Here the velvet-bound family picture album beside the horsehair-covered chair records an individual family, but evokes as well the portrait of a whole era. And so it is also with the whole house of one of our Chief Executives, where we still find the bookcase filled, the Chickering Grand awaiting the skilled hands of the hostess, where we can observe the hunting trophies, the faded campaign banners, the uniforms in which our future Presidents as young men went off to war, their wives' treasured wedding gowns, the still-folded baby clothes, the curious children's toys.

To summon up a sense of the past, we, of course, need to know the basic biographical facts about these Presidents, the nature of their origins, their early struggles, the positions they took on the overriding issues of their day. Much of this lore has come down to us, in letters, biographies, and even in the campaign songs of the day. But only by studying our Presidents against the environment which nurtured them and placing them in the community in which they grew up and emerged into national prominence are we privileged to know them as did their neighbors, representative and outstanding citizens of their communities. Ironically, viewing them from the point of view of their origins, we often find ourselves modifying the opinions of those primarily concerned with evaluating their performance in the White House; William Henry Harrison, for instance, emerges as a far more important man than his brief tenure as President allowed him to prove to history; John Tyler emerges in the direct line of the early Virginians, but living in an age in which the Inevitable Conflict made sectionalists even out of men of national scope.

And in still another sense, these homes are a historic bequest providing us an eloquent link to the past. For whether politics is, as Wendell Phillips said, "but the common pulse," or, as Henry Thoreau would have it, "the gizzard of society, full of grit and gravel," these homes provided each President with a gauge to judge the impact of his policies. For it was in homes very much like these across the nation that men and women met to discuss the issues of the day. This grass-roots fact the Presidents bore in mind as they mapped their political strategy. And it was to these front porches that their cheering fellow citizens came in torchlight procession with bands playing to hail the victor, or, more quietly, to console the loser. As such, these Presidents' homes have all known the limelight of history. For us today they can also be beacons, guiding us to the hearthstone of our great national heritage, quickening our awareness of the great personalities of the past, and vividly recreating our own history; which, as President Kennedy reminded us, is but prologue to the future.

Homes of the American Presidents

ONE

George Washington

*First in war, first in peace, and first in the hearts
of his countrymen, he was second to none in the humble
and endearing scenes of private life.**

OF ALL AMERICA'S historic houses, none but the White House itself summons up such a wealth of association as does George Washington's Mount Vernon. On its gentle eminence overlooking the placid Potomac, famed even in its own day, it is the goal of patriotic pilgrimages by over one million visitors a year. As they quietly move through the halls, rooms, and corridors built by Washington, they can almost hear Washington's own standing invitation, issued in 1794: "I have no objection to any sober or orderly person's gratifying their curiosity in viewing the buildings, Gardens &ct about Mount Vernon."

Washington was exceedingly proud of the mansion, which he enlarged from a single-story building, and of its surrounding five farms, totaling some 8000 acres. "No estate in United America," he wrote, "is more pleasantly situated than this. It lies in a high, dry and healthy Country 300 miles by water from the sea, . . . on one of the finest Rivers in the world." Mount Vernon's land had been in the Washington family since 1674, when Washington's great-grandfather, John Washington, had acquired title to it with a friend. George Washington himself was born on February 22 (February 11, Old Style), 1732, at Wakefield, the old Washington plantation at Bridges Creek, Westmoreland County, Virginia, in a primitive dwelling with steep roof and projecting eaves.† His mother, Mary Ball, was the second wife of widower Augustine Washington, and the accumulated children of the fast-growing family soon outgrew Wakefield. When George was three his parents moved to the small house then situated on the site of the present Mount Vernon.

During the three years the Washington family lived there, George's father built a fine grist mill, and about 1740 erected a house (the center of the present mansion) for Lawrence, his eldest son by his first marriage. George was eleven when his father died at the Ferry farm, near Fredericksburg, and at the age of sixteen George went to live again with his half-brother at the estate—now called Mount Vernon in honor of the British Admiral Vernon, under whom Lawrence had served at Cartagena in South America. Washington as a youth at Mount Vernon loved outdoor sports, fox-hunting and—when in Williamsburg—cards, dancing, and the theater. As a young man he

* "Lighthorse Harry" Lee, December 26, 1799.
† Wakefield burned in 1780. In 1932 an approximate replica was built there which is maintained by the National Park Service.

The mansion's east front, from an engraving published in 1804, five years after the death of General George Washington.

became a surveyor for William Fairfax. Outdoor life developed Washington's rugged physique—he was six feet tall, weighed slightly over 200 pounds by the time he reached manhood, and had phenomenal strength in his arms and shoulders. His face, however, was pitted for life from the smallpox he contracted in Barbados, where he went with Lawrence in hope of gaining back his half-brother's health.

Lawrence died in 1750, and two years later Washington, at twenty-two, inherited the house and 2126-acre estate. He had little time for farming. The next year Governor Dinwiddie made him a lieutenant colonel in the Virginia militia and sent him to the frontier. At Fort Necessity he was forced to surrender to the French, but it gave him a taste for fighting. "I heard the bullets whistle, and, believe me, there is something charming in the sound," he wrote with a young man's bravado to his younger brother. Later, serving with Braddock, he reported, "I had four bullets through my coat and two horses shot under me." Having helped to take Fort Duquesne from the French in 1758, he was at twenty-six a seasoned veteran and held the rank of colonel.

As Colonel Washington was hurrying to the colonial capital at Williamsburg, he was invited by the plantation owner of Poplar Grove to meet "the prettiest and richest widow in Virginia." She was Martha Dandridge Custis, three months younger than Washington and the mother of two small children. He was too much the gentleman to reveal details of his courtship, but we do know that he set to work adding a second story to the one-level Mount Vernon he had inherited. (As a good squire of English stock he also sent to London for his coat of arms, which later would adorn his carriage as well as a mirror and mantel in Mount Vernon.)

In September 1759, Washington noted, "I am now I believe fixd at this Seat with an agreable Consort for Life and hope to find more happiness in retirement than I ever experienc'd amidst a wide and bustling World." Washington's high hopes were crowned by marriage to Martha on January 6, 1759, and soon the young proprietor was writing to his overseer: "You must have the House very well cleaned and Were you to make Fires in the Rooms below it we'd Air them. You must get two of the best Bedsteads put up, one in the Hall Room, and the other in the little dining Room that used to be, and have beds made on them against we come. Enquire abt. in the neighbourhood, and get some Egg's and Chickens, and prepare in the best manner you can."

Martha Washington proved to be a perfect consort. In appearance, Washington Irving reports, she was "rather below the middle size, but extremely well shaped, with an agreeable countenance, dark hazel eyes and hair, and those frank, engaging manners, so captivating in Southern women." Martha chose to describe herself modestly as an "old-fashioned Virginia housekeeper, steady as a clock, busy as a bee, cheerful as a cricket."

The Philadelphia painter Charles Willson Peale, who came to Mount Vernon in 1772 to paint Colonel Washington in his militia officer's uniform* (and incidentally turned out the miniature locket of Martha that Washington was to carry with him through the Revolution), has left us an entrancing picture of the forty-year-old Washington, then about to embark on an unknown destiny:

> One afternoon several young gentlemen, visitors at Mount Vernon, and myself were engaged in pitching the bar, one of the athletic sports common in those times, when suddenly the Colonel appeared among us. He requested to be shown the pegs that marked the bounds of our efforts; then, smiling, and without putting off his coat, held out his hand for the missile. No sooner did the heavy iron bar feel the grasp of his mighty hand than it lost the power of gravity, and whizzed through the air, striking the ground far, very far, beyond our utmost limits. We were indeed amazed, and we stood around all stripped to the buff, with shirt sleeves rolled up, and having thought ourselves very clever fellows, while the Colonel, on retiring, pleasantly observed, "When you beat my pitch, young gentlemen, I'll try again."

Mount Vernon, under Washington's watchful eye, was steadily growing. In 1773 he began adding to the south end of the mansion and, despite threatening war clouds, proceeded to join the kitchens to the new wing by an arcade. Building was to continue throughout the Revolution—the north banqueting hall in 1776, the glorious piazza overlooking the Potomac in 1777—but Washington was to see little of it, leaving it to his overseer and cousin, Lund Washington. For eight winters during the Revolution, Martha traveled north to

Mount Vernon, 1757

With second story, 1759

Completed, 1787

---

* The painting now hangs at Washington and Lee University.

The mansion's west front is the formal façade of Mount Vernon. The arcade leads, left to Washington's office, and, right, to the spacious kitchens. On March 31, 1785, Washington noted in his diary, "Planted the Scarlet or French honey suckle (as my Gardener calls it and which he says blows all the summer) at each Column of my covered ways."

stay with her husband, the Commander-in-Chief of the Continental Armies, returning each spring as the campaigns were resumed. Only once, en route to and from Yorktown in 1781, was Washington able to see his home with his own eyes. That the separation from Martha and Mount Vernon was painful he left no doubt: "I should enjoy more real happiness in one month with you at home than I have the most distant prospect of finding abroad, if my stay were to be seven times seven years."

On December 23, 1783, Washington, now fifty-one and a tall, commanding figure in his buff-and-blue regimentals, entered the old State House at Annapolis and surrendered his commision to Congress. On Christmas Eve he was back at Mount Vernon, and was soon writing with profound satisfaction, "At length I am become a private citizen on the banks of the Potomac; and under the shadow of my own vine and my own fig-tree, free from the bustle of camp, and the busy scenes of public life." "Agriculture," he announced, "has ever been among the most favored of my amusements." And again, "I think that the life of a husbandman of all others is the most delectable. It is honorable, it is amusing, and, with judicious management, it is profitable. To see plants rise from the earth and flourish by the superior skill and bounty of the laborer fills a contemplative mind with ideas which are more easy to be conceived than expressed."

The days were indeed busy at Mount Vernon. Washington was soon ordering flagstones for the piazza, stables to be enlarged (to include, of course, a stall for "Nelson," the horse that had seen

Washington through so many battles), and a spacious greenhouse erected. For the banquet room there was a handsome marble mantelpiece, carved by the fashionable Antonio Canova and presented by an English admirer, Samuel Vaughn. "The chimney-piece is arrived," Washington wrote his benefactor, "and, by the number of cases [ten] too elegant and costly by far, I fear for my own room and republican style of living." Finally, in 1787, the cupola, with a dove of peace for its weathervane, was finished, and Mount Vernon as we know it today was completed.

In the same year, Washington presided over the Constitutional Convention in Philadelphia. Two years later, civic duty called again, this time to guide the destinies of the newborn United States of America as its first Chief Executive. "I call Heaven to witness I most heartily wish the choice may not fall on me," Washington protested. When, inevitably, it did, Washington was aware, "The eyes of Argus are upon me and no slip will pass unnoticed." For as President, Washington knew, "My station is new . . . I walk on untrodden ground . . . there is scarcely any part of my conduct that may not hereafter be drawn into precedent." Wishing to dignify the office, he patterned his behavior on that of the courts of Europe, wearing black velvet at state levees, a white leather scabbard and state sword, and even the title "Your Serene Highness" was considered. But he wrote privately, "I can truly say I had rather be at Mount Vernon with a friend or two about me, than to be attended at the Seat of Government by the Officers of State and the Representatives of every Power in Europe."

On March 4, 1797, with the inauguration of John Adams, Washington was at last able to return to Mount Vernon and peace. Despite his long absences from Mount Vernon, Washington had managed it well, increasing it from just over 2000 acres to five farms of 8000 acres in all (of which his own survey map shows 3260 acres were tilled). In all, he had the labor of some 300 slaves, of whom ninety were at the mansion house. It was as nearly a self-supporting community as Washington could make it, with its own cobblers, weavers, ironmongers, miller. But even with all of Washington's diligence, the five-farm estate barely made a profit; his wealth, which came to between $500,000 and $750,000 at the time of his death, was largely in terms of real estate (he owned 63,000 acres, of which 40,000 were in Virginia).

Although in his final years he became slightly stooped and suffered from his ill-fitting false teeth, he remained a striking figure. "Washington had something uncommonly majestic and commanding in his walk, his address, his figure, his countenance," wrote architect Benjamin Latrobe. An old friend and former aide-de-camp, Richard Kidder Meade, wrote, "You will meet, sir, with an old gentleman riding alone, in plain drab clothes, a broad brimmed white hat, a hickory switch in his hand, and carrying an umbrella with a long staff which is attached to his saddle horn. That person, sir, is General Washington."

As a planter, Washington rose at dawn to give his overseers their orders, returned for breakfast (tea, coffee, and Indian corn cakes with butter and honey), then on horseback he rode to each of his farms, returning to dress for a two-o'clock dinner. The menu for such a repast has been preserved by a grateful guest: "The dinner was very good, a small roast pig, boiled leg of lamb, roasted fowl, beef,

Washington's desk and chair, purchased in Philadelphia, and globe, made in London, were used in Mount Vernon library.

peas, lettuce, cucumbers, artichokes, etc. etc. We were desired to call for what drink we chose." There was tea in the late afternoon, supper was often at ten, followed sometimes by music; Nelly Custis (Martha's granddaughter) was proficient at the harpsichord. Although Washington cheerfully confessed "I can neither sing one of the songs nor raise a single note on any instrument," he apparently greatly enjoyed these evening musicales. And the General was a hospitable host; at least one guest noted that "At twelve I had the honor of being lighted up to my bed room by the General himself."

Guests arrived in an endless procession at Mount Vernon, from the distinguished Marquis de Lafayette to mere curiosity seekers. As early as 1787 Washington had protested, "For in truth [Mount Vernon] may be compared to a well resorted tavern, as scarcely any strangers who are north to south, or south to north, do not spend a day or two at it." To aid him in handling all this entertainment, the former President in the final years invited his nephew, Lawrence Lewis, to act as a kind of social secretary. Romance flourished, and on Washington's last birthday the halls of Mount Vernon were made festive for the marriage of Lewis and Nelly Custis.

Washington kept to his planter's routine until the very end. On December 12, 1799, he noted in his diary "Morning snowing." Though he had a sore throat, bad cold, and weak lungs, he insisted on his morning inspection ride. The next day quinsy developed. Doctors were summoned and, as was the custom, bled him profusely. "Doctor, I die hard," Washington said, "but I am not afraid to go." At ten that evening he said, "I feel myself going. I thank you for your attentions," and, a few minutes later, was dead. Martha Washington closed the second-floor bedroom they had shared so long and until her death in 1802 lived in a small upper room with a view of Washington's tomb.

So overpowering was the majesty of Washington's presence and in such veneration has his memory been held as the Father of His Country that Mount Vernon has come to seem the epitome of excellence. Even judged by colonial Tidewater plantation-house standards, however, Mount Vernon is less than that. In its own day it was surpassed in splendor by half a dozen other Virginia mansions. To Benjamin Latrobe, the architect for the U.S. Capitol, Mount Vernon was "by no means above what would be expected in a plain English country gentleman's house on £500 or £600 a year."

Latrobe's evaluation overlooks the originality of the front portico, the ingeniousness of sanding the paint to make pine siding appear stone, the exquisite plastering of the dining room, and such details as the Palladian window in the banquet hall. But over the years, Mount Vernon has become more precious, as the home of our First President and for its evocation of a way of life that was passing even as Washington lived it; nowhere else does the whole panorama of an eighteenth-century planter's life become so vivid as in Washington's mansion house overlooking the Potomac.

In 1853, the Mount Vernon Ladies' Association was formed by Miss Ann Pamela Cunningham of South Carolina, and in 1858, on the eve of the Civil War, Mount Vernon was purchased from Colonel John A. Washington, Jr., great-grand-nephew of the First President. Under Miss Cunningham's direction, the ladies labored for years to preserve and restore the home of General George and Martha Washington. It is largely thanks to them that today Mount Vernon continues to open wide its doors in hospitality to a grateful people.

Locket with portrait of Martha Washington by Charles Willson Peale was worn by Washington through the Revolutionary War.

The Adamses

I will give you, "Independence Forever!" *

ALL OF US as Americans are constantly bemused and astounded by this extraordinary golden age in our history which produced so many men of exceptional talent," President John F. Kennedy said on the publication of the first four of the proposed ninety volumes of correspondence of the first three Adamses. "I have not heard, nor I suppose is there, a rational explanation for the fact that this small country, possessed of a very limited population, living under harsh circumstances, produced so many, many brilliant and extraordinary figures who set the tone of our national life and who, really, represent the most extraordinary outpouring of human ability devoted to government than any time since the days of Greece. And any touch we may have in our lives with that period attracts us all. . . .

"The record of the Adams family—this tremendous devotion to the public interest, this vitality which goes from generation to generation down to the present is, really, the most exceptional scarlet thread which runs throughout the entire tapestry of American political life.

"I think the quality I find interesting in the Adamses is their constant dissatisfaction with their own record. In a sense it was their self-love and self-esteem, rather than any rather synthetic sense of their inadequacy, that made them work so hard, and yet made them feel that they had failed to achieve what they were capable of and what the time demanded. I think therefore that we can consider that they have bequeathed to us two extraordinary and important qualities: conscience, Puritan conscience, and courage—the courage of those who look to other days and other times."

For those who, like the thirty-fifth President of the United States, would like to come "closer to the tables where the record was written," there is, apart from the Adamses' own voluminous writings, no better touchstone to history than the two simple farmhouses where the second and sixth Presidents were born and Peacefield, or The Old House, as John Adams' descendants came to call it. For in this old and venerable mansion in the once-rural city of Quincy, Massachusetts, lived four consecutive generations of Adamses, all distinguished in letters, learning, and the service of their country.

No house in America can offer, for sustained historical associations, a room the equal of the Old House's second-story study. Here at his desk the second President penned his long correspondence to Thomas Jefferson; on the same desk his son, the sixth President, kept

Cradle, made in Quincy in 1715, and used by five generations of the Adams family.

* John Adams' proposed toast for the fiftieth anniversary of the Signing of the Declaration of Independence, July 4, 1826.

the journal which he began at the age of eleven in Paris and continued until near his eightieth year, when he commented in one of his last entries, "There has perhaps not been another individual of the human race of whose daily existence from early childhood to fourscore years has been noted down with his own hand so minutely as mine." In the third generation, in this same study, Charles Francis Adams prepared his articles for the *North American Review* and edited the letters of his grandmother, Abigail Adams. And it was here that Brooks Adams, last of the family to occupy the mansion, labored over his many books, as did Henry Adams, his even more brilliant brother. As the visual record of how four gifted generations of distinguished Americans lived, Peacefield is unique—as unique, indeed, as the Adamses themselves, a family that one historian unhesitatingly called "this most important family in American history."

The Adams family had already been in New England for four generations before John Adams was born on October 30 (October 19, Old Style), 1735, the eldest son of Deacon John Adams, a farmer, and Susanna Boylston, in the small house on the old Country Highway that had connected Plymouth and Boston since 1648. This house (John Adams was born in the east chamber) is typical of the third generation of houses built by New England yeomen, as far a cry from the Pilgrims' primitive lean-tos and mud wattle Plymouth houses as they were from the fine residences being built of brick in the eighteenth century up Boston's Beacon Hill.

Such houses as Deacon Adams', framed with massive beams, joined carpenter-fashion and secured by wood pegs, and floored with two-foot-wide planks, have brick-filled walls, covered with clapboards on the outside to ward off weather and plastered within. At the center is the massive fireplace, used for both heating and cooking. When the house was built, sometime between 1675 and 1681, it had two lower rooms and two minute chambers above on the second floor. Sometime before Deacon Adams bought the house in 1720, a lean-to had been added (or rather superimposed, since it had its own set of roof-rafters). This effectively doubled the size of the house, adding two more rooms on the ground floor and two chambers plus attic room above.

Life in such a house in John Adams' boyhood in Braintree (as it was called until 1792, when the name was changed to Quincy) was hard, even a little humdrum; the last Indian raid had been in 1675; the outcroppings of granite (later to furnish the stone for the Bunker Hill Monument) made farming difficult, but the sea was full of fish and the marsh grass made luxuriant hay. Almost lyrically, John Adams himself described the round of toil in words that presage those of Robert Frost: "Sometimes I am at the orchard ploughing up acre after acre, planting, pruning apple-trees, mending fences, carting dung; sometimes in the pasture, digging stones, clearing bushes, pruning trees, building walls to redeem post and rails . . . sometimes I am at the old swamp, burning bushes, digging stumps, cutting ditches across the meadows and against my uncle; and am sometimes at the other end of town, buying posts and rails to fence against my uncle, and against the brook. . . ."

Given his choice between digging ditches or studying Latin, John Adams chose the latter, becoming the second Adams to go to Harvard (class of 1755), then taught school, then studied law. Far less of a fire-eating Son of Liberty than his second cousin Sam Adams, he still

John Adams' birthplace in Quincy is typical New England salt-box with lean-to addition. It was built between 1675 and 1681.

argued against the royal governor in 1765 that "no freeman should be subject to any tax to which he has not given his consent." And he found the Boston Tea Party magnificent: "The sublimity of it charms me!" In 1770 he had defended, on request, the officer-in-charge at the Boston Massacre and won his acquittal (only two of the British soldiers were branded on the hand and sent back to England); he was nonetheless chosen one of Massachusetts' four delegates to the first Continental Congress in Philadelphia in 1775.

On October 25, 1764, John Adams had married Abigail Smith, daughter of a Weymouth Puritan divine; Abigail proved to be a delightful mixture of common sense, high spirits, and wit, a woman who all her life held dour John Adams in her spell and even fascinated the gallant Virginian Thomas Jefferson. The newlyweds first moved into the house next door to Adams' birthplace, a dwelling Adams had inherited three years before from his father. It had room enough for his growing library and, with a door cut in the old front kitchen, for a law office as well.

It was from this house that Abigail Adams wrote that on June 17, 1775, she had that day climbed the hill behind the house with her seven-year-old son Johnny (John Quincy Adams) to see the Battle of Bunker Hill, ten miles away. "Dear Friend Dr. Warren is no more but fell gloriously fighting for his Country," she wrote her husband in Philadelphia, adding, "The constant roar of the cannon is so distressing that we cannot Eat, Drink or Sleep." From the Continental Congress, John Adams could report that troops would soon be on the way and that he had nominated Colonel Washington for Commander-in-Chief of the Continental Army, noting, "Mr. Washington, who happened to sit near the Door, as soon as he heard me allude to him, from his Usual Modesty darted into the Library Room."

On March 2, 1776, Abigail is interrupted in mid-letter, "But hark! The House this instant shakes with the Roar of Cannon. . . . No sleep for me tonight." Washington's men, she soon discovered, had arrived and were cannonading the British in Boston from Dorchester Heights. "I went to bed after 12 but got no rest," Abigail

Desk used by the two Adams Presidents (top) in the Old House, Quincy, Massachusetts. Double sewing chair (below) was added by Mrs. Charles Francis Adams and placed in the "Long Room" beneath portraits of President John Adams, left, and her husband, right.

The Old House as it appeared in 1828, showing the extensive barns and stables, since removed. The Adamses never forgot that they were farmers.

Abigail Adams, painted by Gilbert Stuart, was the only American woman who was wife of one President, mother of another. (Below) John Adams, also painted by Gilbert Stuart.

wrote the next day, "the Cannon continue firing and my Heart Beat pace with them all Night." On March 17 she wrote exultantly that the British were abandoning Boston: "From Penns Hill we have a view of the largest Fleet ever seen in America. You may count upwards of 100 and 70 sail. They look like a Forrest."

John Adams, who was on the committee to draft the Declaration of Independence, proved, in Jefferson's words, to be "the colossus" and "the pillar of its support on the floor of Congress." As the newly created United States desperately needed credit and allies abroad, Benjamin Franklin, Arthur Lee, and John Adams were sent abroad to win recognition from France in 1778. Then Adams went on to The Hague to arrange for financial credits. The power politics of Europe, he saw, were fraught with danger for the new American Republic: "For my own Part I thought America had been long enough involved in the Wars of Europe. She had been a Football between contending Nations from the Beginning. . . ." Then, on June 1, 1785, almost ten years to the day after the Battle of Bunker Hill, John Adams was ushered into the royal bedroom of King George III of England as the first accredited Minister of the United States of America. Both Adams and the King were overcome with emotion. When the King recovered and said, laughing, "There is an opinion among some people that you are not the most attached of your countrymen to the manners of France," John Adams reported that he "assumed as gay an Air as was decent and said, 'That opinion, Sir, is not mistaken, for I must avow to your Majesty that I have no Attachments but to my own country!'"

"The King replied as quick as lightning, 'An honest Man will never have any other!'"

Back in New York, John Adams found himself elected the nation's first Vice-President (1789–1797), and then followed Washington as the country's second President (1797–1801). Placing himself above party, President Adams opposed outright war with France, but asked Washington, then on the verge of death, to don once again his old uniform if war should come. Adams sent the famous frigates *Constitution, United States,* and *Constellation* to sea, where they aided our armed merchantmen in bagging eighty-four French ships in the undeclared war. John Adams was the first President to enter the still unfinished "President's Palace" in Washington (Abigail hung out the washing in the East Room), but never well liked as president and opposed by Congress, he lost his popularity and a second term. So out of sorts was Adams at the end of his term that he rode out of Washington on Inauguration Day before dawn without greeting his successor, Thomas Jefferson.

"Oh! that I might have a home!" he had groaned as President. "But this felicity has never been permitted me. Rolling, rolling, till I am near rolling into the bosom of mother earth!" But after having "trotted the bogs five hundred miles" back to Quincy, Adams found himself in a residence worthy of him. In 1787, while still Minister to England, he had bought for £600 the house built in 1731 by Major Leonard Vassall, a wealthy West India sugar planter. This house, which Adams named Peacefield, was then modest in size, comprising the present house's paneled room, west entry, and dining room on the ground floor; there were only two bedrooms and three smaller rooms in the attic; the kitchen and servants' rooms were in a detached building. To this, while still President, John Adams had built a large

East wall of the Old House study (top) *has a marble fireplace, cut in Philadelphia about 1800, flanked by terrestrial globe and celestial sphere belonging to John Quincy Adams. The kitchen* (below) *has tin roasting oven belonging to Abigail Adams, cast-iron wood-burning stove added about 1850, and gas-burning range installed after the turn of the century.*

gabled ell, containing the Long Room on the main floor, a new entry (the east entry), and above the new drawing room a spacious second-story study. Viewing it through child's eyes, John Adams' great-grandson was to write years later in *The Education of Henry Adams*:

> The old house at Quincy was eighteenth century. What style it had was its Queen Anne mahogany panels and its Louis Seize chairs and sofas. The panels belonged to an old colonial Vassall who built the house; the furniture had been brought back from Paris in 1789 or 1801 or 1817, along with porcelain and books and much else of old diplomatic remnants; and neither of the two eighteenth-century styles . . . was comfortable for a boy, or for any one else. The dark mahogany had been painted white to suit daily life in winter gloom.

When the Declaration of Independence had been signed in 1776, John Adams had written Abigail from Philadelphia, "I am apt to believe that it will be celebrated, by succeeding Generations, as the great Day of Deliverance. . . . It ought to be Solemnized with Pomp and Parade, with Shews, Games, Sports, Guns, Bells, Bonfires and Illuminations . . . from this Time forward forever more." As the fiftieth anniversary of the first Fourth of July approached, John Adams, then nearing his ninety-first birthday, prepared his own toast. "I will give you," he said, "Independence Forever!" Asked by the Quincy townsmen if he would add anything else, he said with true Yankee asperity, "Not a word!" It was a toast he never lived to utter. Stricken two days before, he died on July 4, 1826, in his chair in his spacious study, murmuring, "Thomas Jefferson survives," unaware that a few hours before in distant Monticello his comrade-in-arms and friend of later years had also passed away.

John Quincy Adams, eldest of the five childen born of Abigail to John Adams, began serving his country probably earlier than any other American. As the guns on Dorchester Heights rattled the window panes of his birthplace in Braintree, John Quincy, aged eight, was diligently practicing the manual of arms with his musket; at ten he accompanied his father to Paris; by the age of twelve he had crossed the Atlantic four times, running the British blockade each time, and had been shipwrecked on the coast of Spain; at fourteen he was Secretary of the American Legation in Russia. He studied at Paris and London, returning to go to Harvard (Class of 1787); at twenty-six he was named by Washington as United States Minister to The Hague.

The girl John Quincy chose to marry and eventually bring back to the Old House in Quincy had nearly as exotic a background as his. Louisa Catharine Johnson was the daughter of a Maryland merchant who had been caught in London by the War of Independence and fled to Nantes, France, until the peace. Louisa, when she married John Quincy Adams on July 26, 1797, had thus been French for her first ten years and a Londoner for the next ten. Her grandson, Henry Adams, described her as "charming, like a Romney portrait, but among her many charms that of being a New England woman was not one. The defect was serious." Or perhaps it seemed so only to strong-willed Abigail Adams, the only woman to be wife of one President and mother of another.

Much of John Quincy's early married life was spent abroad, as Minister to Prussia. He was home for a period, serving both in the state and national senates, then overseas again as Minister to Russia, a commissioner at the conference of the Peace Treaty of Ghent in 1814, finally as Minister to England. He returned to Washington, where for eight years he was President Monroe's brilliant Secretary of State, a position in which he heavily influenced the writing of the Monroe Doctrine. But despite John Quincy Adams' brilliant career, old John Adams grumbled in Quincy, "My son will never get a chance at the Presidency until the last Virginian is in his grave."

In 1824, to John Adams' surprise and delight, John Quincy Adams was elected sixth President of the United States by the House when Henry Clay threw his votes to Adams, temporarily frustrating the ambitions of Andrew Jackson. But this combination of "the Puritan and the blackleg" satisfied no one. John Quincy Adams was the last nonpartisan President. When he departed from Washington, the Age of Jackson, the spoils system, political appointees, and the pork barrel began. Wrapping himself in deep and pessimistic melancholy, John Quincy Adams left for Quincy. Depressed by the recent loss of one son, a drunkard whose death was probably suicide, he resolved "to go into the deepest retirement and withdraw from all connection with public affairs."

But the Adams in John Quincy soon showed. Asked to represent the old Plymouth District in Congress, he accepted—with the understanding he would be responsible for his opinions to no one but himself. For nine consecutive terms he was returned to Congress, becoming known as "Old Man Eloquent" as he battled single-handed to repeal the "Gag Resolution" passed to muzzle debate on petitions (mainly from antislavery men) to the House of Representatives. Hands shaking, eyes watering, voice cracking with age, the former President battled like an ancient gladiator. Julia Gardiner Tyler, wife of President John Tyler, witnessed one such occasion; "Mr. Adams was exceedingly bald, and as he sat in the middle of the House, with the immense petition [on the subject of slavery] rolled around

John Quincy Adams, painted by Thomas Sully, and his elegant, London-educated wife, Louisa Catharine, used the bedroom built in 1788 for Abigail Adams. The Sadler tiles were bought by John Quincy Adams and very much pleased his mother, Abigail.

39 THE ADAMSES

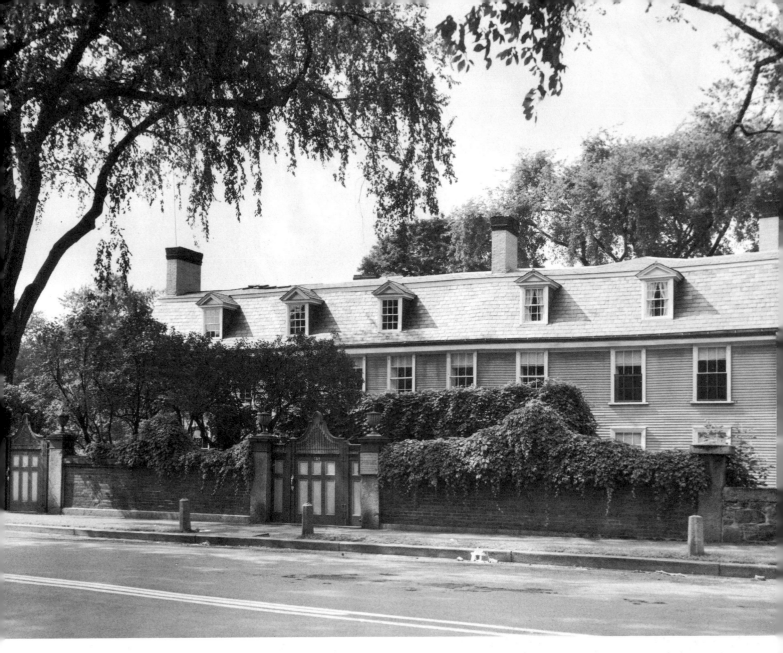

Front view of Peacefield with original house at left, later additions at right.

a kind of windlass to sustain it, his excitement was manifested in the flaming redness of his bald head, which acted a a chronometer to his audience." But, after thirteen years of unrelenting fight, John Quincy Adams won his point. In his diary he rejoiced at his hard-fought victory by writing the simple line, "Blessed, forever blessed be the name of God."

During the summers, John Quincy Adams was a far more homespun figure in the Old House to which he had added a passage in the back to join the two ells. He would rise early, start the fires with his flint-and-steel, then don old clothes to work at haying with his hired hands, lamenting the loss of "the best hours of the day." He meticulously kept up the diary he had started as a boy, and accounted for every minute of his days except for two wasted hours—"This wasted time I have found to be as indispensable as sleep," he wrote. "It must be wasted on trivials—doing nothing." His grandson was later to recall the pleasant autumnal air that pervaded the Old House at this time; Henry Adams wrote of how as a boy he "hung about the library; handled the books, deranged the papers, ransacked the drawers; searched the old purses and pocket-books for foreign coins; drew the sword-cane; snapped the travelling-pistols; upset everything in the corners, and penetrated the President's dressing-closet where a row of tumblers, inverted on the shelf, covered caterpillars which were supposed to become moths and butterflies, but never did."

As Henry Adams discovered, John Quincy Adams could be firm. Once when young Henry was standing at the bottom of the long staircase leading up to the President's library and sullenly protesting that he would not go to school, the door opened, and out walked the old former President. Coming down the stairs, he took the young rebel by the hand and walked with him for a mile through the summer's heat without uttering a word until he had deposited young Henry Adams, paralyzed with awe, inside the schoolroom.

"Madame," as Mrs. John Quincy Adams was called, "was a little more remote than the President, but decorative. She stayed much in her own room with the Dutch tiles, looking out on her garden with the box walks. . . ." Henry Adams, writing in 1905, could still recall her "sitting in her panelled room, at breakfast, with her heavy silver teapot and sugar-bowl and creamjug. . . . To the boy she seemed singularly peaceful, a vision of silver grey, presiding over her old President and her Queen Anne mahogany; an exotic, like her Sevres china; an object of deference to every one. . . ."

An invitation to John Quincy Adams to be guest speaker at the cornerstone-laying of the Cincinnati Astronomical Observatory when he was past seventy-six gave the tottering old man a belated chance to be greeted as a great American in an area long hostile to the Adamses (neither father nor son ever carried a state west of the Alleghenies). As he heard himself cheered from station to station en route, he wrote in his diary, "I cannot realize that these demonstrations are for me; and the only comfort I have is that they are intended to maintain respect, and not hatred." In Akron, his Puritan reserve melted away altogether as one young lady in the reception room kissed him on the cheek. Swept away, he confessed, "I returned the salutation on the lips and kissed every woman that followed." He collapsed on the floor of Congress, dying at his post on February 21, 1848, at the age of eighty, as became an Adams. His last words: "Thank the officers of the House. This is the last on earth. I am content."

The last of the Adams Presidents was gone, but the family and the house in Quincy still lived on. In 1848, Charles Francis Adams, who had been vice-presidential nominee with Martin Van Buren on the Free Soil ticket and Minister to England during the Civil War, added thirty feet to the kitchen ell for servants' quarters, and in the following year he built the stone library next to Abigail Adams' garden to house President John Quincy Adams' library and letters. In turn, his son Brooks Adams, who added the present entrance gates, used the house as a summer residence until his death in 1927. Over the years, the styles of furniture blended, the kitchen changed from open hearth to coal to gas, the lighting from candlelight to electricity. The Adams house in Quincy holds a unique place not as a period piece, but as the continuous record of one great family, a house to which each generation contributed something of itself.

John Quincy Adams, photographed in the "Long Room," or parlor of the Old House, in 1848, the year of his death.

THREE

Thomas Jefferson

ALL MY WISHES end where I hope my days will end, at Monticello," wrote Thomas Jefferson. For all the brilliance of his public career, Jefferson at times doubted his temperamental fitness for office: "The whole of my life has been a war with my natural tastes, feelings and wishes. . . . Domestic life and literary pursuits were my first and my latest inclinations, circumstances and not my desires led me to the path I have trod."

Only on his hilltop estate at Monticello did Jefferson feel free to indulge his natural inclinations in a world ordered to his own liking. And it is because Monticello so precisely expresses the native genius of its designer that it is rivaled in popularity today only by Mount Vernon and Hyde Park as both a symbol and touchstone of greatness.

"Architecture is my delight," Jefferson confessed freely, "and putting up and pulling down one of my favorite amusements." This was nowhere more true than at Monticello, a building he began planning at twenty-four and did not finish until death put an end to his putting up and pulling down. Jefferson was only a boy when he picked out the site for Monticello. (The name, which means "small mountain" in Italian, derives from the 865-foot hill upon which it is built.) He had been born only a few miles across the Rivanna River at Shadwell on April 13, 1743 (April 2, Old Style). His father, Peter Jefferson, was a Welsh-descended engineer and tobacco planter, and his mother was Jane Randolph, a daughter of one of Virginia's first families.

Jefferson was a well-to-do youth. His father died when he was fourteen, leaving him 2750 acres and his slaves. Red-haired, with freckles, hazel eyes, and a somewhat shambling walk (he was six feet two), Jefferson was a popular figure at William and Mary (1762), where he read classics, studied law under George Wythe (the teacher of John Marshall, Monroe, Henry Clay, and Edmund Randolph), cut a splendid figure on a horse, and delighted in playing duets on the violin with the likes of Patrick Henry. While still at college, he had bought his first book on architecture from an old cabinetmaker who lived near the college gate, and in 1763, while studying law, he amused himself by planning his first small house. Two years later he began grafting cherry buds to start Monticello's future orchards. By May 18, 1767, the year he was admitted to the bar, Jefferson "agreed with Mr. Moore that he shall level 250 ft. square on the top of the mountain at the N. E. end by Christmas, for which I am to give him 180 bushels of wheat and 24 bushels of corn." Soon after, Jefferson's ledgers are filled with calculations for his new house; the axis is to be 118.33469 ft., a Doric pedestal 22½ ft., bricks would total 185,000. Indeed, Jefferson's calculations were not only minutely detailed but

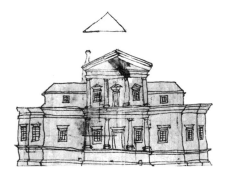

Jefferson's earliest sketch of Monticello, circa 1770.

also highly informed, for he had by now apparently come across Andrea Palladio's *Four Books of Architecture.* In Palladio, plus James Gibbs' *Rules for Drawing* and *Book on Architecture,* and Robert Morris' *Select Architecture* Jefferson found his guides to classic architecture.

In July 1769, Jefferson ordered bricks made and a deep well dug for his mountaintop mansion. The first building was a small outchamber on the south brink of the summit. When, the next year, fire destroyed the family house he had inherited at Shadwell (and with it Jefferson's first library), he stepped up his building program, sketching designs for the slave quarters along the roundabout drive. On November 26, 1770, he triumphantly jotted in his account-book records, "Moved to Monticello." He found the new site exhilarating. Soon he was writing to a friend, "I have here but one room, which, like the cobbler's, serves me for parlour, for kitchen and hall. I may add, for bedchamber and study too. . . . I have hope, however, of getting more elbow room this summer."

Jefferson by now had a new reason for haste. He was courting a slender brunette widow, Martha Wayles Skelton, whose husband had owned Elk Hill on the James River. On January 1, 1772, Jefferson, twenty-nine, and his bride, twenty-three, were married at her father's house, The Forest. Tradition has it that Jefferson and Martha had to make their way on horseback through snowdrifts up the mountain to his bachelor's quarters, now known as the Honeymoon Cottage, and that when they arrived the slaves were asleep and the fires out.

Elevation of the First Monticello, drawn by Jefferson, shows two porticoes, ornamented with columns. The second row of columns may never have been erected, but this design is echoed in southern plantation houses for decades afterward.

It is just possible that part of the mansion was habitable. In any case, the first Monticello soon was—for Jefferson, like Washington, continued to build throughout the Revolution.

The Monticello Martha Jefferson knew, and which she, so contemporaries said, "vivified" by her presence and gay spinet playing, was wide and shallow, only half the size of the present building. There were five major rooms on the main floor: the "Parlour" flanked on the north by the dining room and the "North Bow room" (later called the tea room); on the south there was a large, square "Dressing room" and bedroom on the south bow. On the second floor was found a large library over the parlor, with a bedroom on either side. Across the front façade were Doric columns and on the second floor an Ionic portico, planned but probably never erected.

The Marquis de Chastellux has left us a brief description of this first Monticello as it appeared in 1782:

> The house, of which Mr. Jefferson was the architect and often one of the workmen, is rather elegant, and in the Italian taste, though not without fault; it consists of one large square pavilion, the entrance to which is by two porticoes, ornamented with pillars. The ground floor consists chiefly of a very large, lofty saloon which is to be decorated entirely in the antique style; above it is a library of the same form; two small wings with only a ground floor and attic story, are joined to this pavilion, and communicate with the kitchens, offices, etc., which will form a kind of basement story, over which runs a terrace . . . we may safely aver, that Mr. Jefferson is the first American who has consulted the fine arts to know how he should shelter himself from the weather.

It was to this "square pavilion" that on June 4, 1781, the "British horse came to Monticello." Just in the nick of time, Jack Jouett, a kind of Virginian Paul Revere, galloped up to spread the alarm that Tarleton's Raiders were on their way to capture Governor Jefferson of Virginia. Jefferson, who had sent his family away to

Watercolor portraying Thomas Jefferson, painted from life by Robert Field in Philadephia, 1797, shows Jefferson as Vice President.

From 1796 until 1809 he was busy redesigning the Monticello we know today. Monticello's East Façade, with portico topped by a weathervane and square-faced clock to be read both indoors and out; South Wing, enclosing the conservatory; West Façade is an octagon modeled on a classic temple. To give Monticello the appearance of a one-story structure, Jefferson merged the windows on the first and mezzanine floor, concealed the third story behind a balustrade. Kitchens and other areas were reached by an underground passage, barely visible by the South Wing, at far left.

Enniscorthy, rode down one side of Monticello as the Redcoats swarmed up the other. Left behind was the steward Martin, who finished handing down the silver and valuables to Caesar, the Negro slave, as the British arrived. Caesar found the porch plank dropped into place over his head and remained trapped in the secret hideaway for eighteen hours, until the British finally departed.

Jefferson at the time was sharply criticized for leaving Virginia undefended against such British raids. But at home he was anxiously watching over the health of his wife, who in ten years had presented him with six children (only two of whom survived to maturity). When she died on September 6, 1782, four months after bearing her last daughter, Jefferson was so distraught that he refused to speak for weeks, and never remarried. Martha's death, coupled with Jefferson's departure in 1784 to France with Benjamin Franklin and John Adams to negotiate a commercial treaty, thus marked the end of a period at Monticello. He was not to return until five years later, and when he did, he brought with him eighty-six packing crates and a host of new ideas that he incorporated into the Monticello that we know today.

The Monticello gardens claimed his attention first. Jefferson had always been a landscape gardening enthusiast. In a rush of romantic enthusiasm he had dreamed of cascades, Greek and Chinese temples, and even "the caprice of Gothic is sometimes not incompatible with greatness." He had laid out wild areas with jessamine, honeysuckle, and sweetbrier as a wild-animal preserve, and wondered if he might not afford a peacock or a buffalo. In England he dashed from one great estate to the other to view the gardens, discovered "This, indeed, went far beyond my ideas." Monticello's gardens soon showed the benefits of Jefferson's lessons abroad.

So did Monticello itself. In 1789, Jefferson began pulling down and building up his house to conform to the classic models he had admired in Europe. By 1794 Jefferson complained, "We are now living in a brick kiln, for my house, in its present state, is nothing better," and not until 1808 was the new Monticello finally finished. By then his granddaughter, Ellen Randolph, could write, "I think the hall

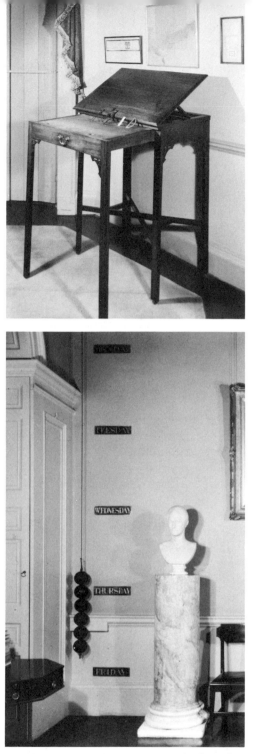

Jefferson's architect's table on which he drew plans for Monticello and the University of Virginia was built, probably by local carpenters, with adjustable table top. Below are the cannonball weights which operate the clock at Monticello. Bust at right exemplifies Jefferson's taste for the classical.

with its gravel colored border is the most beautiful room I was ever in, without excepting the drawing-rooms at Washington. The dining room is much improved; the pillars of the portico are rough cast and look very well; all the railings at the top of the house [are] finished and painted."

To carry out his architectural plans, Jefferson was dependent on his own servants (83 slaves and 34 free men and women) and what few artisians, including one British army deserter, he could hire. From among them he had to train bricklayers, stonecutters, carpenters, cabinetmakers, ironmongers. Some of the furniture made by the craftsman-slave James Hemmings is still treasured at Monticello; two "house-joiners," James Dinsmore, who came from Philadelphia in 1798, and John Neilson, who arrived in 1804, helped build Monticello, and later worked with Madison at Montpelier and at the University of Virginia, where they developed Jefferson's style in buildings of their own, much as Frank Lloyd Wright's apprentices in the twentieth century spread that master's lessons far and wide across the United States.

In expanding Monticello to its present thirty-two room size, Jefferson wanted to make the main pavilion appear only one story tall. This he did by blending the mezzanine and lower windows into one visually connected unit, hiding the upper story behind a balustrade. The stairway was removed from its usual central position in the main hall or passageway, and tucked into narrow corners. This device had been used by Palladio at Malcontenta and other villas, and appealed to Jefferson because it gained a large, impressive central hall of uncluttered space. To connect the mezzanine floors of the two wings a ramped gallery with exquisite detailing crosses a part of the central hall.

Jefferson not only took his delight in mathematics over into architecture but also a lawyer's love for precedents. He had confessed to his good friend of later years, the Comtesse de Tessé, "While in Paris, I was violently smitten with the Hôtel de Salm, and used to go to the Tuileries almost daily to look at it." This building Jefferson had traced back in Palladio to the Temple of Vesta, and used as the model for Monticello's west front, including the dome. He was equally respectful to classical precedent in the orders of his columns, Doric on the exterior, Ionic on the interior. But in building the wings, which form a double-L or three-sided square, he proved himself imaginative indeed; these were placed in semiburied underground galleries which left the views open while providing walkways in wet weather. Here were housed smokehouse, kitchen, dairy rooms, icehouse, stables, and harness rooms, their existence barely suspected by guests.

Jefferson was thus a profound admirer of the classic forms, but he was also as much the inventive American as Benjamin Franklin. Jefferson designed a weathervane that transmits its message to the porch roof; clocks are double-faced (to be read both in and out of the house) and operated by an ingenious cannon-balls-on-pulley arrangement that also marks the days. The upstairs beds were merely wall hooks from which rope springs and mattresses could be hung, and his own bed was fitted in an alcove, which provided a natural breezeway. Even the twin glazed doors opening into the hall were rigged by a sprocket arrangement so that both opened as one. At Monticello, ladders folded up, "whirligig" chairs swiveled, while others came equipped with footrests and writing tables. Music stands folded into small boxes; a dumbwaiter raised a bottle from the cellar at the same time that an empty was being returned.

Nor did Jefferson's accomplishments end there; he was surgeon enough to sew up a wound or set a slave's broken leg; as a mathematician he could calculate an eclipse. He invented a folding chair, a pedometer (to measure his walks), a letter-copying machine, a hemp machine, a two-wheeled carriage, and a plow that once won a gold medal in France. He knew French, Italian, Spanish, German, Latin, and Greek (he was rereading the tragedies when he died). Indeed, the Sage of Monticello had all the earmarks of that much-esteemed man of the eigthteenth century, the universal genius. So various were his interests that they tumbled out all over the house in the most extraordinary disarray, until the halls resembled more Teddy Roosevelt's Sagamore Hill than the rigid formality of Mount Vernon.

The innumerable visitors to Monticello were a burden and expense under which Jefferson groaned. The steward, Bacon, described the voracious demands of this "perfect throng of visitors": "I have often sent a wagon-load of hay up to the stable, and the next morning there would not be enough to make a bird's nest. I have killed a fine beef and it would all be eaten in a day or two. . . . They pretended to come out of respect and regard for him, but I think that the fact they saved a tavern bill had a good deal to do with it."

More cruel yet was Jefferson's declining fortune. For all his republican simplicity that made him walk to his own inauguration, he loved fine books (assembling three libraries), expensive statues, paintings, wines and food. In his last year as President, his expenses were $8000 more than his salary, and, after retirement, his estates constantly lost money.

And yet Jefferson knew no way to halt his creative drive. Three years before he left the White House he began work on Poplar Forest, an estate ninety miles from Monticello in Bedford County, as a "summer haven." The design was nearly as ingenious as that of Monticello, an octagonal house (suggested by William Kent's *Designs of Inigo Jones,* 1737). And in 1816 he wrote to John Adams that he was "mounted on a hobby . . . this is the establishment of a university." As Rector of the University of Virginia, Jefferson was able to design much of the campus, overseeing its construction at Charlottesville, four miles away, through a telescope.

After Jefferson's death, on July 4, 1826, the fiftieth anniversary of the Declaration of Independence that he himself penned, a final financial reckoning was made and Jefferson was found to be all but bankrupt. Jefferson's one surviving daughter, Martha Randolph, was allowed to occupy Monticello, "bare and comfortless," for five years; in 1831 Jefferson's home passed into the hands of a Charlottesville druggist. Not until April 13, 1923, with the establishment of the Thomas Jefferson Memorial Foundation, did the house and 658 surrounding acres become a national shrine. Today it is visited by tens of thousands annually, a fitting homage to one of our greatest Americans, the man who said, "I have sworn upon the altar of God eternal hostility against every form of tyranny over the mind of man," who gave to the University of Virginia its motto, "Ye shall know the truth and the truth shall make you free," and to all mankind held out the prospect of a society based on "Life, Liberty and the Pursuit of Happiness."

Portrait of Martha Jefferson Randolph, Jefferson's eldest daughter and his official hostess in Washington and at Monticello, still hangs in the historic mansion.

FOUR

James Madison

ARRIVED AT MR. MADISON'S country seat, about 110 miles from the City of Washington and situated in Orange County, Virginia, 5 miles from Orange Court House, on one of the mountains forming the ridge called the Southwest Mountain." So wrote Mrs. William Thornton, wife of the Commissioner of the District of Columbia, on her first visit in 1802 to James Madison's country estate.

"It is a wild and romantic country," Mrs. Thornton continued, "very generally covered with fine timber and forest trees. The house, originally built by his father, but added to by himself, is upwards of eighty feet in Length with a handsome (but unfinished) portico of the Tuscan order, plain but grand appearance, rendered more pleasing by displaying a taste for the arts which is rarely to be found in such remote and retired situations. . . ."

The mansion to which Dr. William Thornton and his wife Anna Maria were welcomed was far smaller than the one that stands today, and it was just coming to be known as Montpelier, for the fair city in France. James Madison, diminutive but plucky Secretary of State

Montpelier, Madison's estate, in Orange County, Virginia, as it appeared in the early nineteenth century, was dominated by its classic portico, suggested by Jefferson.

James Madison, called Jemmy by his old friends, was admired for his keen intellect; Dolley (as she spelled her name) Madison was one of the most popular hostesses in Washington history.

to Thomas Jefferson, sniffed disdainfully at what he called the "Yankee trick" of spelling the name of Vermont's capital city with a single *l*. In return Vermonters considered Madison Frenchified, not altogether without reason.

James Madison, or "Master Jemmy" as the hundred-odd slaves at Montpellier called him, was a fifth-generation descendant of Ship Carpenter John Maddison, who had first obtained patent for land in 1653. According to Madison, his "ancestors* on both sides were not among the most wealthy of the country but in independent and comfortable circumstances." Madison's grandfather, Ambrose, had bought the nucleus of the Montpellier estate in 1723 and built there a modest wooden house, half a mile south of the later mansion site. Madison himself was born on March 16, 1751, at the home of his maternal grandmother, Rebecca Catlett Conway Moore, at Port Conway in King George County on a site overlooking the Rappahannock.

Madison was fortunate in having a father, James Madison, Sr.,

Montpelier, as it appears today, is a private estate noted for its fine racing horses. This rear view shows the trees planted by Madison. The original house has been greatly enlarged.

* Including Madison's great-grandfather, James Taylor, one of whose great-grandsons was President Zachary Taylor.

who believed that his son would play a major role in the destinies of this new land. And, although James, Jr., was frail and sickly, he was given a splendid classical education at the hands of a Scottish master, Donald Robertson (whose Scots burr forever after echoed in Madison's French). At the College of New Jersey (soon to be renamed Princeton), young "Jemmy" packed in two years of work in one, studying twenty-one hours a day and driving himself into what historian Irving Brant has suggested was "epiloid hysteria." In the end Madison turned to law and, with the forming of the revolutionary "Committees of Safety" (of which his father was a leader), threw himself wholeheartedly into the great and noble adventure of the eighteenth century, the formation of new governments.

Madison was not a prepossessing figure; Jefferson failed to notice him when they first met in the Virginia House of Delegates in 1776. Nor was he a spellbinder; voters, irked because he would not furnish free barrels of whiskey, did not re-elect their young squire. But Madison's application to detail, his broad grasp of theory, and his quiet wit earned him quick recognition in the Council of State. Madison's qualities burst into prominence under Jefferson, were nourished through service in the Continental Congress, and reached a magnificent flowering in the closed-door sessions of the Constitutional Convention of 1787. There, seated at his secretary's desk, Madison wrote down in his own shorthand the only nearly complete record we possess of that historic occasion. Taking the Constitution to the voters, Madison performed an even more heroic task in outdebating the formidable orator Patrick Henry, and successfully swinging the crucial Commonwealth of Virginia to the side of ratification. And by championing in Congress the first ten amendments to the Constitution, the Bill of Rights, Madison sealed his right to be called "The Father of the Constitution."

James Madison was a figure of respect among his fellow congressmen in Philadelphia, but he fared less well with the ladies. One pretty sixteen-year-old, Catharine Floyd, summarily turned down his suit, signing her letter—so history records—with a seal of rye dough. A widow in New York had held out equally successfully. In May 1794, the forty-three-year-old Madison resolved once again to scale the walls, this time with the help of his friend Aaron Burr. Madison's object was Dorothea (Dolley) Payne Todd, twenty-four, a Quaker widow with one son (her husband and other son had died the year before in a yellow fever epidemic). Hearing of Madison's intended suit, Dolley in a panic had sent off an epistle to her friend Elizabeth Collins: "Dear Friend:—Thou must come to me,—Aaron Burr says that the great little Madison has asked to be brought to see me this evening."

This time Madison won. Four months later, in September 1794, the future President, splendid in a jabot of Mechlin lace to help make up for his slight figure (barely a hundred pounds), married his Dolley at Harewood, the Virginia home of Mrs. George Steptoe Washington, Dolley's sister and the favorite niece of George Washington. In 1798 the couple, seventeen years apart in age but marvelously complementary in tastes, began modernizing the house Madison's father had built in 1760.

Aiding the Madisons were two of the best connoisseurs in the new Republic: their neighbor Thomas Jefferson, who while in France had picked out the marble mantelpiece for the drawing room, and

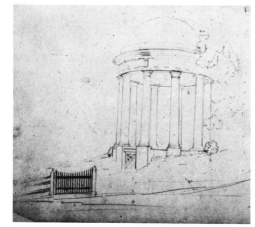

Madison's summer house at Montpelier was a delightful classic pavilion.

Portico-covered porch, 80 feet long, commands vista to the river and Blue Ridge Mountains. Inside is a large central hall, with suite of rooms opening off to right for Madison's mother, and on left, parlor, "Clock Room" with fifty busts and statues, and dining room which normally served dinners for as many as twenty guests.

Massive columns, 30 feet high, support the portico. In 1809 Madison commissioned Thornton and Latrobe, designer and builder of the White House, to enlarge Montpelier, changing walls from brick to Virginia limestone.

James Monroe, who sent back from Paris tablecloths for their eighteen-foot dining-room table and four dozen napkins "not in the least objectionable for having been used," plus chairs, couches, aristocratic fauteuils, even an iron bed from the Tuileries—all then to be had cheaply from the impoverished French nobility. The effect for rural Virginia was striking indeed: "Airy apartments—windows opening to the ground, hung with light silken drapery, French furniture, light fancy chairs, gay carpets,"

Dolley Madison was to leave behind her a legend both at Montpelier and on Capitol Hill as the most popular hostess and First Lady of all time. While her husband served as Jefferson's Secretary of State, Dolley acted for two terms as official hostess at the Executive Mansion for the widower Jefferson. Her own rented house in Washington, at 1333 F Street, contained the most sought-after drawing room in all Washington. When Madison assumed the presidency in 1809, Dolley ushered in a new era of splendor.

Not even fire and disaster could quench Dolley Madison's good spirits. Presidential history has left us no more endearing picture than that of Dolley at the Executive Mansion on August 23, 1814, "turning

Dolley Madison was described by Washington Irving as "a fine, portly, buxom dame, who has a smile and a pleasant word for everybody." When Henry Clay said, "Everybody loves Mrs. Madison," she gaily replied, "Mrs. Madison loves everybody!"

my spy-glass in all directions" hoping to see her husband return, and then, in midafternoon, deciding to pack up and flee the White House just a step ahead of the British redcoats led by Admiral Cockburn and General Ross.

When Madison and Dolley were safely reunited in Washington, the Executive Mansion was a smoldering pile in the wake of the British invasion. The President moved into the Octagon House, New York Avenue and 18th Street, as temporary quarters. Soon the news turned better. Fort McHenry, guarding Baltimore, held out as Francis Scott Key watched the bombardment through the long night and penned the poem published anonymously soon after by the Baltimore *Patriot*:

> *O! Say can you see, by the dawn's early light,*
> *What so proudly we hailed at the twilight's last gleaming. . . .*

Next came the stirring message from Commodore Thomas Macdonough, "The Almighty has been pleased to grant us a signal victory on Lake Champlain, in the capture of one frigate, one brig, and two sloops of war of the enemy"; and finally the splendid victory of General Andrew Jackson at New Orleans.

In April 1817, Madison and Dolley, having, seen their good friend James Monroe sworn in as President, made their way back to Montpelier (as by now even Madison was spelling it), after forty-five years of nearly uninterrupted service to state and nation. Part of the trip was by steamboat, a remarkable experience for this little man in his powdered wig who had served from Lexington and Concord through the end of the War of 1812. Awaiting them was their newly readied home. In 1809 Madison had commissioned William Thornton and Benjamin Latrobe, the designer and builder of the White House, to remodel Montpelier, adding single one-story wings to either side* and changing the exterior walls from brick to Virginia limestone.

Guests, including Lafayette and Daniel Webster, arriving at Montpelier were met beneath the lofty colonnade, thirty feet high and eighty feet across, which by tradition had been designed by Thomas Jefferson. Inside they found the long central hall usual in big houses in the South, and on either side two large salons. Also on the right was a suite of four rooms, set aside for Mrs. Nelly Madison, the ex-President's mother, who lived on to the age of ninety-seven. In the square parlor were "six or eight" paintings by Gilbert Stuart, including his famous *Signing of the Declaration of Independence,* which had been rescued by Dolley Madison from the White House; the stately dining room was also covered with portraits of the great; and the so-called "Clock Room" had a museumlike collection of fifty statues and busts, including a marble medallion of James Madison by the celebrated sculptor Caracchi.

A room of special interest to Madison was his library. His father had started the collection by buying the whole of Royalist Lord Dunmore's confiscated books, and Madison himself was an inveterate collector. In time, the library of nearly four-thousand volumes, eventually willed to the University of Virginia, grew so large it forced Madison to work in the parlor. For Dolley Madison, the dining room was a social center. Her letters abound with tales of generous Virginia

---

* These were raised to two stories over a century later when the property was bought by William Du Pont.

hospitality; she thought nothing of having fifteen or twenty for dinner and in summer once served ninety on the lawn. To keep sufficient food in stock, Madison built Virginia's first icebox. A merry wife, Dolley loved to keep her music box playing, doted on novels ("but not Cooper—too full of horrors!"), and once was observed gaily running a foot race across Montpelier's lawn with Jemmy.

Trade embargoes and the War of 1812, plus declining fertility of the land and the slave economy gradually forced all Virginians to the wall. As early as 1826 Madison confessed his profits barely paid his overseer's salary. To provide for the future, Madison with the help of his wife labored daily from 1821 until his death fifteen years later on his notes of the Constitutional Convention, a masterwork which he confidently believed would bring $100,000 (Congress bought Madison's notes in 1837 for $30,000 and the remainder from his widow in 1848 for $25,000).

The major division of the Constitutional Convention, Madison had noted, was not between large and small states, but slave and free, South and North. And although in retirement Madison served as rector of the University of Virginia and at the age of seventy-eight accepted membership in Virginia's Constitutional Convention, his main preoccupation was with that "dreadful calamity," slavery. Nullification and secession, he proclaimed, were "twin heresies which ought to be buried in the same grave." It was to this overriding issue that Madison devoted his final message to the nation:

> *That the Union of the States be cherished and perpetuated. Let the enemy to it be regarded as a Pandora with her box opened, and the disguised one as the serpent creeping with his deadly wiles into paradise.*

After Madison's death on June 28, 1836, Dolley Madison returned to Washington, living with her sister on Lafayette Square. Her old capital welcomed back its "Dowager Queen," although she was in such financial straits that Daniel Webster regularly dropped off baskets of groceries to help pad out the household budget. Still a personage, Dolley was invited by President Tyler to cruise on board the USS *Princeton* on February 28, 1844, the day the ship's major gun exploded, killing several of the official party but leaving Dolley unscathed, since she and the President had lingered below decks. Dolley was also present when Samuel F. B. Morse demonstrated his new electric telegraph; after seeing the first message come over the wire from Baltimore ("What hath God wrought"), the inventor gallantly asked Dolley to send back a reply. For once Dolley slightly failed a rendezvous with destiny: her reply, the first social greeting ever telegraphed, was, "Message from Mrs. Madison. She sends her love to Mrs. Wethered."

No official occasion seemed quite complete without Dolley Madison, and, until she reached the age of eighty-one, she was included in the capital's great events, among them the dedication of the Washington Monument on July 4, 1848. And when Sarah Polk arrived in Washington to take up her residence in the White House, it was only natural that she should turn to Dolley for advice. The crisis of the moment was whether Mrs. Polk should return calls or be "exclusive" and receive calls only. Dolley, who through the years had developed a fine sense of tact, did the proper thing: she left it up to Sarah.

Montpelier after the Civil War retained a few touches of its former elegance with its marble fireplaces and Empire clock, but new wallpaper, heavy Victorian furniture and fireplace stove canceled out the memory of one of the most elegant of Virginia mansions.

FIVE

James Monroe

JAMES MONROE was the fourth of the great Virginians who presided over the United States for thirty-two of the Republic's first thirty-six years. Lacking the stature of Washington, the genius of Jefferson, or the dry brilliance of Madison, James Monroe could nevertheless boast a longer and more distinguished record than almost any other President: officer in the Revolution, member of the Virginia legislature, Continental Congress, and Virginia constitutional covention; United States senator and envoy to France, England, and Spain (he signed the Louisiana Purchase); Secretary of State under Madison; and, following the burning of Washington in 1814, Madison's Secretary of War. He was twice elected President of the United States, the second time with only a single dissenting vote (New Hampshire's William Plumer, who voted for John Quincy Adams to insure that Washington would be the only President elected unanimously by the Electoral College). His eight years in the White House produced "The Era of Good Feelings" that saw Florida become a new territory, forts eliminated from the U.S.-Canada boundary, the Monroe Doctrine enunciated for the Western Hemisphere, and the way paved for further expansion with the Missouri Compromise.

Monroe emerged from the White House an object of sincere respect. Known as "The Last Cocked Hat," an epithet more of affection than ridicule that referred to his liking for the simple garb of colonial times, he was broad-shouldered and rawboned and somewhat resembled Washington; his features seemed chiseled from rock while his gray-blue eyes seemed to invite confidence. "Neatness and republican sincerity" were the words that came to the tongue of one Yankee.

While Monroe's parentage seems not overly exalted—his father Spence Monroe had been apprenticed to a carpenter; his mother, Elizabeth Jones, was the daughter of James Jones, "an undertaker in architecture"—it was nonetheless the seedbed of Virginia aristocracy in an age when a man could be both a carpenter and a gentleman. His boyhood home in Westmoreland County was primitive indeed, a two-

Monroe's birthplace, Conway House, in Port Conway, Virginia, has since disappeared, leaving no trace.

James Monroe, painted by John Vanderlyn, lived in this white-painted brick residence, now part of the University of Virginia, when he first came to Charlottesville to be near Jefferson in 1790. His law office was in one of the arcaded outbuildings.

story house whose "rafters and beams showed plainly the unskilled art of the craftmanship of the labor of the period," a descendant has written. Here the family dined "in a large living room, in which an oldtime fireplace with a broad hearth was particularly conspicuous with its pots and pans hanging on cranes over a slow wood fire."

From these beginnings Monroe rose rapidly. As a boy he had walked through the forest to Parson Campbell's school with his friend, the future Chief Justice John Marshall. Apparently he learned well. At sixteen he entered William and Mary. It was not long before the college halls reverberated to the repeated oratory of Patrick Henry and the stirring events then moving the colonies rapidly toward open revolt. At seventeen Monroe, with Benjamin Harrison, Jr.,* of Berkeley, raided the royal governor's palace in Williamsburg to seize the cache of ammunition; at eighteen Monroe was a soldier in the War of Independence, an officer in the Third Virginia Regiment.

Monroe was wounded at Trenton, wintered with Washington at Valley Forge, and at nineteen was made a major. But campaigning was long and the commands Monroe longed for were slow in coming. With a career to make he decided to buckle down to the study of law, reading in the chambers of his good friend (shortly to become governor of Virginia) Thomas Jefferson, and soon afterward was writing about the purchase of a lot and house "on the hill" in Fredericksburg. In October 1786, he was admitted to the bar and opened his office on Charles Street, now a historic shrine and headquarters of the James Monroe Memorial Foundation.

The same year that Monroe hung out his shingle he married Elizabeth Kortwright, a haughty New York belle whose father had been a British army officer. It was not long, though, before Monroe began planning for a second house, this one to be much closer to Jefferson's Monticello. In 1786 he wrote Jefferson, "Believe me I have not relinquished the prospect of being your neighbor." It was a prospect that delighted Jefferson as well: "I find friendship to be like wine, raw when new, ripened with age, the true old man's milk and restorative cordial. . . . I wish to heaven, you may continue in the disposition to fix . . . in Albemarle. . . . Perhaps Madison may be tempted to do so. This will be society enough, and it will be a great sweetener of our lives. Without society, and a society to our taste, men are never contented."

By August 1789, Monroe had carried out his promise, having purchased from "Colo. G. Nicholas improvements in Charlotteville & 800 acres of land within a mile, on the road to R. fish Gap—" This farmhouse, now known as Monroe House on Monroe Hill, was later incorporated into the University of Virginia, where it still stands, linked to the adjacent buildings by an arcade.

Six years later, in 1795, Monroe bought a plantation even closer to Monticello and began to construct his "cabin-castle," probably the rear portion of Ash Lawn. Since Monroe was on a diplomatic mission to France, Jefferson agreed to oversee the construction. From Paris Monroe wrote to Jefferson: "I accept with great pleasure your proposal to forward my establishment on the tract adjoining you, in the expectation, however, that you will give yourself no further trouble in it than by employing for me a suitable undertaker who will receive from you the plan he is to execute, that you will draw on me for the money to pay him, & make my plantation one of the routes you take

* Father of William Henry Harrison, the tenth President.

Elizabeth Kortwright Monroe, wife of the fifth President, painted by Benjamin West.

Ash Lawn, in Charlottesville, is modest house within sight of Monticello, which Jefferson oversaw as favor to Monroe, who described it as his "cabin-castle." (Below) Overseer's cottage.

House at 2017 I Street, N.W., in Washington, D.C., occupied by Monroe as Madison's Secretary of State (1811-1817) and for six months as President while the White House was being rebuilt after the War of 1812.

when you ride for exercise, at which time you may note how far the execution corresponds with the plan. With this view I shall look out for a model to be forwarded you as soon as possible, subjecting it to yr. correction & give you full power to place my house, orchards, etc. where you please."

The prospect of such friendly relationship with Jefferson pleased Monroe tremendously, as he showed in a letter to the other great Virginian of the triumvirate, James Madison. On January 20, 1796, Monroe wrote: "Mr. Jefferson proposed to have a house built for me on my plantation near him & to wh. I have agreed under conditions that will make the burden as light as possible upon him. For this purpose I am about to send 2 plans to him submitting both to his judgement, & contemplate accepting the offer of a skilful mason here who wishes to emigrate & settle with us, to execute the work. I wish yrself & Mr. Jones to see the plans & council with Mr. Jefferson on the subject."

Nothing, unfortunately, is known of the two plans, or of the eager mason. Since all this rhetoric, at least, seems overly imposing for the house we now know as Ash Lawn, it has been suggested that the building that has survived may, in fact, be the overseer's cottage. Such at least is the suggestion of Laurence Gouverneur Hoes, head of the James Monroe Law Office Museum. The present owner of Ash Lawn, however, is of the opinion that this is indeed the house that was the subject of so much delightful correspondence between Monroe, Madison, and Jefferson. It served as Monroe's country retreat for many busy years, until he decided to build an even grander house for his retirement after his presidency.

The Washington that was to be the background for so much of Monroe's official life from the time he began serving as Madison's Secretary of State in 1811 was, as Gouverneur Morris remarked at the time, "the best city in the world for a *future* residence. We want nothing here but houses, cellars, kitchens, well-informed men, amiable women, and the other little trifles of the kind to make our city perfect."

In this setting Monroe was fortunate to own one of the few solidly built brick residences. This house on I Street served Madison as a kind of headquarters in 1814 when the British landed, intent on capturing Washington. Monroe had led a scouting party to observe the British advance. After the White House was burned, Madison appointed Monroe his Secretary of War. "I had a couch in my house on which I occasionally reposed," Monroe wrote, "but from which even in the night I was called every two hours when the expresses arrived, to receive the dispatches which they brought."

Oak Hill, in Loudoun County, Virgina, remains one of the South's great mansions. Growing among the locusts and poplars are many of the oaks Monroe himself planted, one for each state of the Union.

When Monroe was elected President, such harried scenes of midnight messengers on horseback dashing up to deliver the latest dispatches gave way to a far more decorous atmosphere. For though unwell, Mrs. Monroe was a regal figure—"the most stately, gracious and regal-looking lady ever to be Queen of the White House." For the first nine months of her husband's term of office, while the White House underwent repairs, she stayed in her own house rather than move into the Octagon House at New York Avenue and 18th Street, which had been serving as Madison's White House.

Few presidents have found the White House more burdensome than did Monroe, and it was with a sense of both relief and anticipation that he and his wife left Washington in March 1825. Awaiting them was their new home, Oak Hill, near Leesburg, Loudoun County, Virginia. In 1806 Monroe had inherited the land from his father-in-law, Joseph Jones, and had prevailed on Jefferson to design a splendid country seat in the Palladian manner, with an immense portico facing south, supported by massive thirty-foot-high Doric columns. To execute it, Monroe had the services of James Hoban, builder of the new White House.

Oak Hill, now the private residence of Mrs. Marion duPont, was completed in April 1823 and furnished with pieces from Ash Lawn and the Monroes' own things from the White House. Among the locusts and poplars, Monroe personally planted the oaks, one for each state of the Union furnished by the respective congressmen. The completed mansion, built of brick kilned on the plantation (without its present wings), became one of the famed architectural showpieces of Virginia.

Perhaps its most splendid moment was the visit on August 7–9, 1825, of General Lafayette, then sixty-eight, and President John

Oak Hill, as it appeared in 1859, twenty-eight years after Monroe reluctantly sold it, retained its original appearance. The high, colonnaded veranda clearly echoes the Greek temple form that inspired it.

Quincy Adams. Unfortunately it was the hottest time of summer; the distinguished guests had to content themselves with what Adams called "desultory conversation" as they gazed out over the magnificent panorama of trees, lawns, and the distant Blue Ridge in one direction, the Catoctin Hills in the other.

Actually Oak Hill, its rooms bursting with daughters and grandchildren and its stately living room and dining room graced with marble fireplaces, the gift of Lafayette, was in perilous financial condition. On July 4, 1826, Thomas Jefferson had died in a state of near-bankruptcy. Monroe's finances were almost as bad, although he proudly turned down Lafayette's offer of a loan while desperately petitioning Congress for his proper back expenses, including money paid to free the Revolutionary Pamphleteer Tom Paine from a Paris prison.

Monroe had already sold 950 acres while serving as an ambassador abroad. In 1825 he advertised the sale of his estate and slaves at Ash Lawn, plus 3500 acres. In 1831, the year after his wife died, Monroe was finally forced to sell Oak Hill. He wrote to Madison, six years his senior, "It is very distressing to me to sell my property in Loudoun, for besides parting with all I have in the State, I indulged a hope, if I could retain it, that I might be able occasionally to visit it, and meet my friends, or many of them, there. But ill health and advanced years prescribe a course which we must pursue."

Monroe moved for his final days to the house of his daughter and son-in-law, whom John Quincy Adams had named postmaster general of New York, at the corner of Prince and Marion streets near the Bowery. It was there that the last of the great Virginians died at the age of seventy-three, on July 4, 1831, five years to the day after Thomas Jefferson and John Adams.

SEVEN

Andrew Jackson

FRIDAY MORNING, May 30, 1806, two men stood by the bank of a small stream in Kentucky, each with his toe marking a peg driven into the ground. One was a brash lawyer, Charles Dickinson, reputedly the best pistol shot in Tennessee. Exactly twenty-four feet away stood a slender, six-foot figure in a loose-fitting frock coat, Andrew Jackson, at thirty-nine already sometime state attorney general, congressman, senator, and now major general in the Tennessee state militia. At the command *"Fire!"* Dickinson raised his pistol; the seconds heard the report and saw a puff of dust fly from Jackson's chest.

"Good God! Have I missed him?" Dickinson cried.

"Back to your mark, sir," bellowed the director of the duel.

As Dickinson stood, eyes averted, Andrew Jackson deliberately took aim. His pistol snapped, halted at half-cock. Methodically Jackson cocked again. This time the pistol fired, and Dickinson reeled backward as the red stain spread over his trousers where the bullet had entered under his ribs. Only then did Jackson's surgeon note with horror that one of Jackson's boots was already filled with blood.

"Oh, I believe he has pinked me a little," Jackson murmured.

It was worse than that. Dickinson's bullet had come to rest inches from Jackson's heart. There it was to rest, a torment to Jackson the rest of his life, just as Dickinson's slow agony and death was ever after to be used as an accusation against Jackson by his political opponents.

Ostensibly the quarrel was over a horse race between "Plow Boy" and Jackson's favorite, "Truxton," a bay stallion named for the commander of the USS *Constitution*. But the real reason was deeper; in

For fifteen years Andrew Jackson and his wife lived in log cabins close to the present Hermitage. In such primitive surroundings they entertained James Monroe.

Major General Andrew Jackson, the "Hero of New Orleans," was painted shortly after the War of 1812 by R.E.W. Earl, a painter whom Jackson befriended and who lived with Jackson at the Hermitage. His wife, Rachel Donelson Jackson, died a few days before Jackson left the Hermitage for the White House. This portrait of her was in Jackson's bedroom, where it was the first object his eyes lighted on each morning.

the public rooms of Witt's Tavern in Nashville, Dickinson had spoken loosely of Jackson's beloved wife, Rachel. And Jackson was never to forgive a slight on Rachel's name, any more than he regretted shooting Dickinson, whom he called a "base poltroon and cowardly talebearer." "I should have hit him if he had shot me through the brain," Jackson said in later years.

Andrew Jackson had never known his father, who died before he was born. He had lost two brothers in the Revolution, and his mother, a North of Ireland lass, had died while nursing wounded American soldiers when Andrew was only fourteen. Young Jackson had picked up the swagger and some of the cockfighting, horse-racing, gaming tastes of the Charleston aristocracy along with a little law before he decided at the age of twenty-one to ride westward. In the stockaded settlement of Nashville, he put up at the cabin of the widow of Colonel John Donelson and had been quite taken with the daughter of the house, Rachel, a young woman then home recovering from a disastrous marriage to Captain Lewis Robards. Under the impression that Robards had obtained a divorce, Andrew Jackson married Rachel Donelson in 1791, only to have to repeat the ceremony again in 1793, when it was learned that the divorce had been delayed. For a woman of stern Presbyterian principles, as Rachel was, it was a humiliating experience—one that Jackson's enemies loved to harp on.

By 1792 Andrew Jackson and Rachel had built their first log cabin at Poplar Grove outside Nashville, Tennessee. Four years later they moved to a finer house on Hunter's Hill, at the same time opening a store where, along with calico, nankeen, and cambric, they sold "Spanish segurs" and whiskey at seventy-five cents a gallon, for Andrew Jackson, like William Henry Harrison, operated his own still. As the protégé of Governor William Blount, Jackson prospered in politics, but he got himself badly into debt. In 1804 he was forced to sell his store and home for $10,000. But he had even better ground

The Hermitage today is unchanged since Jackson's death. The front portico, with its cast-iron capitals (above) and rear porch (below) add great dignity to the final building. The well, detached kitchen and original brick paving are also visible.

in view, and in the same year he put out 1000 apple and peach trees on his new land, a 1200-acre plantation called The Hermitage.*

The cluster of log cabins to which Andrew Jackson was carried after his near-fatal duel with Dickinson was a far cry from The Hermitage of later years. The main building was a two-story log cabin, one that may well have been a blockhouse used as protection against Indians in earlier days. Jackson had left unpartitioned the main large ground-floor room, which measured twenty-four by twenty-six feet, adding out behind a lean-to with two rooms, a pantry and a downstairs bedroom. Behind, Jackson erected smaller cabins for slaves, provision storerooms, and a smokehouse. In this rustic setting Jackson and Rachel lived for fifteen happy years (1804–1819), and here they entertained both President Monroe and Aaron Burr. It was also from here that Jackson left to defeat the Creek Indians at the battle of Horseshoe Bend in Alabama in 1814 and, as a major general in the U.S. Army, again left to drive the Spanish from Pensacola. To this Hermitage Jackson returned in 1818, hero of the Battle of New Orleans.

What prompted the erection of the new Hermitage in 1819 is not known. It was a modest structure, probably designed by the future President himself. With its four main rooms on the ground floor, each with its fireplace and chimney, and large central hallways, opened in warm weather from front to back to form a breezeway, it was a house that adhered closely to a nearly universal ground plan for Southern mansions, from Virginia's Berkeley on.

Jackson's decision to build with brick made the 1819 Hermitage more substantial than most such houses. The materials for the brick came from Jackson's own property. Clay was found close to the surface near the house. The topsoil was removed and lime sprinkled on the clay. A field hand on a mule trod the two into the right mixture, and the bricks, hand-shaped, were put into a kiln on the spot. The foundation of native limestone was also available on the plantation, and Jackson's slaves felled the poplar and cedar trees for flooring, beams, and framing. Gardens were laid out and tenderly cared for by Rachel, and a picket fence, painted white, surrounded the main house. "How often does my thoughts lead me back to The Hermitage," Jackson would write from Washington when he was serving his second term as U.S. senator in 1823. "There in private life, surrounded by a few friends, would be a paradise compared to the best situation here; and if once more there it would take a writ of *habeas corpus* to remove me into public life again."

Jackson's definition of "a few friends" would make sense only to such old-line Virginia gentlemen as Washington and Jefferson. By all accounts, The Hermitage was close to overflowing with guests, with not one person but whole families in each of the four upstairs bedrooms. Roast pig and fine brandy were there for all; the old cook, "Aunt Betsy," was never at a loss in the open-hearth kitchen. In the evenings there would be hymns and sometimes a guitar strumming the General's favorites, "Scots, Wha Hae wi' Wallace Bled" and—best of all—"Auld Lang Syne," while Rachel, sun-tanned and briskly effi-

---

* The origin of the name remains obscure. It may be named for a Virginia plantation owned by the Donelsons, or possibly in honor of the British economist Jeremy Bentham, a favorite of Jackson's, whose estate in England was also called the Hermitage.

Old print, circa 1840, shows the Hermitage as it was rebuilt for the last time in 1834. The guitar-shaped drive, here distorted into a banjo-shape by the artist, was designed by R. E. W. Earl and planted with young cedars by Jackson. To the right is Rachel's temple-shaped tomb; in the distance is another plantation house, Tulip Grove, belonging to Andrew Jackson Donelson. Second print (below) depicts the first Hermitage as it appeared in 1831, after both the wings and central portico had been added.

A high moment in Andrew Jackson's life occurred during Lafayette's visit to the Hermitage in 1824. In the library, Jackson has just shown Lafayette the pistols that the French patriot had given Washington and which now belonged to Jackson.

cient, would light up her evening corncob pipe or a "segur" for a contented smoke "to fight off the asthma."

Of the famous and casual visitors, none caused more stir in the brick-walled Hermitage than the Marquis de Lafayette, who arrived on May 4, 1824, disembarking at the river-boat landing three miles away and riding up in time for a many-course 3 P.M. dinner. After the feast Jackson showed Lafayette his war trophies, a congressional sword, his New Orleans saber, and finally a pair of pistols.

Lafayette's eyes lighted up when he saw the last, for they were the same ones he had presented to General Washington in 1778; Washington's nephew, Bushrod Washington, had in turn given them to Jackson. When Lafayette exclaimed how delighted he was to find them in such worthy hands, Andrew Jackson is said to have blushed for the only time in his life. "Yes, I believe myself worthy of them," Jackson cried, clasping the pistols and Lafayette's hand to his breast, "if not for what I have done, at least for what I wished to do for my country."

Visitors apart, what delighted Jackson and his wife most were the youngsters. Included among the children being reared by the childless Andrew Jacksons were his adopted son, Andrew Jackson Jr., and Andrew Jackson Hutchings, the orphan of an old war companion, Andrew Jackson Donelson, a nephew who later was nominated for the vice-presidency with Millard Fillmore, and a Creek Indian orphan, Lyncoya. Lyncoya had, as a one-year-old, been brought from the breast of his dead mother to Jackson's tent after the "Battle of Tallushatches" and kept alive by the General with brown sugar, water, and bread crumbs. The General found a warm spot in his heart for Lyncoya—an unusual attitude for an Indian fighter on the frontier—reared him, and finally apprenticed him to a saddlemaker, only to have the Indian boy die, probably of tuberculosis, at The Hermitage.

Jackson swept into the White House in 1828, but his beloved Rachel witnessed only the bitterness of the campaign, not the final victory. She died on December 22, 1828, at the age of sixty-one, a few days before Jackson was to leave for Washington. Jackson, who could not believe she had gone, ordered blankets kept handy for hours afterwards in hope that she should revive, then finally watched her burial in a corner lot of her flower garden. Broken and sorrowing, Jackson began negotiations for a "monumental tomb" which was to serve as his own, as well as Rachel's, and is still venerated at The Hermitage.

Two years later Jackson began planning from the White House the enlargement and embellishment of The Hermitage. The project was completed by 1831, but soon after fire, starting in one of the chimneys, swept through most of the house. Much of the furniture was destroyed, along with such mementoes as the Lafayette-Washington pistols. In 1834, Jackson courageously gave the order to rebuild The Hermitage once again. This time, on the advice of friends, the rooms were made higher and more spacious, and the 1819 brick walls, which had withstood the fire, were painted white to hide the smoke stains (much as the Executive Mansion in Washington had been painted white for the same reason in 1816).

Jackson insisted that the present Hermitage be kept at the site originally picked by Rachel. When it was completed, he authorized his daughter-in-law to go to Philadelphia to buy the rather heavy pieces now at The Hermitage. Jackson's only stipulation was that the bedposts be plain, to facilitate cleaning; as the bedroom furniture still demonstrates, his wishes were carried out. The value of the furnishings, divided among seven Philadelphia furniture stores, came in 1836 to exactly $2203.77. But Jackson's tribulations were not over. Half the goods were lost on board the river steamer, the *John Randolph* which burned at the wharf in Nashville. Jackson reordered, this time

The front parlor of the Hermitage was redecorated by Jackson in 1836, after he had left the White House. He ordered mirrors, tables, chairs and settees bought at seven Philadelphia furniture stores, shipped by steamer to New Orleans, then upriver to Nashville. Jackson was not fussy about style; he purchased what was then in fashion, heavy and ornate versions of eighteenth-century modes.

General Jackson's bedroom (above), *in which he died, was on the ground floor. Jackson had a practical eye for furnishings, wanted them kept simple to expedite dusting. His office in the Hermitage* (below) *was for decades the center of power for the Democratic Party. Here were planned the campaigns of Van Buren and Polk. When Jackson's doctor asked him what he would have done had Calhoun and the Nullifiers persisted in their threat to leave the Union, Jackson roared, "Hang them, sir, as high as Haman!"*

substituting American-made wallpaper with scenes of Telemachus for French paper, which would have cost double the price.

The expense of refurbishing the Hermitage was considerable, and when he left the White House Jackson needed loans from his friends to get his affairs back in order. But under his supervision The Hermitage soon was brought back into full production. His stud farm, which he had begun with the great champion "Truxton," was a handsome money-earner. The guitar-shaped entrance drive was laid out with the help of Ralph E. W. Earl, a painter who made The Hermitage his home, and Jackson himself supervised planting the cedar trees which still stand there. The house soon rang with the shouts of Jackson's grandchildren, little Rachel and Andrew Jackson, III. Jackson, whose oaths could—and did—quell a mutiny and whose "By the Eternal!" made the rafters shake, was curiously gentle with children. On some Sundays, they were allowed to accompany the old President himself on his drive in the great carriage drawn by four handsome bays, attended by Negro servants in livery with brass buttons and glazed hats with silver bands.

Hospitality, too, revived, including one stupendous feast for the 900-man regiment of Texas Volunteers. And with entertainment came the politicians, first to plot a second term for Van Buren (unsucessfully), finally to prepare for the victory of Polk. When the "glorious news" of Polk's election reached The Hermitage, Old Hickory held a magnificent celebration barbecue and climaxed the event by appearing on the second-floor balcony and, waving his cane, delivered one of his most rousing old-time harangues.

But Jackson's active life was fast drawing to a close. Though his last days were made pathetic by dropsy, he faced the end courageously. Commodore J. D. Elliott, U.S.N., had offered Jackson a Roman sarcophagus from Palestine. Jackson replied, "My republican feelings and principles forbid it; the simplicity of our system of government forbids it. Every monument erected to perpetuate the memory of our heroes and statesmen ought to be an evidence of the economy and simplicity of our republican institutions and of the plainness of our republican citizens...."

As his strength ebbed, Jackson sat huddled in the chair of his ground-floor bedroom. Over the fireplace was his favorite painting of Rachel; by his side was her Bible. When a friend arrived at the last moment, Jackson greeted him wryly: "Major, I am glad to see you. You like to have been too late." To the slaves gathered outside the two bedroom windows, Jackson gave his last words, "Don't cry. Be good and we shall meet." He was buried beside Rachel in the garden. Old Hickory's final resting place was marked simply, as he wished it:

GENERAL ANDREW JACKSON
BORN MARCH 15, 1767
Died June 8, 1845

Despite all Jackson's efforts, his adopted son remained a heedless spendthrift after the President's death. By 1856 Andrew Jackson, Jr., had run through his inheritance, and The Hermitage's 1200 acres were reduced to 500. When even these and the mansion were put up for sale, Tennessee's governor Andrew Johnson, a future President himself, had the state legislature pass a bill buying it in the hope of making it an extension of the U.S. Military Academy at West Point, with Andrew Jackson, Jr., to remain a "tenant at will." During the Civil War, Tennessee Confederate troopers paid their respects, found the ladies celebrating Jackson's 9th of January Victory of New Orleans, and joined in the picnic. Days later Union cavalry arrived to safeguard the house from molestation, and in the process their horses trampled Rachel's flower garden into a quagmire.

The Civil War dealt less kindly with the inhabitants of The Hermitage; of the five young men who left to fight for the Confederacy, only one, Colonel Andrew Jackson, III, returned. And in 1888, it was his wife, Ohio-born Amy Jackson, who, inspired by the success of the Mount Vernon Association, urged the founding of the Ladies' Hermitage Associates. This group, officially formed on May 15, 1889, has been the custodian of The Hermitage ever since, reassembling the General's dispersed possessions and repairing the damage of wind and weather. Today The Hermitage is once again largely as it was on the day Jackson died, a fitting memorial to America's greatest general between the Revolution and the Civil War and the President whose administration ushered in the Age of the Common Man.

Portrait of Andrew Jackson taken by Brady shortly before he died, displeased Jackson, then aged seventy-eight, who thought it made him "look like a monkey."

EIGHT

Martin Van Buren

The land is the finest for cultivation that I ever in my life set foot upon and it also abounds in trees of every description. The natives are a very good people for when they saw that I would not remain, they supposed that I was afraid of their bows and taking their arrows, broke them in pieces and threw them into the fire.

W HEN HENRY HUDSON made this entry in his log aboard his ship *Half Moon* on September 18, 1609, he was so delighted with the spot he had found on the Hudson River that he named it *Kinder-Hoeck—* "Children's Corner." Some forty years later a group of indentured Dutch settlers were to make good the explorer's prediction. Among the emigrants was one Jan Martense van Aelsteyn, who purchased an estate from the Indians for beaver skins and grain. On December 5, 1782, Martin Van Buren, Jan's great-great-grandson, was born in the small town on the Albany–New York Post Road, known by then as Kinderhook.

Martin Van Buren, for all his long lineage, was born far from the purple; his father, Abraham Van Buren, was a small farmer and innkeeper; his mother, Mary Hoes Van Alen, was a Dutch widow of equally humble background. Rotund, blond, blue-eyed Martin Van Buren reached his full growth of five feet six inches when he was fourteen. By this time he had also finished his formal education in the frame schoolhouse soon to be made famous by a visiting writer, Washington Irving, whose portrait of the harried schoolmaster Jesse Merwin has come down in literature as Ichabod Crane of Sleepy Hollow.

As a scholar, Martin Van Buren had little claim to fame. His handwriting and grammar could barely pass muster. As Governor De Witt Clinton once sharply put it, after reading a message from Van Buren: "It is equally offensive to grammar and truth." Van Buren's real education came from the political gossip in his father's tavern and from such dashing figures as Aaron Burr, who often lolled away his time there, leaving behind memories of his racy ways and laying the ground for a rumor, started in Washington years later, that he was in fact Van Buren's natural father.

There was little to sustain this rumor, apart from a certain physical resemblance, but it gained currency (and was delightedly confided to his diary by John Quincy Adams), largely because there was nothing in Van Buren's background to account for his rapid ascent and natural brilliance—nothing, except a mighty ambition backed by

Martin Van Buren's Birthplace, Kinderhook, New York.

Martin Van Buren, born the son of an innkeeper, returned to Kinderhook as a squire after his Presidency, hoping in vain that the Nation would call on him again. His wife and schoolmate died at the age of thirty-six, and Van Buren never remarried.

natural guile. Van Buren used his law training to mount the ladder of politics as he moved surely from Columbia County surrogate to state attorney general, from state senator to U.S. senator, from governor of New York to Secretary of State to Andrew Jackson and, in 1832, became the Vice-President to Old Hickory.

In vain did Van Buren's enemies froth; he was called heartless, a hypocrite, selfish, and an intriguer. Under Andrew Jackson he introduced the spoils system with a vengeance: "We give no reason for our removals." Jackson found him "a true man with no guile"; his opponents dubbed him "The Flying Dutchman," "The Red Fox of Kinderhook," "The Little Magician." Despite it all—or perhaps because of it—Martin Van Buren in 1836 became eighth President of the United States, only to lose to William Henry Harrison on their rematch in 1840.

After his defeat Van Buren returned slowly and reluctantly to Kinderhook, to recoup and win again if possible. He had married his cousin, Hannah Hoes, in 1807; in time the family had grown to four sons, but Hannah Van Buren died young, in 1819, before Van Buren's national career had begun. From then until his defeat in 1840, Van Buren had hardly known a home. The role of hostess in the White House had been played by his daughter-in-law, the beautiful Angelica Singleton, a niece of Dolley Madison from South Carolina who had married his third son, Martin, Jr. But he had observed how Washington's Mount Vernon, Jefferson's Monticello, and Jackson's Hermitage had become national shrines and rallying points. To provide a similar setting for himself, Van Buren bought the 200-acre Van Ness estate, on which Irving and Burr had been guests in his youth.

Van Buren at first wanted to call the large brick mansion "The Locusts" for its trees, but was dissuaded when it was pointed out that James Fenimore Cooper had already used the name in *The Spy* and

Lindenwald, as Van Buren called his renovated Hudson River mansion, was redesigned after 1840 by Richard Upjohn to take on the appearance of a Venetian Villa, with carpenter scrollwork (not shown) hanging from the eaves and a ninety-nine stair campanile in the rear. A notable innovation was the installation of furnaces and central heating in 1849.

called it Lindenwald. The original house was two stories tall, built by the Van Ness family in 1797, as its knocker still proudly proclaims, on land once owned by Van Buren's ancestor, Jan Martense van Aelsteyn. The mansion was originally of red brick and built in a kind of Palladian–Hudson River style. All this Van Buren intended to modify. He summoned the New York architect Richard Upjohn, designer of New York's famous Trinity Church, to give it a "Venetian villa look," adding an extra story, two wings, and a loggia tower incorporating ninety-nine steps, a heavy trim of Victorian foliage along the eaves, and a preposterously heavy Victorian porch. On the exterior the red brick was plastered and painted yellow. To give it a noble approach, Van Buren himself laid out the half-circle drive with carriage circle before the house and mounted ornate gatehouses at either entrance.

To prepare for the horde of well-wishers he hoped would soon be beating their way to his thirty-room mansion, Van Buren added two kitchens, a new well, and, for appearance sake, a library wing on the south end of the house. The central hall, 47½ ft. long and 17½ ft. wide, was papered with sportive French wallpaper, *Paysage à chasse* by Jean Zuber, and furnished with an expandable table capable of seating sixty-five guests. To provision it, there was a root cellar, wine cellar, and vinegar cellar, plus trout, pickerel, and perch from the two artificial ponds, and the rich harvest from the fields and orchards of pears, peaches, plums, and apples. A notable improvement in 1849 was the installation of a furnace, one of the first American instances of central heating.

Van Buren lived to see his anticipated guests come and go, including General Winfield Scott and old Henry Clay. All were impressed, including Senator Thomas Benton from Missouri, who made his first acquaintance with fingerbowls at Lindenwald. "I am very chary of new customs," the senator confided later, "but when I saw Mr. Van Buren dip the tips of his fingers in the bowl and wipe them daintily on a napkin, I just raked back my sleeves and took a good plain Republican wash."

Unfortunately for Van Buren, the campaign slogan "Van, Van, the used-up man!," that had downed him in 1840 was revived, and again defeated him. He contested the Democratic nomination for the presidency, lost to Polk because he opposed the annexation of Texas. In 1848 he ran for President on the Free Soil Ticket and lost again, with Daniel Webster's remark ringing in his ears: "That the leader of the Free Spoils Party should become leader of the Free Soil Party, is a joke to shake my sides and his."

It was a defeat from which Van Buren never really recovered. Faced with the inevitable, he accepted it, traveling abroad for months on end, or, back at Lindenwald, gossiped with cronies in the taproom of the Stranahan Hotel and dozed through the long Dutch Reformed services with a large fur glove covering his bald pate in winter and a footstove to keep him warm. Van Buren had proposed marriage to Margaret Sylvester, a forty-year-old Kinderhook spinster, who had stiffly refused. But Van Buren's youngest son and literary executor brought his wife, Harriet Irving, daughter of Washington Irving, to gladden the echoing rooms of Lindenwald, and their children added warmth and cheer to the aging ex-President's final years. Van Buren, afflicted with gout, depressed by the Union forces' long string of defeats, and putting his faith in a President not of his party, Abraham Lincoln, died quietly in his eightieth year.

Van Buren's heirs made little attempt to keep Lindenwald as a national legacy. Soon after Van Buren's death, his furniture was auctioned off, including the rug in his study which was worn threadbare from his habit of practicing speeches while pacing back and forth before the full-length mirror. The house was sold to strangers. New York state seems little interested in its first President. The house was most recently bought by Mrs. Kenneth Francis Campbell in 1957 and the already-much-maligned brick mansion has had its Victorian frills removed only to acquire an even more incongruous white-columned portico.

The presence of Van Buren, who proudly began his will "I, Martin Van Buren . . . heretofore Governor of the State and more recently President of the United States, but for the last and happiest years of my life, a Farmer in my native Town," is an elusive ghost in his old mansion. The mantels, mirrors, and the time-damaged wallpaper in the great hall remain, but little else that can be ascribed with certainty to the eighth President. The most Machiavellian of politicians has disappeared with scarcely a trace, little honoring, and no discernible glory.

The mansion, as it was originally built by the Van Ness family in 1797, was a Georgian house in quiet good taste. Van Buren brought it "up to date" by stuccoing the exterior brick and painting it a dark yellow.

NINE

William Henry Harrison

What has caused this great commotion
All the country through?
It is the ball a-rolling on
For Tippecanoe & Tyler too!*

THE NAME OF William Henry Harrison summons up the figure of the Indian fighter, frontier hero, and soldier whose Whig campaign emblems were the log cabin, a keg of hard cider, and a buckeye cane. In vain his opponents protested, "He is not a poor man." One Democrat declared in exasperation. "He does not live in a log cabin. He is a rich man; he lives in a magnificent frame house, is surrounded with a princely estate. So, sir, all this story about the log cabin is falsehood. It is a mean fraud." But it was the Jackson–Van Buren Democrats who had wished the myth on Harrison, for it was in a partisan Baltimore newspaper that the remark was first quoted: "Give him a barrel of hard cider and a pension of two thousand a year . . . he will sit the remainder of his days in a log cabin . . . and study moral philosophy."

General Harrison was the new West's own candidate, but he was also a Virginia gentleman from one of the Tidewater's first families. The first Benjamin Harrison had emigrated to Virginia at some time before 1632 and was prominent enough to become clerk of the Virginia Council. Benjamin, III, was prosperous enough to buy the James River farm lands of Richard Berkeley of Stoke, England, a plantation in Charles City County known originally as Berkeley Hundred. Benjamin Harrison, IV, increased the family fortunes even further by marrying Anne Carter, daughter of Robert "King" Carter, the wealthiest man of his day in the American colonies. Perhaps with the assistance of "King" Carter, this Harrison between 1725 and 1726 erected the still standing mansion at Berkeley where his grandson William Henry Harrison was born on February 9, 1773, to Benjamin Harrison, V, a Signer of the Declaration of Independence.

Young William Henry was old enough to remember the day his father led his Virginians into battle at Yorktown, and more particularly the dreadful day when the family fled Berkeley just ahead of the traitor Benedict Arnold and his army of Tories and Hessians then on their way to take Richmond. Arnold did not overlook The Signer; on the way back the Redcoats so pillaged the house, burning all the furnishings and stealing forty Negroes and all the horses, that Benjamin, V, by then governor of Virginia, was unable to move back into Berkeley for four long years.

Berkeley was not to be so misused again until the Civil War, when General McClellan used it as a headquarters during the sum-

William Henry Harrison (1773-1841)

President Harrison made his reputation as the "Eagle of the West" as an Indian fighter, but actually "Old Tippecanoe" was born at Berkeley, an aristocratic Virginia plantation house overlooking the tranquil James River.

* Campaign song, 1840

mer of 1862* (the Union troops called it "Harrison's Landing"). Foraging Union soldiers all but denuded the estate of its magnificent stands of trees in their search for firewood. Now restored and refurbished by the present owners, Mr. and Mrs. Malcolm Jamieson, it is a magnificent historical landmark, the oldest brick mansion in Virginia and one of the most handsome.

The two-and-a-half-story, thirteen-room Georgian house is flanked by two lesser buildings, to the south by Bachelor's House, used variously as an office, school, or extra guest space, and on the north by the kitchens and servants' quarters, connected to the Big House by an underground passage called the Whistle Hole, a name derived from the eighteenth-century practice of having servants whistle along the way so that they would not taste the food they were carrying.

It was in Bachelor's House that William Henry Harrison, with his brothers and sisters, was tutored in the three *R*s, with some Latin and Greek. William Henry set his mind on being a doctor, but when his father died, he found that his inheritance added up to only a pittance in ready cash, and he could not afford to complete his medical education. Virginia's Governor Richard Henry Lee appealed to the President, and in 1791 Washington signed young Harrison's commission. The neophyte officer, then only eighteen, was jubilant: "In 24 hours from the first conception of the idea of changing my profession," he later recollected, "I was an Ensign in the 1st U.S. Regt of Infantry."

In October 1791 Harrison, footsore and weary, led a company of eighty recruits overland from Philadelphia to Fort Pitt (Pittsburgh), then took them by flatboat down the Ohio to Fort Washington, Cincinnati. It was a fateful remove. Once on the frontier, Harrison was never to return permanently to the eastern seaboard. In the company of such eager young officers, and later explorers, as Ensign Meriwether Lewis and Lieutenant William Clark, he served under the dashing General "Mad Anthony" Wayne at the outset of the hard Indian fighting that was to stretch out over twenty years.

Once, while back on leave in Virginia, Harrison permanently cast his lot with the West, transferring his Berkeley legacy to his brother in return for a large tract in Kentucky and $1500 in notes. Harrison by now had met and fallen in love with Anna Tuthill Symmes, daughter of a New Jersey Revolutionary officer and former chief justice of the New Jersey supreme court. Judge John Cleves Symmes had also yielded to the spell of the Western frontier and contracted for the purchase of one million acres of land between the Great and Little Miami rivers. But an impecunious Virginian officer

* At Berkeley, in April 1862, General Daniel Butterfield, commanding the 3rd New York Brigade, First Division, composed a new bugle call for "extinguish lights," and "Taps" was heard for the first time. It quickly spread to other Union camps, and, by the end of the Civil War, was adopted officially.

Berkeley's high-ceilinged rooms, restored by the present owners, reflect the eighteenth-century tastes of Benjamin Harrison, a signer of the Declaration of Independence, who built the plantation house in 1726. Here Union troops, camping near the James River, first played bugle call "Taps."

was not his idea of a proper son-in-law. With General Wayne's blessing, the two romantic lovers had a runaway marriage (November 25, 1795). Two weeks later, when Judge Symmes caught up with his son-in-law, he demanded, "How do you expect to support my daughter?" In dashing fashion Harrison grasped his scabbard, exclaimed, "My sword is my means of support, sir!"

Apparently it was an answer to the judge's liking. For, though the newlyweds began housekeeping in a log cabin that was the southeast bastion of Fort Washington, within two years Judge Symmes had sold his son-in-law 160 acres of land for $450 at North Bend. There on a high terrace of land some three-eighths of a mile back from the Ohio, Harrison built a cabin with logs cut on the site. It was modest indeed for the young couple and their first daughter: three rooms on the ground floor and two on the second. But this humble cabin served as a kind of cornerstone for the great rambling Big House that Harrison in later years constructed around it.

This early cabin structure, incorporated into the Big House, was sum and substance of Harrison's log-cabin campaign emblem. Contemporary illustrations (the house burned to the ground on July 25, 1858) show a structure wholly without architectural graces except

Berkeley Plantation, birthplace of William Henry Harrison, is one of Virginia's finest Georgian mansions, built between 1725 and 1726. Underground passageways, presaging Monticello, connect the main thirteen-room house with outbuildings, which contained the kitchen and servants' quarters.

At North Bend, Ohio, Harrison built the log-and-wood frame Big House, a rambling structure but no log cabin.

The "log cabin and hard cider" campaign of 1840 capitalized on Harrison's victory over Tecumseh at Tippecanoe.

for small gable windows and lights over the main entrance. The plan of the house was rambling, only one room in depth, with no corridors connecting bedrooms, parlors, drawing room, and dining room. The kitchen was an extension of the back hall, with servants' quarters for the domestic slaves behind. One tin tub, painted black, was kept in the wash house, ready to be filled with hot water, a long process of which Mrs. Harrison complained often until finally she acquired a small portable tub of her own, shaped like a sleigh.

It was from this house that Harrison left for his unsuccessful campaign against Van Buren in 1836 and his final victory in 1840. But almost as permanent a home for the Harrisons—and one far grander in proportions—was Grouseland, known during the years that Harrison was governor of the Indiana Territory (1804–1812) as the White House of the West. As a young officer, Harrison had been appointed by John Adams to be Secretary of the Northwest Territory and at the age of twenty-six he was elected to Congress. There, a few days after his twenty-seventh birthday, he sponsored Harrison's Land Law, a bill that divided half the virgin territory into 320-acre tracts, thus heading off the wholesale land grab of wealthy land speculators. To Adams, Harrison had qualified himself as the obvious candidate to govern this new territory, and in January 1801 he arrived at the frontier settlement of Vincennes to take up residence.

"I am much pleased with this country," Harrison wrote a friend. "Nothing can exceed its beauty and fertility." From Colonel Francis Vigo, with whom Harrison at first stayed, he bought a 300-acre farm and soon in the midst of the fine walnut grove a brick mansion, called Grouseland, was going up. Two and a half stories tall, with four chimneys and thirteen large rooms, it bore a marked resemblance to the Berkeley of Harrison's youth and reputedly cost $20,000; to pay for the brick alone, Harrison bartered 400 acres of land estimated to be worth $1000.

Harrison meant Grouseland to be worthy of his rank and title; when the house was finished in 1804, it was as fine as any in the West. But he was also mindful that his family by now numbered five children, and Vincennes still lay under the threat of Indian attack. The outer walls, eighteen inches thick, were slit for portholes, and the attic had windows designed for sharpshooters, while the roof originally had a lookout post. Massive double shutters closed the great windows in time of attack and a powder magazine was constructed in the cellar. For emergency escapes, there was a trapdoor on the second floor leading to a hidden closet on the ground floor, as well as an underground passage leading to one of the rear buildings. Such precautions were highly necessary; tradition has it that one night when Harrison was walking the floor with his baby son, John Scott, an Indian's bullet crashed through the rear shutter of Grouseland, narrowly missing one future President and the father of yet another President, Benjamin Harrison.

Perhaps Grouseland's most harrowing time began on August 12, 1810, when the great Indian Chieftain Tecumseh arrived with some 400 warriors "painted in the most terrific manner," to parley. For four days the long speeches continued, while Harrison, who had taken the precaution of stationing a company of soldiers out of sight inside Grouseland, sought to outlisten Tecumseh. At the end, the proud Indian warrior is reported to have told the unyielding governor, "The

1840 campaign scarf depicted Harrison as combined farmer, frontiersman, bold negotiator and dashing soldier. Log cabin at top bears no resemblance to Harrison's own house, but it set "the ball a-rolling on for Tippecanoe and Tyler too!"

Great Chief [Madison] is so far off he will not be injured by the war. He may still sit in his town and drink his wine whilst you and I fight it out."

Tecumseh's words were prophetic. The next year, on November 7, 1811, the two opponents were to meet in battle at Tippecanoe, a small river up the Wabash, from which Tecumseh fled in dishonor. The final account was not reckoned, however, until Tecumseh's death in the Battle of the Thames on October 15, 1813.

The end of the war also concluded Harrison's military career; he resigned his commission as major general on May 11, 1814, and left Grouseland to return to the Big House at North Bend. From there he went to the Ohio senate and then the U.S. Senate (1825–1828) and was briefly Minister to Colombia. It was, on the whole, an undistinguished aftermath to his long service. Sober, honest and plain-speaking, Harrison received his friends at North Bend in a very humble setting indeed. Mrs. Harrison, who allowed no politics on Sunday, struck one visitor as "one of the handsomest old ladies I ever saw . . . a perfect beauty and such a good person." Horace Mann, the Massachusetts abolitionist and educator, described disparagingly, the North Bend house's interior: "The furniture of the parlor could not have drawn very largely on anyone's resources. The walls were ornamented with a few portraits, some in frames, some disembodied from a frame. The drawing-room was fitted in more modern style; but the whole furniture and ornaments in these rooms might have cost $200 to $250."

The popularity of Harrison's Land Law, which was thumbed through endlessly by settlers along the frontier, combined with the loyalty of Harrison's old soldiers and even their sons, made plain General Harrison, Hero of the West, the answer to "aristocratic" Van Buren. Harrison was twice the Whig candidate, the second time victoriously so, in one of the most raucous campaigns in history. But at sixty-five, the honor had come too late for Mrs. Harrison, who still mourned the loss over the years of eight of her ten children. Sitting in the Big House at North Bend, she said, "I wish that my husband's friends had left him where he is, happy and contented in retirement." Worn and ailing, she was still preparing to leave for the White House

Grouseland, at Vincennes, Indiana, was the "White House of the West" between 1804 and 1812 while Harrison was Governor of the Indiana Territory. Beneath the elms, Harrison parleyed with Chief Tecumseh while Harrison's troops stayed out of sight within the house. Built to withstand attack, Grouseland had heavy double shutters, rooftop lookout (not shown), and cellar powder magazine. While walking the baby one night, Harrison narrowly escaped being hit when an Indian took a pot shot at him through a window.

At Grouseland, kitchen was in basement and contained escape tunnel (top); Council Chamber (below) was scene of many meetings with Indian chieftains, who squatted on floor. Bricks were made nearby, but glass for window panes came from England, furniture, mantels and wainscoting were brought downriver from Pittsburgh.

Anna Symmes Harrison (circa 1840).

when the news came that President Harrison had died.

Between election and inauguration, Harrison had returned to Berkeley, where he retired to his mother's old room, laboriously penned his long inaugural address, so full of classical references that when Daniel Webster finished editing it, the Yankee legislator remarked to his landlady, "Madame, within twelve hours I have killed seventeen Roman proconsuls—dead as smelts, all of them." As the son of a founder of the Republic, Harrison tried to play the soldier's role in the midst of a rabble of office-seekers. For a man of his age, it was a losing battle. As the Concord philosopher Ralph Waldo Emerson was to note, "He died of the presidency in one month."

Most of President Harrison's meager personal possessions were lost when the Big House at North Bend burned. Harrison's eldest son had been appointed receiver of the land office in Vincennes by Monroe, and in 1812 moved into Grouseland, living there nearly a decade. The house served for a time as a library, later as a hotel, then as a storage shed for grain, and was finally abandoned. The Vincennes Chapter of the Daughters of the American Revolution rescued the house from demolition in 1909. It has been a memorial and museum since 1911 and is furnished as nearly as possible with pieces of the period of Harrison's residence, if not the actual family furniture.

TEN

John Tyler

PRESIDENTS are nominated for their national appeal, Vice-Presidents usually to promote interparty harmony and to broaden the spectrum of sectional appeal. Such a candidate in 1840 was Virginia's John Tyler, hand-picked by Henry Clay to run with the aging war hero General William Henry Harrison and make the winning Whig ticket "Tippecanoe and Tyler Too." When Harrison died a month after his inauguration, even Clay was aghast. No President of the United States had died in office, and there was even strong feeling that Tyler should call himself only Acting President and stay out of the White House. But when Tyler showed, by taking the oath as President in Brown's Hotel in Washington, that he intended to be Chief Executive in name as well as deed, the vain, confident Clay only smiled. "Tyler dares not resist." Clay said scornfully. "I will drive him before me."

Henry Clay, as it turned out, had reckoned without his man. Tyler was proud, stubborn and opinionated, probably the closest thing to the Virginia Cavalier of romantic fiction that history has produced and submitted to the intense limelight of high office. In Tyler's case, background and family were all-important. Born on a plantation called Greenway in Charles City County, Virginia, on March 29, 1790, he was the fourth generation in America to bear the name of John Tyler, a fact he never forgot. The family had been prominent from the start, and Tyler's grandfather had crossed political swords with Benjamin Harrison, his Charles City County neighbor, Signer of the Declaration, and father of "Old Tippecanoe."

Young John Tyler was a fine-spirited, attractive, and highly intelligent lad. Best scholar in his class, he also led the student revolt against the sadistic teacher, Master McMurdo, tied him up and left him locked in the schoolhouse. When the schoolmaster had wriggled free, he rushed angrily to John's father, Judge Tyler, demanding that the boys be whipped. Judge Tyler drew himself to full height, dispatching the bullying master with the classic *"Sic semper tyrannis!"* But such high jinks did not interfere with young Tyler's scholastic progress. He entered William and Mary, the traditional family college, at thirteen, graduated at seventeen, was admitted to the bar while still in his teens, and at twenty-one was elected to the state legislature, the same time that his father was elected governor. Only one vote in the whole county was cast against the fledgling politician (Master McMurdo?).

With a brilliant career assured, John Tyler, twenty-three, married a wealthy planter's daughter, Letitia Christian, of Cedar Grove, Virginia, a striking young woman exactly his own age. It was a happy marriage, with seven children, although Letitia Tyler was struck down with partial paralysis toward the end of her life, and died while her

Tyler's birthplace, Greenway, was a plantation house in Charles City County, Virginia, built about 1750.

John Tyler (1790–1862) was the fourth generation bearing the same name to be born in Virginia. His first wife, who came from the same planter aristocracy, died in the White House while Tyler was President. His second wife, Julia Gardner (below), married him in one of the most talked-about June-and-September romances in White House history.

husband was at midterm in the White House. John Tyler meanwhile continued to rise; he was elected to Congress, twice to the U.S. Senate, and twice governor of Virginia.

The one setback in his political career came in 1836, when he was defeated for Vice-President on the states'-rights Whig ticket. Exhausted from his political labor, he returned to the quiet streets of Williamsburg, then rapidly drifting toward becoming a provincial backwater since Jefferson had moved the capital to Richmond. There in 1837 Tyler bought the roomy house of N. Beverley Tucker and resolved to enjoy good conversation, his old friends from college days, and his children.

Yet he ran again for Vice-President and won. He expected but a minor role. He was outside his Williamsburg house, down on his knees in the dust playing "knucks" with his children, when the messenger from Washington arrived breathlessly to tell him that President Harrison had died. Tears streamed down Tyler's face as he rose from the game of marbles and went inside to inform his semi-invalid wife. The situation in the national capital was more confused than even he could imagine. Not only was he the first Vice-President to be called on to fill the highest office because of the death of the incumbent; it soon appeared that Tyler was a President without a party. A onetime Jacksonian Democrat who had left the party to join the Whigs, he completely alienated the Whigs by vetoing the Clay-sponsored bill to revive the Bank of the United States. His whole Cabinet resigned in protest, with the lone exception of Daniel Webster, then Secretary of State and engaged in negotiating the Maine–Canada boundary dispute with England.

Tyler's states'-rights position was in many ways an anachronism, but this fact we know only in retrospect through the smoking battle-fields of the Civil War. So was Tyler's optimistic hope that slavery would wither away through the dispersion of the Negro population throughout the Union. But they were opinions held by other of the Virginia gentry, and maintained with courage and conviction. Tyler himself, as a senator, instructed to reverse his vote of censure, had preferred to resign instead. Now faced with no party of his own, and jokingly referred to as "His Accidency," he preferred to govern in hope of creating a personal following. It was a hope doomed to failure, but his administration was not without its victories. The boundary dispute with Canada was finally settled by the Ashburton Treaty; Tyler's envoys opened China's ports to Western trade, and in the last weeks of his administration, Tyler had the satisfaction of seeing the Congress vote for the annexation of Texas.

Toward the end of his term, on February 28, 1844, the President decided on a trip to Mount Vernon aboard the warship the USS *Princeton* which with its heavy armor and a new gun was the most devastating ship afloat. The gun known as the "Peacemaker," was capable of throwing a 225-pound shell some 5000 yards. Before lunch the presidential party witnessed a trial firing of this awe-inspiring weapon. At the end of the outing, the party wanted to hear the mighty "Peacemaker" roar once more; the gun exploded, killing the captain, two members of the cabinet, and Mr. David Gardiner, of Gardiner's Island, New York.

Tyler escorted Gardiner's grieving daughter Julia back to the White House. His kindness at the moment reinforced the widower President's suit already in progress, and in New York, on June 28,

Sherwood Forest has a 300-foot-long façade, made by joining the kitchen and laundry (left) and office and ballroom (right). The parlor is unchanged from President Tyler's time, as are the clavichord and Chinese garden seats (above). Beside Tyler's law books is the music box that chimed when one of Tyler's sons returned to the deserted mansion after the Civil War.

1844, the President, fifty-four, and Julia, twenty-four, were wed in a January–May wedding that had all Washington agog and talking. Julia Tyler proudly rode to the inauguration of Polk at the end of her new husband's term, wearing about her neck the gold pen with which John Tyler at the last moment had signed the admission of Texas to the Union.

In 1842 President Tyler had purchased for $12,000 a rundown estate of some 1200 acres just three miles from his childhood home at Greenway. This estate he decided to call Sherwood Forest, thinking of himself as by then something of a political Robin Hood. The estate, between the Chickahominy and James rivers, was ideally situated, thirty miles east of Richmond and twenty miles west of Williamsburg. A conscientious farmer, Tyler labored hard to bring the plantation back, using thirty to forty slaves and putting in the ground 8000 bushels of lime in one year alone.

The original house, when Tyler bought the plantation, was a clapboard structure built in 1790. This Tyler renovated and doubled in size, connecting the old kitchen and laundry to the east wing by a covered colonnade, and adding a corresponding wing on the west for his office and the ballroom. Completed, the house, although only one room deep and three stories tall merely in the central portion, has a 300-foot façade, one of the longest house-fronts in the U.S.

The second Mrs. Tyler proved as prolific with offspring as the first; both wives presenting Tyler with seven children. It is interesting to note that the first Tyler child was born in 1816, the last died in 1935, a time span of 119 years! Not only was the house filled with children; the Tylers also entertained extensively. Guests were invited to ride in the fine coach with liveried footmen, or travel in the Tyler barge, which Julia Gardiner Tyler described enthusiastically in her letters: The four oarsmen wore "bright blue with white calico shirts—white linen pants—black patent leather belts—straw hats painted blue, with 'Pocahontas' upon them in white—and in one corner of the shirt collar (which is turned down) is worked with braid a bow and arrow (to signify the Forest) and in the other corner the President's and my initials."

Entertainment within the house was of as high an order. Wrote Mrs. Tyler's sister while a guest at Sherwood Forest, "We danced incessantly until one o'clock when the first supper was announced.... The mottoes and confectionery were of the most expensive kind—candied fruits, ices, etc. in abundance. This over we danced again until three, when the second supper was announced.... Such turkeys and such saddles of mutton! the fat on the former three inches thick—there was venison, wild duck, etc., etc. Champagne flowed unceasingly —of the nicest kind."

For seventeen years the former President enjoyed this idyllic life,

President Tyler purchased an estate near his birthplace and named it Sherwood Forest, since at that time he thought of himself, ruefully, as something of a political outlaw.

The long narrow ballroom of Sherwood Forest once echoed to the music of the waltz when ante-bellum belles whirled in hooped dresses. It is still used for fashionable coming-out parties by the Tyler family.

Empire-style hallway has slender colonial spindles supporting the steamed-wood banister, and original carving on the door panels.

occupying himself with his correspondence and his duties as chancellor of William and Mary, an office vacant since it had been last held by George Washington; occasionally the Tylers went to the seashore, or to White Sulphur Springs or Saratoga Springs to take the waters. But in Virginia and throughout the South war clouds were gathering. Tyler struggled to keep the peace. He condemned South Carolina's nullification and secession and, as Virginia's commissioner to Buchanan, tried to keep Fort Sumter neutralized. As a final move, born more of desperation than of hope, he presided over the peace conference called by Virginia in Washington. When this "palaver of Peace," as James Russell Lowell sarcastically called it, failed, Tyler became an enthusiastic supporter of the new Confederate States of America. "The whole state is clad in steel under the command of the most accomplished leaders," he wrote. "In a week from this time, James River will bustle with fortifications, and Charles City will be far safer than Staten Island." Tyler went so far as to propose the occupation of Washington by the Confederacy, and the appropriation of the Stars and Stripes as the Confederate flag to emphasize that the South was the true Union, and that it was the North that had seceded from its principles!

Such high hopes were possible up to the day Tyler died, January 18, 1862. Five of Tyler's sons went off to fight under the Stars and Bars, but war was to obliterate the world Tyler so loved. Soon Yankees were encamped under the trees of Sherwood Forest, and had actually stuffed hay under the plantation house in preparation for burning when a Union general ordered the men away. Julia Gardiner Tyler, who had already hidden the china and silverware, made her way, with her younger childen, to live out the war with her mother in New York.

Kept in the house, which still remains in the hands of the Tyler family, is the Swiss music box which rests now as always on the piano. Family tradition has it that when sixteen-year-old David Gardiner Tyler came trudging home from the defeated Confederate Army, his footsteps on the ravaged, deserted hall set the music box to playing, telling him that, at last, he was truly home.

The present owner of the family mansion, Mr. J. Alfred Tyler, and his wife, Katharine Thomason Tyler, maintain Sherwood Forest as both a home and a historic site. Children swim in the spring-fed, sun-dappled pond where President Tyler once kept his decoy geese, and Tylers still hunt over the ancestral acres for game birds and deer as they have for over a hundred years. In the house, the relics of the President are kept on display, including the portrait of the President by G. P. A. Healey which hangs over the Italian marble mantel in the parlor, where the wallpaper dates from 1844. Facing him across the hall is the portrait of Julia Gardiner, who died in 1889. Among the original pieces are a pair of porcelain garden seats given to Tyler by Caleb Cushing, Commissioner to China; a silver pitcher sent to John Tyler by the ladies of Brazoria County, Texas; and in the dining room, the original Duncan Phyfe table which once groaned with turkey and saddles of lamb, while overhead the original crystal chandelier still shines. The body of the President, however, is no longer buried (as he had directed) at Sherwood Forest, but has been removed to Hollywood Cemetery, Richmond, Virginia, where the fifth, and last, of the Virginia Presidents rests beside James Monroe, fourth of the Great Virginia Dynasty.

ELEVEN

James Knox Polk

James Knox Polk (1795-1849), a staunch, determined Presbyterian, was called "Little Hickory," and is ranked as the only strong President between Jackson and Lincoln.

WHO IS JAMES K. POLK?" the Whigs chanted gleefully during the 1844 campaign. And well they might. Even Polk's own party, the Jacksonian Democrats, and his fellow politicians, were hard put to it to explain to the country at large just why their man from Tennessee should win. But James K. Polk, or "Little Hickory" as he was sometimes called, had favored for the annexation of Texas, with California and Oregon thrown in as well. So, it seemed, did the American people, and Polk at the age of forty-nine was swept into office.

Who is James K. Polk? Historians today would place him among the near-great Presidents, men of the caliber of Theodore Roosevelt, Grover Cleveland, and John Adams. In many ways history could not have picked a more unlikely spokesman for Manifest Destiny. James Knox Polk was born on November 2, 1795, the eldest of ten children, into a strict Presbyterian world, the son of a prosperous farmer and slave-holder in Mecklenburg County, North Carolina. His mother, Jane Knox, who was to outlive him, made the future President a strict Sabbatarian, but also a scholar. The family moved to Middle Tennessee when James was eleven, and there he studied first at Murfreesboro Academy and later at the University of North Carolina. He was salutatorian of his University class (1818), and earned first honors in mathematics and classics. He began studying law in Nashville with Judge Felix Grundy (later senator and attorney general under Van Buren), was admitted to the bar, and, at twenty-eight, elected to the Tennessee legislature, where he enjoyed the friendship of Andrew Jackson.

On January 1, 1824, the young legislator married Sarah Childress, also a strict Presbyterian and a strikingly handsome woman. Politics soon became the be-all and end-all of Polk's life. A gifted, precise and stirring orator, he was soon known as the "Napoleon of the Stump." Elected in 1825 to Congress, he served there for fourteen years, the last four as Speaker of the House. He was the backbone of the Jacksonian Democrats, serving as floor leader and leading debator. When Andrew Jackson decided to kill the Bank of the United States, it was to Polk he instinctively turned. "The hydra of corruption is only *scotched, not dead,*" Jackson wrote Polk in a confidential letter on December 16, 1832, and added, "Attend to this." Polk did.

Polk was the first "dark-horse" candidate in American politics, the secret candidate of the group who clustered in aging Andrew Jackson's Hermitage office and plotted the Democratic road to victory. Polk was also the only Speaker of the House to become Chief Executive, a rare compliment. But once in the White House, he

Polk's boyhood home in Columbia, Tennessee, was built, and perhaps designed, by his father shortly after 1816. The fan-shaped transom in this solidly built farmer's house testifies to family's taste and affluence.

wrote, "In any event I intend to be *myself* President of the U.S." He set himself four goals: reduction of the tariff; establishment of an independent Treasury; settlement of the Oregon boundary dispute; and acquisition of California. All four goals he achieved, fighting one war with Mexico and narrowly avoiding another with England (by compromising in Oregon on the demand of "54–40 or Fight!" and settling instead for the 49th parallel).

Polk governed with a single-minded energy, and it left him prematurely white-haired and aged before his time. For his retirement he had bought the colonnaded mansion of his old law mentor, Judge Grundy, which with its extensive formal gardens occupied a whole city block in Nashville, Tennessee; but he lived only three months after his retirement to "Polk Place," passing away on June 5, 1849, in his fifty-fourth year. His wife (there were no children) lived on there almost into the twentieth century, dying at Polk Place on August 14, 1891, a few weeks short of her eighty-eighth birthday.

It is one of the tragedies surrounding America's great historic houses that Polk Place, despite Polk's own explicit instructions to

hand it over to the state of Tennessee, was allowed to be demolished after Mrs. Polk's death. The Polk shrine has thus become the ancestral home in Columbia on land bought by President Polk's father, Samuel, on May 18, 1816. Adjoining it is the home of the President's two sisters, also a historic shrine.

Polk's boyhood home is modest, built of handmade brick, and may well have had Polk's father as architect as well as owner. Surrounding it were flower and kitchen gardens, a carriage house, stable, smokehouse, and slave quarters. On the inside the arrangement is typical of the well-off Tennessee farmer's abode, with a double parlor off the hall, and a porch (now a museum). To the rear, the original brick paving that led to the detached kitchen and servants' room has been recently uncovered and restored. Fortunately much Polk memorabilia has been preserved, including such personal items as Mrs.

The Polk House interiors at Columbia are largely decorated with pieces from Polk's own mansion in Nashville (since destroyed). The double parlor (top, left) has a rosewood sofa. The French gilt candelabrum, beneath Sarah Polk's portrait, was used in the White House. The French mahogany étagère (above), was imported from New Orleans and displays a marble inkstand from Italy, and the fan, presented to Mrs. Polk at her husband's inaugural ball, with eleven miniatures of the Presidents up to that date. Massive mahogany bed stands in the east bedroom.

Polk's inaugural fan, a satin evening gown from Worth of Paris, her lace mitts and eyeglasses. Much furniture associated with the President has been placed in the house, including the parlor furniture from Polk Place, two large rosewood sofas, and matching mahogany armchairs. On one marble-top console table is a French gilt clock under glass, a type much admired by Polk. Of particular interest is the colored-marble mosaic table with an American eagle bearing the arms of the United States, a present from a friend in Tunis, one of the last gifts received by Polk before his death. On the flag are thirty stars, a reminder of the Union's growth during an adminstration that saw the United States at last reach from one coast to the other and increase its territory by 552,568 square miles to attain the status of a great continental power.

TWELVE

Zachary Taylor

THERE HAVE BEEN many Presidents with distinguished war records, from General Washington to Lieutenant John F. Kennedy, U.S.N.R. But career officers are a rarity; there have been only four: Wm. Henry Harrison, U. S. Grant, Dwight D. Eisenhower, and Zachary Taylor. "Old Rough and Ready," as Taylor's adoring troops called this plain-spoken, roughly dressed general, was also one of our great frontiersmen and Indian fighters. Early breveted major for his heroic defense of Fort Harrison overlooking the Wabash against Tecumseh's braves in 1812, "Zach" Taylor was made a colonel for his services in the Black Hawk War (1832) and a brigadier general after his rout of the Seminole and Mikasuki Indians in the dense cypress swamps and hammocks around Lake Okeechobee in 1837. As historian Claude Bowers has pointed out, "No single servant of the Republic did more, or as much, in negotiations or in battle to open the settlement of the white man of the rich commonwealths of Indiana, Illinois, Missouri, Wisconsin and Michigan."

Born a Virginian in Orange County on November 24, 1784, Zachary Taylor was transported over the Appalachians while still an infant by his mother to join Revolutionary Colonel Richard Taylor. Their first home was a log house on Muddy Fork of Beargrass Creek, five miles east of the swampy frontier settlement of Louisville, Kentucky. The setting was primitive indeed. A contemporary account of the Taylors' first house in Springfield describes "a small log cabin, about twelve feet square . . . belonging to Colonel Richard Taylor. . . . This residence was on the edge of a dense canebrake. Here we were saluted at night by the howling of wolves."

On this new frontier three factors early entered into Zachary Taylor's life: the menace of hostile Indians, the presence of Negro slaves (by 1800 his father owned twenty-six), and the life on the Ohio River, for which Beargrass Creek served as a sheltered anchorage. In such a primitive setting Zachary Taylor's schooling was of necessity minimal—spelling was an enduring torment all his life—but he did learn how to load a rifle on the run, ride a horse, and grow to admire plainness in speech and appearance and, above all, physical courage. About 1790 Taylor's father began building the three-story brick house which still stands at 5608 Apache Road, Springfield, Kentucky. The house was then the center of a 400-acre farm overlooking the Ohio and was Taylor's home until he joined the Army as a first lieutenant at twenty-three. A substantial house, the Taylor homestead had quarters for Negro house servants in the basement, a thirty-foot hallway which ran from double front doors to the back, dividing the twin parlors. On the second floor were four spacious bedrooms; on the top floor were housed the Taylors' coachmen. It was more than sub-

Zachary Taylor (1784–1850) was born in Virginia but grew up in Kentucky, becoming one of our leading soldier-Presidents. His daughter eloped with Jefferson Davis, later President of the Confederate States of America.

stantial for the frontier, a fact underlined by the handsome carved walnut paneling.

When Taylor's father died in January 1829, Zachary's childhood home was sold, a fact Taylor lamented at the time in a letter to his brothers-in-law: "It would have been very gratifying to me if it had been in your power to purchase the old family establishment . . . I was very desirous that it should have remained in the family." Taylor, at the time, was stationed at Fort Snelling. He was to return only briefly to farm nearby the homestead, and wrote, in April 1816, "I have comenced making corn and tobacco & am now in my own cabbin where I will always be extreamely happy to take you by the hand. . . ." It was a brief civilian interlude. For almost all of the thirty-nine years from 1808 to 1847 that Taylor was in the U.S. Army, he and his Maryland-born wife, Margaret Mackall Smith, moved constantly from one frontier Army post to the next, raising over the years five daughters (of whom three died) and a son.

Merely listing the posts Taylor commanded gives some indica-

Taylor's boyhood home in Springfield, Kentucky, was built by his father between 1785 and 1790. Slave quarters were in the basement, coachman's in the attic.

Margaret Smith Taylor (1788-1852).

tion of the rugged frontier life this family endured—Fort Howard, Michigan Territory; Cantonment Bay, St. Louis; Fort Jessup, Louisiana; Fort Snelling, unorganized territory (Minnesota); Fort Crawford, Michigan Territory. But even in log-cabin posts, life continued; it was at Prairie du Chien, Wisconsin, that one of Taylor's junior officers, Lieutenant Jefferson Davis, fell in love with Taylor's eighteen-year-old daughter, Sarah Knox Taylor. The gruff father set his face against the courtship, telling a fellow officer, "I will be damned if another daughter of mine shall marry into the Army. I know enough of the family life of officers. I scarcely know my own children, or they me."

The two lovers persisted; three years later they were married in Springfield, Kentucky, in the absence of Sarah Knox's parents. It was a brief and tragic honeymoon; three months later Sarah Knox died of malaria at Locust Grove, Louisiana, at the plantation of Jeff Davis' sister, a tragic blow that made Davis a near-recluse for eight long years. Only ten years later did the handsome Jeff Davis and Taylor, then on his way to command his army in New Orleans on its way to the Rio Grande, finally meet, on a Mississippi River packet. By then their sorrow was a common one; the two men greeted each other fondly, and after Taylor's victory against overwhelming odds at Buena Vista (1847), the doughty old warrior was proud to report to Washington, "Colonel Davis, though severely wounded, remained in the saddle until the close of the action."

The General Zachary Taylor who rode into history during the Mexican War at Palo Alto, Resaca de la Palma, Monterey, and Buena Vista was a curious one. A far cry from the punctilious General Winfield Scott ("Old Fuss and Feathers"), Taylor was often mistaken for a farmer; short and bandy-legged, barely five-foot eight-inches tall though powerfully built, Taylor wore a "blue checked gingham coat, blue trousers without any braid, a linen waistcoat and a broadbrimmed straw hat" in the field. According to one soldier, "On horseback [he] looks just like a toad." But in battle, astride his war horse Old Whitey, he coaxed the utmost from his troops. When Taylor ordered Captain Bragg "Double-shot your guns and give 'em hell," his remark became legend. Bullets knocked off buttons, ripped his sleeve, and—as his soldiers sang—

> *The shot flew about him as thick as any hail,*
> *And the only injury he there received*
> *Was a compound fracture of his brown coat tail.*

"Old Rough and Ready" was a soldier's soldier through and through. Stubborn and courageous, as a host of junior officers from Grant, Meade, and Bragg to Sherman and Jeff Davis testified, he remained for all his Regular Army rank a civilian at heart. Or, as Taylor frankly confessed to Jefferson Davis, "It would be much more congenial to my feelings to be sitting with you under your own vine & figtree discussing the best mode of raising cotton."

As a planter Taylor was only mildly successful. On April 21, 1842, he had bought Cypress Grove Plantation with its 1923 acres and eighty-one slaves for $35,000 in notes and $60,000 in cash. This plantation in Mississippi, ten miles below Rodney, then on the eastern bank of the Mississippi (the river has since shifted its bed), was well and humanely operated, but constant river flooding, followed by droughts, had brought crop failures and diseases; the modest planta-

Hallway of Taylor's boyhood home, Springfield, Kentucky.

After the Mexican War, General Taylor retired to his Spanish Cottage in Baton Rouge (left) *to take up life of a planter. Mrs. Taylor recruited soldiers on the sick list from the barracks to ready this simple, four-room house with its wide veranda. He looked forward to simple peace and quiet. Instead he was sent to the White House and, worn out from fever and campaigning, died sixteen months after becoming President.*

tion house with its "capital parlor" and "colonnaded verandah" remained modest indeed.

The house to which Taylor retired after the Mexican War, and from which he left for the White House, was the "Spanish cottage" in Baton Rouge, only a few steps from The Barracks. A simple elevated wooden structure with a wide encompassing veranda gallery, it had only four rooms, but Mrs. Taylor, with the help of Negro servants and soldiers recruited from the sick list, made it homey, with a garden of roses and honeysuckle and a pasture for the General's horse, Old Whitey.

Taylor's regret at leaving for the White House was genuine. His gracious wife, ailing but a far cry from the old crone puffing her pipe by the open fire political opponents pictured her, dreaded it, and with reason. Taylor was worn out by years of frontier living, fever, and campaigning. He died in 1850, a few days after dedicating the Washington Monument on a broiling July Fourth, only sixteen months after taking office. His last words were "I expect the summons soon—I have endeavored to discharge all my official duties faithfully—I regret nothing, but am sorry that I am about to leave my friends." He is buried in a plot in Springfield, Kentucky, in the small family graveyard that he himself had ordered fenced with stone near his boyhood home whose sale he had so regretted.

THIRTEEN
Millard Fillmore

Millard Fillmore's house on Franklin Street, Buffalo, was the future President's home during his fifteen years as state legislator and Congressman. While not nearly as grand as campaign literature indicated, it stood for solid respectability.

ILLARD FILLMORE arrived at the presidency by inadvertence. When Zachary Taylor ("Old Rough and Ready") agreed to be a Whig and run, second place went to the rotund, florid party regular from Buffalo, New York, simply as a way to round out the ticket and placate several minor factions. Yet Fillmore fulfilled the role fate awarded him by being superlatively the average man, and on the whole this was enough to produce a reasonably good President.

Indeed, it was probably Fillmore's averageness that made him such a sympathetic figure. Like many in his generation he was born in a log-cabin farmhouse on a recent frontier in Cayuga County, New York. The land in west-central New York state had been cleared by his father. A poor boy, Millard had a scant education, bought his first book—a dictionary—at the age of eighteen. Later campaign biographers were to make much of his early hard years apprenticed to a wool-carder, of how as an apprentice he bought his freedom for thirty dollars to study law, paying his way as an itinerant schoolteacher.

He was helped mightily by his wife, Abigail Powers, a Baptist minister's daughter, two years his senior and herself a schoolteacher, from Stillwater, New York. He persevered until he was admitted to the bar in 1823 at the age of twenty-three, practicing first in East Aurora and later in Buffalo. He was well-enough thought of to catch the eye of political boss Thurlow Weed, and he put in fifteen years as a state legislator and congressman. The couple, with their daughter Mary Abigail and young son, Millard Powers Fillmore, were the essence of respectability. And if their Buffalo house at 180 Franklin Street (since torn down) was not quite as grand as campaign illustrators would have it, nonetheless it stood for solid respectability.

Unhappily, Abigail Fillmore never lived to return to Buffalo. During the emotional inauguration speech of Franklin Pierce, she became chilled; she died four weeks later in Washington's Willard Hotel. Fillmore had planned a splendid retirement for them, buying the Hollister House on Buffalo's Niagara Square, then the city's most exclusive residential quarter. There within a year Fillmore had to endure another sharp blow when his only daughter, Mary Abigail, who had served as White House hostess, died, turning the high gabled Gothic manse into a house of long mourning.

That Millard Fillmore at the age of fifty-three should choose to retire in elegance was an acceptable ending to the log-cabin-to-White-House dream of every schoolboy. That he should choose to live in such baronial splendor was also part and parcel of the times. For in the wave of eclecticism that swept into fashion after 1820, Gothic (or Gothick, as its adherents preferred) was evocative of mystery, high

Abigail Powers, a minister's daughter and schoolteacher, helped her husband Millard Fillmore, (left) overcome his poor early education, and become a prosperous lawyer and successful politician.

romance, and splendid ennoblement. James Fenimore Cooper, whose novels were read eagerly, scorned classic temples, remodeled his own Otsego Hall in Gothic and convinced Samuel F. B. Morse, inventor of the telegraph, to do likewise.

Gothic was considered somehow a more "religious" architecture and at the same time the only proper style, with its battlements and crenelations, for West Point, Virginia Military Institute, even the Smithsonian Institution in Washington. Nor was the style necessarily retrograde. The Fillmores had been one of our most up-to-date First Families, installing the first kitchen range as well as the first outsized soldered zinc bathtub. And as they, and other patrons of wealth, took for granted, Gothic was to evoke a sense of the moss and patina of history—and was also meant to include modern plumbing. Indeed the very antic shapes, towers, belvederes, and turrets allowed by the style actually disguised a far freer internal organization of spaces than had been possible in the four-square plans of the Federal period, so much so, in fact, that the architectural historian Wayne Andrews has stated that "the modern concept of the free plan might be said to date from this period."

The sense of mourning that surrounded the Fillmore mansion on Niagara Square lifted in 1858 with the marriage of the ex-President to Mrs. Caroline Carmichael McIntosh, the forty-five-year-old widow of an Albany merchant. The wedding itself caused a pretty flutter at

Campaign biographers made much of Fillmore's early struggles to earn a living as a youth, when he was an apprentice wool carder and farm hand educating himself in his spare hours and "at the nooning" studying his books.

After the White House, former President Fillmore returned to become Buffalo's First Citizen, purchasing the Gothick Manse on Niagara Square. For all its turrets and gables, it was known to be "a home of industry and temperance, with plain diet, no tobacco, no swearing." Here Fillmore and his second wife, Mrs. Caroline McIntosh, entertained such dignitaries as Presidents Lincoln and Johnson. The house was later converted to the Castle Inn, finally demolished in 1929 to make way for the Hotel Statler.

the time, for Fillmore romantically chose to be married in the room of the Schuyler mansion in Albany where some seventy-five years before Alexander Hamilton had taken to wife the beauteous Elizabeth Schuyler.

The new lady in residence did little to change the plain, simple living pattern of Millard Fillmore. As one of Fillmore's biographers described it, "It was a home of industry and temperance, with plain diet, no tobacco, no swearing." The Fillmores entertained ponderously, but well, such visiting dignitaries as President Lincoln and President Johnson. Naturally public-spirited, Fillmore himself became an indefatigable benefactor and philanthropist, freely gave his time to the YMCA, the Humane Society for the Prevention of Cruelty to Animals, the Buffalo Bar Association, Fine Arts Academy, the University of Buffalo (which he helped found), and served as chancellor of the Buffalo Historical Society, which he had helped establish in 1842.

Only once did the sharp tempers and tensions of the period come close to boiling over in his presence. When all of Buffalo went into deep mourning on Lincoln's death, draping their houses in black

crêpe, an angry mob gathered in Niagara Square on April 27, 1865, and started pelting the Fillmore mansion, noticeably undraped, with bottles of ink. It was an indignity Fillmore little merited; he was deeply concerned at the time with a grave illness in the family and had simply not heard of his neighbors' plans to deck their walls in mourning.

In many ways history has dealt shabbily with Fillmore. The house from which he left Buffalo for the White House has since been torn down. The Gothic manse was sold, made into the Castle Inn, and later demolished. On its site is the present Hotel Statler. Even Fillmore's own possessions were put on the auction block, including an unopened cask of Madeira, a gift of Commodore Perry nearly a half-century before, which the abstemious Fillmore had never tapped. Perhaps the worst blow of all was the decision of Fillmore's only son and heir to burn all of his father's letters, papers, and journals. Fillmore's reputation thus must rest on his own plainly written autobiography and the contemporary evidence of a none too sympathetic, ever-partisan press.

FOURTEEN

Franklin Pierce

The Father and The Son
The one fought to make,
The other labors to
PRESERVE the Union

THIS CAMPAIGN SLOGAN—emblazoned on a faded flag now to be found in Franklin Pierce's birthplace in the quiet rural New Hampshire town of Hillsboro—is as fitting a key as any to unlock the secret of the Young Hickory of the Granite Hills who in 1852 defeated his august opponent, General Winfield Scott, by a comfortable margin, but who today remains the least-known of American Presidents, scarcely acknowledged even in his home state. It may well be argued that New Hampshire's Pierce merits better from posterity.

The harsh judgment of history is that Franklin Pierce owed his nomination and election to the presidency to the fact that he was willing to temporize on the slavery issue, thus gaining the support of the Southern Democrats. This vacillation in the face of what now appears an inevitable conflict did not grow from lack of courage. We have the word of General Ulysses S. Grant that Pierce was "a gentleman and a man of courage." Faced with the horror of a civil war Pierce considered slavery the lesser evil. He resolved to be a strict constitutional President and set his star by the larger concept of the Union. It is one of the tragic ironies of history that his effort to defend and preserve the Union should have been taken in retrospect as a failure of will. For if the drift toward civil war could have been averted, Franklin Pierce would have been reckoned one of the principal authors of concord among the states.

Franklin Pierce was born November 23, 1804, the sixth of eight children of Benjamin Pierce and Anna Kendrick, in the just-finished house which still stands in the village of Hillsboro, New Hampshire. The future President owed much to his bluff, strong-willed, determined father Benjamin, who had been orphaned at the age of six. As the elder Pierce wrote, he was himself "without any learning except what I had gathered . . . by attending school from the age of ten to sixteen years, three weeks in each year." When the news of Lexington and Concord reached Chelmsford, Massachusetts, Benjamin Pierce, then eighteen, was one of the first to enlist in the Massachusetts militia. Soldiering apparently was to Benjamin's liking; he stayed with the colors through the entire war, fighting at Saratoga, enduring the winters at Valley Forge, ending up the Revolution in New York. "On account of the

Pierce homestead in Hillboro Upper Village, New Hampshire, was finished in 1804, the year Franklin Pierce was born there. The house also served as a wayside inn and mustering spot for militia in War of 1812.

Living room of the Pierce Homestead has Healey's portrait of Franklin Pierce, donated by the niece of Caleb Cushing, a member of Pierce's Cabinet. The broad paneling was made from logs cut on the farm. The plaster walls were decorated with stencils; brick for the fireplace was made in kilns on the site.

depreciation of continental money," he wrote, "finding myself without funds . . . I accepted the appointment of agent to explore lands owned by Col. Stoddard in New Hampshire."

The task of surveying opened Benjamin's eyes to the possibilities along what was then the frontier:

> When I had finished my business, passing from Stoddard through Hillsboro, I called at a log hut and, after a few words, asked how he lived? As other farmers. Where do you get your meat? In yonder brooks. Where your meal? At Litchfield. I asked him if he would sell—he replied he would. I asked him to go along with me to a Justice of the Peace and I would purchase his farm, which was about fifty acres.
>
> After the deed was executed, I continued my journey to Chelmsford, and the spring following, in company with a soldier, my companion in the army, I came to Hillsboro and took up my residence in the log hut I had lately purchased. Here I commenced cutting and clearing away the trees, lying on a blanket with my companion, and living as best we could.

99   FRANKLIN PIERCE

Benjamin Pierce was not alone for long. Soon other English and Scotch-Irish farmers began leaving their Massachusetts homes for the virgin forests. In 1790 Benjamin, whose first wife had died, married Anna Kendrick, and in 1804 they were able to move into their new big house, a far cry from the Indian cabin Benjamin had bought with its fifty acres for fifty dollars. The farm grew to 250 acres and Benjamin farmed them well; he was also selling graphite from the mountain to Dixon, one of the first lead-pencil manufacturers.

In a New England town the size of Hillsboro, the Pierce homestead was automatically called The Mansion House, and to it came the local citizenry for balls, meetings, and (since Benjamin also ran a tavern there) for relaxation. It was here that young Franklin Pierce got his first lessons in politics and patriotism. In 1807 the father had been asked to form the militia of Hillsboro County, New Hampshire's largest, and received the rank of colonel, later of brigadier general. Franklin Pierce was only eight when he watched his father demonstrating the manual of arms and new firearms to the recruits in the ballroom where General Benjamin Pierce's commission still hangs. Even more exciting to a romantic young boy was the double marriage that took place in the ballroom on Christmas Day, 1812, when Franklin's two sisters, Elizabeth and Nancy, married the two McNeil brothers just before they rode off to war. There must have been a glint of pride in the eyes of the old Revolutionary soldier, General Pierce, as his two sons and two sons-in-law marched off to defend their country. But, as young Franklin was to learn early, war has its price. Handsome young John McNeil, a hero of Lundy's Lane, was struck by a poisoned arrow in the Everglades and returned a cripple.

Rugged, unlettered, dominating, and patriarchal, General Pierce was determined that his son should enjoy the benefits denied him, and in 1820 young Franklin duly enrolled in Bowdoin in the class of 1824, along with such distinguished collegemates as Calvin Ellis Stowe (husband of Harriet Beecher Stowe), Henry Wadsworth Longfellow, and young Pierce's particular friend, Nathaniel Hawthorne. Pierce apparently brought some of the rough, roistering habits of his father's tavern with him to college. In his junior year Pierce found himself at the very bottom of his class. Pierce's young Maine roommate, Zenas Caldwell, prayed nightly with Pierce. The change was dramatic. Hawthorne tells us that Pierce rose at four in the morning, worked unrelentingly until midnight for three months, finally graduated third in his class. His strict Sabbatarianism also stayed with him; when Pierce became President, he insisted on grace before each meal and read nothing but the Bible on Sunday. So intense did his religious conflicts become that only at the end of his life was he able

The best parlor, with its French block-wallpaper depicting "The Bay of Naples" by Joseph Defeau, was redecorated in 1824. The mahogany furniture, covered in horsehair, and Brussels carpet, were brought from Boston and installed to greet young Franklin Pierce when he returned home from Bowdoin College. Upstairs is the ballroom where manual of arms was demonstrated to recruits in War of 1812. Curved table was originally in State Legislature when Pierce was its Speaker.

Pierce Homestead had kitchen added at later date; it connects with stable (right). Large barns, since torn down, were placed across the roadway.

to join a church (Episcopal); until then he had felt unworthy of any church. Sad to report, his resolution was not always marked by victory. In his later years, after the death of his wife, he too often found solace in the bottle.

While at Bowdoin, Pierce fell in love with Jane Means Appleton, daughter of Congregationalist minister Jesse Appleton, the former president of Bowdoin, who had died of tuberculosis, a disease his daughter apparently inherited. It was ten years before Pierce married (on November 19, 1834), a long engagement necessitated by Pierce's feeling that he must be able to support his wife adequately. To prepare himself, Pierce studied law in Portsmouth and Northampton, was admitted to the bar at Hillsboro in 1827, and set up his office across the street from his father's house, where he was close to the intense politicking that sent his father to the governor's chair in 1828 and again in 1829. In the latter year, Franklin Pierce accompanied his father to Concord, New Hampshire, as a member of the legislature, where he fast made his mark, became speaker for 1831–32, and in 1834 was elected to Congress as a supporter of Andrew Jackson. This position seemed to Pierce sufficiently remunerative to provide a sound basis for the marriage. He bought the house of his brother-in-law, the crippled War-of-1812 veteran John McNeil, in Hillsboro, and carried his wife across the threshold in the crisp autumn of 1834.

While Pierce was serving his second term as congressman in Washington his wife gave birth to their first son, a frail infant who died three days later. Mrs. Pierce slowly recovered, but her dislike of Hillsboro became so extreme that Pierce moved their household to Concord, borrowing $500 to make the move, and installed the family in 1837 on Montgomery Street. From there Pierce was elected senator, at thirty-two the youngest member of that national legislative body. But national honors did not bring happiness. A second son, born in 1839, died at the age of four from what was then called typhus fever. Mrs. Pierce came to dread Washington as a place of exile. Pierce cut short what had begun as a brilliant career to return to Concord to resume law practice.

The Healey portrait of Franklin Pierce shows us the figure of a handsome man, slightly under medium height, who was known for his military bearing. There is a touch of vanity: his naturally wavy hair is roached high on his head to gain extra inches. His presence both on the platform and in the courtroom was one that gained instant sympathy. But in response to his wife's wishes, Pierce forswore political office for a decade (1842–1852), declining a position in Polk's cabinet, an appointment as interim senator, and the nomination in 1848 for the governorship of New Hampshire. Only the Mexican War, in which he served with distinction, interrupted his retirement.

Pierce enlisted as a private, was appointed colonel, then brigadier general, leading an army from Vera Cruz to join General Winfield Scott in the capture of Mexico City. While charging directly into enemy artillery emplacements, he was thrown from his horse and suffered a fractured pelvis. A fellow officer called him a "damned coward," a grossly unfair accusation but one later used by Pierce's political enemies, although it was refuted by Grant himself, as well as by such celebrated fellow officers as Regular Army Captain Robert E. Lee and Captain Jefferson Davis, of the Mississippi Rifles.

Franklin Pierce's nomination for the presidency grew from a

stalemate in the 1852 Democratic Convention. Introduced by Virginia on the thirty-sixth ballot, he won nomination from an exhausted convention on the forty-ninth. Although a Mexican War hero in his own state, Pierce had been inconspicuous as a senator and in retirement for a decade. "Hereafter," quipped Stephen A. Douglas of Illinois, "no private citizen is safe." Pierce's acceptance was fatalistic: "I accept . . . relying upon a Power superior to all human might. . . . Weak myself, faith and hope repose there in security."

In fact, Pierce accepted the nomination because he thought he had no chance of winning against General Winfield Scott, his old Mexican War commander. Mrs. Pierce was opposed, and even the Pierces' third son, Benjamin, wrote from school that he certainly hoped his father would lose. The outcome was an unexpected and complete victory, with an electoral vote 254–42 for Pierce. The explanation would seem to be that in the pause before the storm, the American people wanted compromise, and this Pierce, "Young Hickory of the Granite State," offered them. As Pierce's Bowdoin classmate and campaign biographer, Nathaniel Hawthorne, wrote, Pierce looked "upon slavery as one of those evils which divine Providence does not leave to be removed by human contrivances but which in its own good time, by some means impossible to be anticipated, but of simplest and easiest operation, when all its uses shall be fulfilled, it causes to vanish like a dream."

Washington was to prove a bitter experience. Almost as if to prepare Pierce for this came yet another family tragedy. Returning from a funeral in Lawrence, Massachusetts, Pierce and his wife, accompanied by their sole surviving son, Bennie, thirteen, were in a railroad wreck when the axle of the coach in which they were riding broke. Both Pierce and his wife were injured; Bennie was killed. Overwhelmed by a grief from which she never fully recovered, Mrs. Pierce was convinced that the derailment was an act of God, one that freed her husband from all cares other than his great office. For his part, Pierce brought tears to the eyes of his listeners when at his inaugural he said, "My countrymen: It is a relief to feel that no heart but my own can know the personal regret and bitter sorrow over which I have been borne to a position so suitable to others rather than desirable to myself."

Pierce went through his four years of the presidency trying to conciliate at home, act forcefully abroad. His harmonious cabinet, which included Jefferson Davis as Secretary of War, remained unchanged and much of his foreign policy was commendable. He signed a reciprocity treaty with Canada, approved the Gadsden Purchase from Mexico in 1853, and firmly supported Commodore Perry's Open Door policy in the Orient. But at home his attempts at compromise earned him the reputation of being a pro-slavery Yankee.

Most galling to the north was his approval of the Kansas-Nebraska Act, which left slavery an open question in these territories to be decided by "squatter sovereignty;" his appointment of a pro-slavery governor of Kansas threw open "bleeding Kansas" to the "border ruffians"; it probably made the Civil War inevitable. Pierce saw his mandate melt away as the new Republican Party sprang to life, cutting his Democratic representation in the House by half midway in his term. When he left office, the war was only four years away. As Pierce wrote to Jefferson Davis in January 1860, "The

The original, high-ceilinged kitchen was once a busy scene as it served eight children and thirteen servants and farm hands, all from pots and pans in this single, large, all-purpose fireplace.

Pierce Homestead's acres, bought for $50 in 1788, have largely been reforested. In 1825 this fertile soil produced 500 bushels of potatoes to the acre.

The kitchen entrance to Pierce's Concord house in happier times opened onto a garden and lawn where Pierce entertained his old college friend and companion of his old age, Nathaniel Hawthorne.

fighting would be not only along the Mason and Dixon line, but within our own borders and in our own States."

Pierce returned home from Washington a bitterly disappointed man. Concord canceled its official homecoming reception out of dislike for what it took to be his pro-slavery sympathies. But Pierce was not without admirers. People from the surrounding towns swarmed into town to cheer Pierce as, mounted on a horse and escorted by the Manchester Veterans, he rode up Main Street to the state capitol grounds. It was a rousing popular tribute, but it was to be Pierce's last honor.

While in Washington, Pierce had begun building at 52 South Main Street, Concord, a spacious mansion in the prevailing French manner, with mansard roof and stucco finish. Acting as housekeeper was Willard Williams, a foreman in the coach-building factory of Abbott Downing, then Concord's main employer and maker of the famed Concord Coaches used by Wells Fargo in Omaha and Salt Lake City. The ex-President and his wife used the parlor, wide hall, sitting room, and dining room on the first floor. On the second floor, the southeast front bedroom was occupied by the Pierces, while Mrs. Williams presided over the spacious pantries and large kitchen in the rear of the house.

In 1863 Jane Pierce lost her long battle against consumption and melancholia. With her death, Pierce became more dependent on his few old friends. Hawthorne, whom Pierce had repaid by appointing him U.S. consul in Liverpool in 1853, dedicated his last work, *Our Old Home,* to Pierce in 1863. As Hawthorne explained to his Boston publisher, "If Pierce is so exceedingly unpopular, there is so much the more need that an old friend should stand by him." Pierce also stood by Hawthorne. Pierce was taking Hawthorne on a much-needed vacation in the White Mountains when Hawthorne died en route in an inn in Plymouth, New Hampshire, on May 19, 1864.

Yet even at the end there were elements of tragic grandeur in Pierce's life. A year before his death, although barely recovered from a near-fatal illness, Pierce made it a point of honor to attend the annual meeting of the Order of the Cincinnati in Baltimore. There he stood up to make his last speech, one of praise for the officers of the Revolution and their descendants who were still struggling to maintain "an undivided Union." But what was perhaps Pierce's finest hour had come a few years earlier. When the news of Lincoln's assassination had swept through Concord, an unruly mob looking for a scapegoat had remembered Pierce's reputation and stormed through the streets to his house, demanding that Pierce hoist Old Glory from the flagpole. "To the porch," historian Bliss Isely has written, "came a slight, erect man, whose proud roach of hair was grizzled and thin. But his voice sounded as clear as it had in the old years when it had swayed juries, convinced senators and led soldiers into battle at Contreras and Molino del Rey.

" 'It is not necessary for me to show my devotion to the Stars and Stripes,' he cried. Turning on his heel, he re-entered his home while the mob slunk away."

Franklin Pierce died October 8, 1869, and was buried in Concord's old North Cemetery beside his wife and three children. Not until 1914 did the state erect a bronze statue to Pierce on the southeast corner of the New Hampshire capitol grounds, and not until 1946 was a granite memorial erected by the state at his grave. The house at 52 South Main Street, where Pierce lived from 1857 to 1869, has suffered severe depredations. It was in use as the Swedish Baptist Church until 1941, when it was bought by John and Muriel Gavelle as a private home and furnished with period pieces evocative of the Pierce period.

The historic homestead at Hillsboro Lower Village was deeded to the state in 1925 by Captain Hayward Kendall, U.S. Army, and largely restored by the New Hampshire Federation of Women's Clubs between 1947 and 1950, when it became the responsibility of the State Recreation Division. The Hillsboro birthplace has been presided over graciously by its official hostess, Miss Susan Pierce, grandniece of the fourteenth President.

Jane Means Appleton, daughter of the President of Bowdoin and Pierce's ill-fated wife, died in Concord in 1863.

FIFTEEN

James Buchanan

IN THE CAVALCADE of American history, the elegant, rotund figure of fair-haired James Buchanan casts barely a shadow, so intense was the lurid glow of events to come. During his four-year administration (1857–1861) every omen pointed toward the outbreak of the "Irreconcilable Conflict," and every action of the President seemed ineffectual and temporizing. At a time when there was a desperate need for effective action, Buchanan placed his faith in concession and compromise, which only seemed to speed the inevitable aggression.

"If you are as happy, my dear sir," Buchanan greeted Lincoln on inauguration day, 1861, "on entering this house as I am on leaving it and returning home, you are the happiest man in the country." The remark was courtly, worldly, and obviously sincere, but it expressed an emotion which Lincoln, grim-faced and strained, could hardly be expected to share. "Mr. President," Lincoln replied slowly, "I cannot say that I shall enter it with much pleasure, but I can assure you that I shall do what I can to maintain the high standards set by my illustrious predecessors who have occupied it."

Although Buchanan must rank near the bottom in any comparative weighing of America's Chief Executives, yet he illustrates impressively the remarkable caliber of man selected to hold the highest office, even when it was held with little distinction. Indeed, measured by his achievements over forty-two years of political life, Buchanan can claim a distinguished record in all but the presidency. Like a score of other Presidents, Buchanan was born in a log cabin. But, reared as he was, well back from the frontier, he was vastly more favored in his upbringing and education than, for example, Lincoln. His father, a North of Ireland Scot and a Presbyterian, was a prosperous farmer and later a wealthy iron manufacturer. Buchanan had a sound primary and academy education at Mercersburg, Pennsylvania, the town near which he had been born on April 23, 1791; he graduated from Dickinson College (1809) and was admitted to the bar in Lancaster, Pennsylvania, in 1812.

Within three years Buchanan was elected to the Pennsylvania legislature and could claim a law practice of $11,298 a year, nearly ten times the earnings of Lincoln after a similar time at the bar. He had fallen in love with a local belle, Anne Coleman, the daughter of

Buchanan's birthplace in 1791 was the frontier cabin, now at Mercersburg Academy, Mercersburg, Pennsylvania, and furnished in authentic Early American style. Buchanan's father later became a wealthy iron manufacturer, sent Buchanan to academy and college.

a Lancaster millionaire ironmaster. Her parents, put off by his reputation for carefree ways and somewhat irresponsible companions, disapproved. An ugly rumor of Buchanan's amorous behavior in Washington, D.C., where he had gone to try a case, caused further misunderstanding. When Anne Coleman died in December of the same year (1819), Buchanan was inconsolable; he kept her portrait with him until the day he died, when a packet of her letters was found with his notation, "Please do not open these." His wishes were respected and the letters burned.

Buchanan remained a bachelor all his life, but it proved little hindrance to his advancement, largely because of his strikingly beautiful niece, Harriet Lane. Orphaned at the age of nine and asked to choose her guardian, she picked Uncle James Buchanan. As Buchanan steadily mounted the political heights, Harriet Lane accompanied him to Washington, where he was first congressman, then Minister to Russia, then senator, Secretary of State in Polk's cabinet, and then Minister to the Court of St. James's.

James Buchanan (1791-1868), painted by George P. A. Healey.

Perhaps no U.S. Minister has had a more attractive official hostess than Harriet. Indeed, her extraordinary popularity abroad had an ironic aftermath. While Buchanan was in the White House, the British ambassador presented Harriet with lithographs of Queen Victoria, Prince Albert, and the Prince of Wales as a memento from the Prince of Wales (Edward VII) of his successful state visit to the White House in 1860. These royal portraits were framed in gold-leaf frames and hung in the White House Red Room. When Buchanan left, the likenesses and frames went with him as a matter of course.

A huge outcry arose in the press that Buchanan had stolen them from the White House. On December 19, 1861, Buchanan was urgently writing to his niece to clear the matter up: "Lord Lyons, by whom I believe they were sent to you, ought to correct this. I remember they came to you in loose sheets without frames and whether they were framed at your expense or mine I know not. Miss Hetty has found a bill on file against you, receipted for Francis Lamb and dated Dec. 2, 1860, for four gilt frames amounting to $18.00. Were these frames for the pictures?"

It turned out they were, and the framed likenesses remained where they still are, in Buchanan's home, Wheatland, a mile and a half outside Lancaster, Pennsylvania.

The estate and house at Wheatland superbly mirrors Buchanan, his way of life, and the manner of living in mid-nineteenth-century America. Wheatland is distinctly gentry; to curry political favor with the Democratic South it was sometimes referred to at the time as a "plantation estate." In fact, it is as Pennsylvania as Dutch craftsmanship could make it. The original house was built in 1824 by William Jenkins, Lancaster's richest banker, and sold by him to William Morris Meredith, a prominent Philadelphia lawyer in 1845. On December 2, 1848, it was purchased by Buchanan (then Polk's Secretary of State) for $6750, plus $75 for the bookcases that still remain in the library over a century and a quarter later.

Wheatland, so named for its expansive view of the surrounding wheatfields, seems at first sight to be three houses rather than one. In fact, it was designed all of a piece, and, although we know the name of neither the builder nor the architect (if any), a close enough prototype has been found in Asher Benjamin's *The American Builder's Companion; or a New System of Architecture* (Boston,

1806) to suggest that if this manual, so instrumental in spreading the influence of the Greek Revival style, did not actually furnish the master design for Wheatland, it certainly heavily influenced it.

Colonial architecture, from the Harrisons' Berkeley, Washington's Mount Vernon and Jefferson's Monticello, had been built by men with a passing knowledge of the principles of classic architecture laid down by Vetruvius and codified by Palladio. But from the time of Jackson's second Hermitage, with its cast-iron capitals, the classic orders and ornament became increasingly a matter of caprice, to be changed and modified at the pleasure of the builder or carpenter.

Wheatland exhibits many of the peculiarities of this approach, the beginning of a kind of eclecticism that was soon to make all classic ornament mere trimming. A basic symmetry is maintained in Wheatland's over-all design, which includes such familiar features as the front-to-back central hall with balanced parlors on either side. But the house sits high and awkwardly, the portico with its overly small Tuscan columns and wood stairs lacks a certain dignity and repose, although the lunette over the door is well proportioned.

What a mansion like Wheatland lacked in detail, it more than made up for in spaciousness, and this, after all, was what concerned Buchanan, who meant this to be his base of operations for his drive for the Presidency. A great advantage that Wheatland had as a seat for political operations in the mid-nineteenth-century was its central location halfway between Philadelphia and Gettysburg. More important, it was serviced by a railroad. And on June 1, 1849, we find Buchanan making this point in writing to Governor Issac Toucey of Pennsylvania (later to serve as Buchanan's Secretary of the Navy):

I am now residing at this place which is an agreeable country residence about a mile and a half from Lancaster. If you should

Wheatland's library, as shown in Leslie's Newspaper, *1857, was Buchanan's main work room and indicates a certain bachelor untidiness. Bookcases were mahogany, as was sofa with red damask pillows. Ladderback chair by stove was Buchanan's favorite. Green venetian blinds were then considered old-fashioned.*

BRIGHTLY. SC

at any time visit Washington, I hope you may not fail to come this way. There is a better railroad from Philadelphia to Baltimore, via Lancaster, than by the direct route; and you should pass through a beautiful country. . . ."

Guests arriving at the station would be met by John Giles, Buchanan's twelve-dollar-a-month gardener-coachman, atop the square carriage and driving the master's "excellent pair of bays." One guest in 1856 has left us his description of the short ride to the house through the "rich undulating landscape":

> Viewed from the gate, Wheatland is picturesque and elegant. A circular path, hidden by forest trees and shrubbery, leads to the mansion. A carriage drive is composed of tanbark, which completely deadens the sound of approaching footsteps and carriage wheels. . . . A large portico supported by substantial columns, adorns the front of the house. In the center of the lawn is a small white house, the dwelling of the gardener. In front of the house is a beautiful spring which gurgles out of the earth, clear as crystal, glistening like diamonds, under the shade of a magnificent willow tree. This spot is quite a favorite of Mr. Buchanan, and to it, when at leisure, he often leads his casual visitors. Walking in stately dignity over the grounds are two majestic eagles, presents to Mr. Buchanan from a friend living in California.

Guests were sometimes invited to see Buchanan's strawberry patch or the grape vineyards, of which he was particularly proud; and one guest recalls, "We saw clusters of the Malaga grapes which weighed upwards of six pounds." But basically most visitors came to discuss politics, and in Buchanan they found an inspiring, dignified, and handsome professional. "He looks like an English noble-

Buchanan's bedroom had a large double bed with heavily turned posts and scroll headboard typical of early nineteenth century. The walls were painted dull green with white moulding; the floor had a geometrically patterned Brussels carpet. Chest (behind bed) and side chairs are American Empire style, and were bought in Philadelphia.

Wheatland's parlor, in 1857, presented this Victorian interior, with Brussels carpet, flock wallpaper, and double curtains hanging from long French rods. Chairs and walnut sofa with cabriole legs and heavy scrolls were mid-nineteenth-century version of Louis XV. Between the windows is a pier table; on mantel an ormolu clock.

man of thirty or forty years ago when the grave and dignified bearing of men in power was regarded as an essential attribute of their office," one Englishman exclaimed. "The fair and delicate, though fresh complexion of Mr. Buchanan, his eyes of light blue, and full blooded system, attest unequivocally his Anglo-Saxon descent."

Once inside the door, the interior of the house was impressive.

> Upon entering [wrote a newspaper correspondent], you find yourself in a broad hall with the parlor opening on the right, Mr. Buchanan's sitting room or study being on the left. This "cabinet" is occupied by two or three desks, and its walls are well crowded with books.

To the left and at the end of the transverse hallway in the rear was Buchanan's library:

> On the left hand side of the room is a large and crowded book-case; there are two mahogany book-cases in other parts of the room. The mantel-piece is covered with books and papers. The chair always occupied by Mr. Buchanan is to be partially seen at the head of the table. . . . On the right hand is a handsome writing desk covered with newspapers and letters. A large mahogany sofa with damask pillows is also covered with papers. The floor is covered with a dark Brussels carpet, with large red figures. The windows are darkened by the old-fashioned green Venetian blinds; the chairs are of mahogany, with horse-hair seats. . . . Many of the works in the library were of a religious character. Odd numbers of the *Presbyterian* lay strewed about. . . . Various stumps of cigars around the fire-place indicated addiction to the weed. . . .

A New York *Daily Times* correspondent described the ritual of dinner:

> Before each meal a gentle knock at the door of each guest announced that . . . dinner would be served in half an hour. At the precise moment came the word that the meal was served. Our

host was always first in the dining room to welcome each one as he entered. He remained standing in his place, with old fashioned courtesy. The table was beautifully arranged, laid with rare china and silver and supplied with all the luxuries of the fertile country and tropical delicacies.

With the aid of Miss Hetty Parker, his faithful housekeeper, and his niece, Harriet Lane, Buchanan became increasingly famous as a host. The mahogany table, specially built for the room in 1828 and never removed from the house, could be extended to seat twenty-five, and was laid with the handsome silver flatware that Buchanan had purchased for £50 in London in 1855. For the gentlemen after dinner he served sixty-five-year-old madeira, rye, or his favorite John Baer whiskey. After tea or dinner, and always on Sunday afternoons, Harriet Lane would play on the Jonas Chickering grand piano which also is still to be seen in the parlor at Wheatland. When, at long last, the nomination for President was his, Buchanan in 1856 wisely decided to campaign from home, his was the first of the many famous "front-porch campaigns" to come. Wheatland itself became his campaign emblem, and loyal Democrats across the land busied themselves founding Wheatland Clubs to foster the election of "Old Buck."

Before and after his presidency, Buchanan attempted to keep his house up to date. In 1850 he installed a furnace with central heating, and in the same year a cast-iron kitchen range replaced the open hearth in the basement kitchen. On his return from the White House, he ordered that newfangled object, a refrigerator (although he worried when mild winters came that he would harvest no ice for the icehouse). Perhaps the most startling modernity was the paneled bathroom that was reportedly installed in imitation of the one which President and Mrs. Millard Fillmore had introduced into the White House. That in Wheatland featured an enormous tin hip tub, a shower, and—even more unexpectedly—a flush-type bidet.

After his White House term, Buchanan—as Pennsylvania's only President—remained a hero, at least in his own home town. He arrived back in Lancaster to the roar of saluting cannon, thirty-four salvos, one for each state in the Union, a parade, and the inevitable patriotic speeches. But as the years rolled on, fewer and fewer guests showed up at Wheatland. His niece had made a brilliant marriage to a wealthy Baltimore banker, Henry E. Johnson, and Wheatland had known one of its greatest days. But as Buchanan filled up his hours reading his papers, playing cards, or gossiping, time often hung heavy. Now and then he would go to Bedford Springs for the mineral waters to cure his gouty rheumatism and there would try his hand at flirting decorously with the young ladies. But perhaps his greatest pleasure was serving on the Board of Trustees of Franklin and Marshall College in Lancaster, a task he performed until his death on June 1, 1868.

The great charm in visiting Wheatland is that so much of the tang and aroma of this pastoral existence can still be sensed. So magnificently are the rooms maintained, with their Lancaster hostesses in period crinolines, that one almost expects to catch sight of Miss Hetty tidying up the parlor, Harriet Lane once again adjusting her skirts before her fingers ripple the first chords on the Chickering grand, or find elegant and reserved President Buchanan himself standing at the head of the table, ceremoniously greeting each guest in turn.

Rear porch of Wheatland intimately relates the house to the broad acres surrounding it. Hostess in period costume is a member of the Junior League of Lancaster.

SIXTEEN
Abraham Lincoln

AS ABRAHAM LINCOLN rode slowly into Springfield, Illinois, on April 15, 1837, to make it his new home, he was twenty-eight—and at almost the exact midpoint of his life. Just twenty-eight years later to the day, Lincoln would breathe his last in the Petersen house, across the street from Ford's Theater, the most mourned and beloved President in United States history and a figure of veneration the world over.

But in 1837, Lincoln, a lanky country lawyer no more distinguished than hundreds of others, could hardly be said to stand even on the threshold of history as he reined in his borrowed horse at Joshua Speed's general store and asked the price of bedclothes for a single bed. Grocer Speed figured it would come to seventeen dollars. Said Lincoln, "Cheap as it is, I have not the money to pay. But if you will credit me until Christmas, and my experiment here as a lawyer is a success, I will pay you then. If I fail in that I will probably never pay you at all." As Speed recalled in later years, "The tone of his voice was so melancholy that I felt for him. I thought I never saw so gloomy and melancholy a face in my life." But Lincoln could make a friend fast. Speed waved aside payment, invited Abe Lincoln to share his double bed. Down at Sangaman Circuit Courthouse, William Butler, clerk of the court, allowed as how Lincoln could board free at his house. "Well, Speed," said Lincoln, as his face lighted up, "I'm moved!"

Yet, Abe Lincoln had already come a remarkable way by the standards of the frontier. He had been born in a cramped log cabin on Sunday, February 12, 1809, on the south fork of Nolin Creek, Hogdenville, in Hardin County, Kentucky, the second child of dirt-poor frontiersmen. His father, Thomas Lincoln, was descended from the Lincolns who, in 1635, came from Hingham, England, to Hingham, Massachusetts; his mother, Nancy Hanks, was the natural daughter of Lucy Hanks. For all the mystery surrounding her parentage, she was "shrewd, highly intellectual, spiritually inclined," albeit illiterate. Abe was named for his paternal grandfather, Abraham, who had been shot by Indians while working in the field and died before he could see his own son in turn shoot and kill his assassin.

The land was poor and, when Abe was two, the Lincolns moved some ten miles away to Knob Creek, hard by the Cumberland Trail. Lincoln as a lad walked four miles to learn "readin', writin' and cipherin'," but, as he was later to say, all of his schooling throughout boyhood "didn't amount to one year." Then, as Lincoln recounted, "partly on account of slavery, but chiefly on account of the difficulty in land titles," the family pulled up stakes in the winter of 1816 and made the bitter-cold trek to Indiana. There, as squatters, they built

As the Lincoln family moved along the frontier, they cleared land, built their own log cabins. Old print shows one-room cabin near Gentryville, Indiana, that for fourteen years was Lincoln's boyhood home. Here his mother died, his stepmother came to live, and nine people lived in cramped quarters. Old photograph taken in 1891 shows house Abe Lincoln helped build when family first moved to Illinois in 1830.

an eighteen-by-twenty-foot cabin with split logs, wattle and daub (wet clay and grass) on the banks of Pigeon Creek, a mile and a half east of Gentryville, in Spencer (then Perry) County.

Young Abe at seven could tote a gun, kept his powder dry, and, when he hit a turkey gobbler, he would not stop boasting until Paw told him to shut up. Then, in 1818, when Lincoln was nine, Nancy Hanks Lincoln came down with "milk sickness" and died. "Oh, Lord, oh Lord, I'll never furgit it, the mizry in that cabin in the woods when Nancy died," said Dennis Hanks, Nancy's cousin. Abe manfully whittled the pegs for the coffin. Life went on, and a little over a year later, Tom Lincoln rode off to Elizabethville and came back with his new wife, a widow, Sarah Bush Johnson, and her three children. It meant nine living in the tiny cabin, so confined that the women had to get undressed first and then the men. It was now that Abe Lincoln mastered "that most useful instrument," the axe, and in the evenings lay on his stomach by the fire writing, or reading aloud to the family. At sixteen he was almost his full height (6 ft. 4 in.), dressed in buckskins and moccasins, tow linen shirt and coonskin cap, and, as one contemporary remembered, "He can sink an axe deeper into wood than any man I ever saw." He was also willing to walk thirty miles to hear and see lawyers and politicians, practiced speechifying by himself as he split logs. At eighteen he earned his first dollar, helping some passengers with their luggage aboard a New Orleans-bound river boat.

Lincoln was nineteen when his sister died in childbirth, an ordeal that, combined with the early loss of his own mother, made him shy of women for years. When he got a chance to ride a flatboat to New Orleans, he took it. He picked up a scar over his right eye in a knife fight with runaway Negroes who tried to steal the raft. In the slave markets of New Orleans Lincoln saw slavery at its worst and rebelled violently: "By God, boys, let's get away from this. If ever I get a chance to hit that thing, I'll hit it hard!"

In 1830 Lincoln was twenty-one and free to strike out on his own, but first he saw the Lincolns through yet another move, this time to Macon County, Illinois. Tom Lincoln and the rest of the fam-

Lincoln's house in Springfield, Illinois, which he bought for $1,500 in 1844, was his home for seventeen years until he left for the White House. He is seen (opposite) as he appeared in 1857, when he had already been mentioned as Vice President and was about to begin the great debates with Douglas that made him a national figure. A second floor had been added to the house in 1856 (below), and a fence built to Lincoln's own design. In May 1860, he was nominated by the Republican Convention, and throngs of enthusiastic townspeople surged to his house (opposite, below), where Lincoln stood, a commanding figure in white by the front door, while Mary Todd Lincoln sat more decorously on the window ledge of the second story almost directly above her husband.

ily survived the first hard winter, then moved on to Coles County; Lincoln decided to settle on his own in New Salem, a town on the Sangamon River founded only two years eariler. It was here, in Denton Offutt's New Salem general store, that Lincoln became known as "Honest Abe," a man who would walk six miles to return a few pennies overcharged, or miles to deliver four ounces of tea. And here Lincoln proved his manhood by wrestling Jack Armstrong, the champion of Clary's Grove, to a draw, and then said, "Jack, let's quit. I can't throw you—and you can't throw me."

And it was in New Salem that Lincoln made his first try for the state legislature (and lost). Here, too, he enlisted in the Black Hawk War (voted company captain by the boys, he made Jack Armstrong his first sergeant), a war in which Lincoln learned what it was like to eat pork raw, sleep in the rain, witness the huddled bodies of the scalped. But, as Lincoln said, the only blood he shed was to the mosquitoes, and that was quite a lot. Here too he studied surveying "to keep body and soul together," shyly kept company with Ann Rutledge while she waited for someone else to return, which he did, but only after Ann had died. In 1834, he finally made it to the legislature as a Whig, and in 1836, at twenty-eight, his years of reading law bore fruit when he was admitted to the bar to practice on the Eighth Judicial Circuit.

Today the New Salem Lincoln knew, or something very like it, has been rebuilt. The land was bought by William Randolph Hearst in 1906, and in 1933 the village, restored by the Illinois general assembly, opened as a patriotic shrine. However the Illinois state capital of Springfield that Lincoln knew is hardly to be found now; the small town of 1200 people has long since been swallowed up, evoked only by old photographs. Poor though he was Lincoln rode into town a lawyer and floor leader of the Whig party in the legislature—a far cry from the "piece of floating driftwood" he called himself when he had first arrived in New Salem. He set up a law partnership with a Black Hawk War friend, John T. Stuart, and business came slowly. Sometimes Lincoln found "the thing of living in Springfield is rather a dull business, after all." At times he gave way to deep melancholy, telling friends he never carried so much as a penknife on his person lest he be tempted by suicide. One love affair with the plump and plain Mary Owens came to nothing. Then he met Mary Todd, a belle from Lexington, Kentucky; plump, swift of movement, with light-brown hair, a finishing-school education, and ambition. At the ball where they met, Lincoln awkwardly approached, said, "Miss Todd, I want to dance with you the worst way." Mary Todd recalled gaily, "He certainly did."

But nothing came easily to Lincoln. The marriage date was set,

The Lincoln family in 1861 was composed of Mary Todd Lincoln, left; young William, then eleven, who died in the White House a year later; the eldest son, Robert, a student at Harvard; and Thomas, known as "Tad," who is looking at the book in Lincoln's lap.

then broken. Lincoln in a black mood said that he "had done nothing to make any human being remember he had lived."

Nearly a year later, Lincoln, thirty-three, and Mary Todd, twenty-four, were married on November 4, 1842, in the Ninian Edwards' mansion by the Episcopal rector, the Reverend Charles Dresser. The newlyweds moved directly into the Globe Tavern, paying four dollars per week. At the Globe, on August 1, 1843, their first son, Robert Todd, was born.

With a family, Lincoln began casting about for a house. He had greatly admired the Reverend Dresser's story-and-a-half house on the northeast corner of Eighth and Jackson streets, and in 1844, for $1500 in cash (about the equivalent of Lincoln's earnings in a year) he bought the five-year-old house. With it came a 50-by-152-foot lot, a cistern, well, privy, a 30-by-13-foot barn, and an 18-by-20-foot carriage house. As houses went in Springfield, it was a good buy indeed. The frame of the house is oak, the siding and flooring of black walnut. The cornices and trim reflect the Greek Revival style as it appeared on the frontier. As contrast to its green shutters, the house was painted "a Quaker tint of light brown." Lincoln's office was only a few blocks away and a few hundred feet behind the house began the open farmlands. Although it is not mentioned in the deed, there

In Lincoln's Springfield house is this dresser with two bottles of Lincoln's favorite medicine placed on it. At right is Lincoln's secretary in the back parlor. Beside it is a standing globe.

was a $900 mortgage still outstanding. Lincoln raised no objection; he is supposed to have said that he "reckoned he could trust the preacher that married him."

Except for the term Lincoln spent in Washington as a U.S. representative in Congress when he lived in Mrs. Sprigg's boarding house, his Springfield house was to be Lincoln's home for seventeen years, and, as events turned out, the only home he ever owned. Here three more sons were to be born, and one to die. And it was against this homely background that Lincoln was slowly to emerge from local politician and minority floor leader in a state legislature to President of the United States.

"Only events can make a President," Lincoln said. But Mary Todd did her stormy best to goad and support her awkward, brooding, lanky husband. She was delighted when Lincoln added a two-foot brick retaining wall before the house and designed the front yard fence that still stands. In 1856, Mrs. Lincoln used a small inheritance to add a second floor to make the house more commodious and, of course, more respectable.

What was life like in this house? Most of its secrets are still well kept. We know that Mary Todd had a quick temper. "Money!" she once exclaimed, "he never gives me any money; he leaves his pocket-book where I can take what I want." And Lincoln could be a most trying husband. He would revert to his log-cabin days, lie on the front-room carpet to read. He would come to the table in his shirtsleeves and gulp down his food absent-mindedly. When the doorbell rang, Lincoln would answer in his carpet slippers, tell the visiting ladies, "She'll be down as soon as she gets her trotting harness on."

But gradually Mary Todd Lincoln prevailed on her husband to improve his dress; Lincoln began to wear broadcloth, white shirts and collars with a silk cravat, clothes that hung from his gaunt frame as from a hatrack. Some of his country-isms may have been purposeful; photographers noticed that just before the picture was taken, Lincoln would muss his hair. There was something in Lincoln that liked his old, weather-stained umbrella and his six-inch-high stovepipe hat which served him as a filing cabinet and brief case (holding his memorandum book, bank book, and letters tucked in the hatband), just as he liked sprawling on sofas, his long legs propped up on any chair handy.

On weekdays, Lincoln would uncoil from his great height to play marbles or spin tops with his boys. On Sundays he let Willie and Tad tag along to the office, where the two youngsters piled up books and pushed them over, made quivers of arrows out of pencils and aimed at the spittoon while Lincoln lay on the old, battered couch and played with the kittens. When the carriages and churchgoers once again filled the street, Lincoln would gather up his sons, cutting through the pasture to the house. Lincoln could be a disciplinarian, but only rarely. Once neighbors saw him lugging home the howling Willie and Tad, asked, "Why, Mr. Lincoln, what's the matter?" Replied Lincoln, "Just what's the matter with the whole world. I've got three walnuts and each wants two."

Mary Todd could entertain as many as two hundred at a time, and Lincoln could study late into the night on his law cases. But it was to be politics that would confront Lincoln with his own destiny. He observed "Bleeding Kansas" and talked of "The Family of Man." In Chicago he gave the toast, "The Union—the North will maintain it—the South will not depart from it." From Springfield he went for the great debates with his opponent from his earliest legislature days, "the Little Giant" Stephen A. Douglas. Lincoln said, "A house divided against itself cannot stand," and the Nation pondered what he meant. There was talk of the Presidency. "It's too big a thing for me," Lincoln wrote. "Mary insists, however, that I am going to be a Senator and President of the United States, too." When he won a plurality of over 4000 votes, but lost the election to the Senate in the state legislature vote, Lincoln said he felt like the Kentucky boy who stubbed his toe: "I am too big to cry about it, but it hurts too awful bad to laugh!"

But by 1860 Lincoln was becoming the Republican candidate. After the Cooper Union speech in New York he was tagged as "The Prairie Statesman," and Noah Brooks of the New York *Herald* allowed, "He's the greatest man since St. Paul." At the Illinois Republican Convention, he became "The Rail Splitter." And in the temporary "Wigwam" in Chicago on May 18, 1860, Abraham Lincoln on the third ballot became the Republican nominee.

Lincoln then, as he did when the election finals were coming in, went down to the Springfield telegraph office, lounging on a sofa, shrouded in calm. When the good news came, he hurried home to Mary

Lincoln's parlor, as it appears today, with Tad's wicker-back rocking chair beside the stereopticon and Lincoln's favorite horsehair-covered rocker. Below is the parlor as it appeared to contemporaries, with its high bookcase-desk. At the end of the room are globe and sphere still to be seen in Lincoln's Springfield house (see page 117).

Todd. Brass bands marched up to the house to serenade them, and Lincoln waved as he said he wished his house was big enough to ask them all in. On November 6, 1860, he was able to announce triumphantly, "Mary, we're elected." Mary Todd had arrived at last. "We are pleased with our advancement," she told her well-wishers. "Well, wife, if nothing else comes of this scrape, we are going to have some new clothes," Lincoln said, and packed his wife off to New York to buy bonnets, ribbons, and dresses with the help of their eldest son, Robert Todd, then finished with Phillips Exeter Academy and a smartly dressed freshman at Harvard. Quietly, under the care of "Billy the Barber," Springfield's Haitian barbershop favorite, Lincoln began to let his whiskers grow. On February 6, the Lincolns had their goodbye party; it was time to pack up and label the luggage:

> *A. Lincoln*
> The White House
> Washington, D.C.

On February 11, Lincoln walked to the rear of the train about to pull out from Springfield. In the drizzling rain he could see face after face from the past, all silently turned toward him. Slowly, haltingly, Lincoln began to speak, and as he did tears streamed down the faces of his listeners: "No one," said Lincoln, "not in my situation can appreciate my feeling of sadness at this parting. To this place, and the kindness of these people, I owe everything. Here I have lived a quarter of a century, and have passed from a young to an old man. Here my children have been born, and one is buried. I now leave, not knowing when or whether ever I may return, with a task before me greater than that which rested upon Washington. Without the assistance of that Divine Being who ever attended him, I cannot succeed. With that assistance I cannot fail. Trusting in Him who can go with me, and remain with you, and be everywhere for good, let us confidently hope that all will yet be well. To His care commending you, as I hope in your prayers you will commend me, I bid you an affectionate farewell."

Seven days before, on February 4, 1861, the Confederate States of America were formed with the Senator from Mississippi, Jefferson Davis, as their new president. Lincoln was not to come back to Springfield alive. Only the cortege, draped in mourning, would carry his body to its temporary resting place in the vault in Oak Ridge Cemetery in the Illinois capital. Lincoln's home on that sad occasion was draped in crêpe by a local carpenter, but Mrs. Lincoln never returned to live in Springfield. The house was rented until 1887, when Robert Todd Lincoln was prevailed upon to deed the house to the State of Illinois.

No changes have been made in the interior since Mary Todd Lincoln used her small inheritance to repaper the rooms and raise the level of the house one story. Unfortunately, most of the original furniture was destroyed by the Chicago fire of 1871, where it was in the possession of the widowed Mrs. Lincoln. But much remains— Lincoln's favorite rocking chair, the cupboard he used as a bookcase, Mary Todd's sewing chair, some old medicine bottles, and Lincoln's stovepipe hat in which letters would be stored, and, as Lincoln himself once confessed, be "lost sight of for a while." Still his great spirit broods over this place. It is felt by the thousands who each year reverently visit the home of our greatest President.

SEVENTEEN

Andrew Johnson

I KNOW we have an illegitimate, swaggering, bastard, scrub aristocracy who presume to know a great deal, but who, when the flowing veil of pretension is torn off from it, is seen to possess neither talents nor information on which one can rear a useful structure. . . . Sir, I vindicate the mechanical profession."

The speaker was none other than Tennessee's fighting-mad Andrew Johnson; his tormentor across the debating aisle that aristocrat of Mississippi, Jefferson Davis, a slave-holder, plantation-owner, and true gentleman of the South. No two men could be more opposed; yet it is reassuring, and somehow in keeping with the deepest instincts for fair play in the American character, that years later, when Jeff Davis was incarcerated in the prison of Fortress Monroe, the leader of the defeated Confederate States of America could recast the balance sheet and say of Johnson: "His faith in the judgment of the people was unlimited, and to their decision he was always ready to submit. One of the people by birth, he remained so by conviction. . . . He was eminently faithful to his word, and possessed a courage which took the form of angry resistance if urged to do, or not to do, anything which might clash with his convictions of duty."

Plebeian, politician, patriot—Andrew Johnson was "The Great Commoner." He was born in the meanest of surroundings, a small clapboard house attached to Casso's Inn, in North Carolina's capital city of Raleigh (population 1000). His father was the porter at the inn, church sexton, and town constable; his mother, known as "Polly the Weaver," worked as maid and seamstress. When Andrew was four, his father died after rescuing two friends from drowning. This loss left the family bereft; schooling was out of the question. Only academies existed and they required tuition money far beyond poor Polly's means. At fourteen, Andrew apprenticed himself to a tailor named James J. Selby. Young Andy proved an apt learner. "An attractive, harum-scarum boy," the foreman of the tailor shop called him, and added, "he had no unhonorable traits. Among the lads of the town he always led the crowd. If he said go swimming, they went swimming. His piercing black eyes and his will to do or die set him above his surroundings."

Young Andy's scrapes, however, got him in trouble. After one stone-throwing escapade, he ran away from the tailor shop, tried his new-learned trade in nearby towns, then finally, at the age of eighteen, took a cart and the old horse, loaded his mother, brother, and step-father in it, and set off for Tennessee over Daniel Boone's Wilderness Road. The struggling family ran out of funds in Greeneville, Tennessee, and decided to stay put. Andy was to be their mainstay, and with his needle and thread flying, he was soon the best tailor in the county.

Andrew Johnson.

Elizabeth McCardle Johnson.

Sweet young Eliza McCardle, herself a seamstress and daughter of the town's Scottish shoemaker, was the first to befriend the family, and Andrew married her before the end of his first year in town.

By tracing letters in the dust, or on the back of a shovel, Andrew Johnson could barely make out enough to read. This his bride Eliza set out to correct, reading to him by the hour as he mastered reading, writing, and arithmetic. Later, when Eliza's time was taken up with their children, Johnson hired a boy at fifty cents a day to carry on with the reading. Johnson would walk four miles to debate with local college boys; with practice he developed into a superb and fiery stump orator, a fact his fellow citizens applauded. He was also not above mixing a little self-advertising with his campaign oratory. One of the favorite jingles of his followers was a song:

> *If you want a brand new coat*
> *I'll tell you what to do*
> *Go down to Andrew Johnson's shop*
> *And get a long-tail blue.*
>
> *If you want the girls to love you*
> *To love you good and true*
> *Go down to Andy's Tailor Shop*
> *And get a long-tail blue.*

Apparently the voters responded. They elected their conservatively turned-out tailor alderman at twenty, mayor at twenty-two, then sent him to the state capital as representative and senator and finally to Congress in Washington. At forty-five, town tailor Andrew Johnson was governor of Tennessee, and in 1857 he was elected U.S. senator.

During these years, Johnson had prospered at home as well. In 1830, he had acquired a small frame tailor shop on College Street, and eight years later built a small two-story brick house across the street, both of which still stand. But it was a time for the Johnsons to rise even further. On September 10, 1851, while serving his fourth term in Washington as a representative, Andrew Johnson bought a new brick house on Main Street, completed except for the interiors, from James Brannan, a builder-bricklayer who had furnished Johnson with his first house thirteen years before. The cost was $950, a reasonable price indeed, considering that the lot had a 114-foot frontage on Main Street. As part of the deal Johnson also threw in his first house.

But though this house, now a national monument (along with Johnson's original tailor shop), was to become Johnson's final home, his acquaintance with it was fleeting at first. An ardent Jacksonian Democrat and a small slave-holder who had supported John C. Breckinridge against Lincoln in 1860, with the approach of the Civil War Johnson decided to stand by the Union on constitutional grounds. When Tennessee, following South Carolina and the other Southern States, seceded from the Union, Johnson declared in the Senate, ". . . I intend to stand by the Constitution as it is, insisting upon a compliance with all it guarantees. . . . It is the last hope of human freedom." Nor did Johnson stand alone; some 13,000 "Andy Johnson Democrats" from eastern Tennessee promptly entered the Union Army as volunteers, and Lincoln in 1862 appointed Johnson military governor of Tennessee with the rank of brigadier general.

It was a far-from-enviable position; in Nashville, Johnson's life was constantly threatened; in Greeneville, a mob waved the banner *ANDREW JOHNSON, TRAITOR*. When the Confederate armies swept over east Tennessee in August 1861, Johnson's daughter stored most of the furniture with friends and managed to escape through the lines to Union territory. "Your house is now a rebel hospital and

Andrew Johnson's home in Greeneville, Tennessee, was finished in 1851, but during the Civil War it had served as both barracks and hospital. When Johnson returned from the White House in 1869 he ordered a modest classical portal for the front, added the double verandas on three sides of the rear. The new house had ten rooms on three levels; the kitchen was in the basement and was reached by exterior stairs.

the rebels are cutting up Greeneville, " Martha Johnson Patterson wrote her father. On the same day in the U.S. Senate, Johnson thundered, "My wife and children have been turned into the street, and my house has been converted into a barracks, and for what? Because I stand for the Constitution!"

Worse was to befall the house before Johnson finally returned home eight years later. Both Yankees and Rebs scrawled messages on the white painted plaster walls. "This is Greeneville, Tennessee, the Yankees' hole of all holes," wrote one Confederate for posterity's sake. Another celebrated Lovejoy: "Andy you had better skedaddle from Nashvill for Lovejoy is after you and if he git you you are a gonner sartan." The house gradually fell into a state of disrepair; *Frank Leslie's Illustrated Newspaper,* on September 23, 1865, said: "The fences of the lot and windows of the house show evident signs of dilapidation, the consequence of rebellion and rebel rule. A number of panes of glass are broken out and their places supplied with paper. . . . This is the residence of Andrew Johnson, President of the United States."

Johnson's term in the White House following the assassination of Lincoln developed into a long, bitter stalemate with the Congress. Picked by Lincoln in 1864 for the number-two spot in order to give the Republican ticket* a national character, once in the White House Johnson declared an amnesty to all Confederate soldiers, excepting only certain leaders, for the purpose of restoring the seceded states to the Union. Southern states, however, added anti-Negro amendments which enraged Congress. Congress in retaliation restored military control over the South, which infuriated Johnson. Relations between the president and his Congress were further strained when he removed his Secretary of War, Edwin M. Stanton, without consulting the Senate, thus repudiating the tenure-of-office act. The House promptly impeached Johnson, the first President to suffer this humiliation. After long-drawn-out proceedings, the Senate failed by a single vote to find Johnson guilty.

When Johnson left the presidency on March 4, 1869, he was still smoldering under the sting of the accusations against him, and ostentatiously refused to accompany General Grant to the inauguration. But if President Johnson's tenure was stormy, he and his family— including his invalided wife, his daughter Martha, who acted as hostess, and his sons, two of whom served in the Union Army—were liked for their homely ways. "Of these plain people from Tennessee," editorialized one Washington newspaper, "it must be said that they leave Washington with spotless reputations, they have received no presents, no carriages, no costly plate; they have dispensed a liberal hospitality."

Johnson's homecoming on March 20, 1869, was even more heartwarming. A huge civic parade was formed to greet his return down Greeneville's Main Street, over which now hung the banner, *WELCOME HOME: ANDREW JOHNSON, PATRIOT.* Orators harangued the throng of some 15,000 cheering citizens, and Johnson himself rose magnificently to the occasion. Drawing himself to his full six-foot height and sweeping the crowd with his flashing dark eyes, he shouted, "I stand before you unscratched, and I have put the whole pack to defiance. . . . Thank God, I can stand before the peo-

* At Johnson's request called "National Union" rather than "Republican."

ple of my state, and lift up both hands, and say, in the language of Samuel, 'Whose ox have I taken, or whose ass have I taken? At whose hands have I ever received bribes, and had my eyes blinded? If there is any, let him answer and I will return it!' Thus I return to you, feeling in my conscience that I have discharged my duties as a faithful man."

The house to which he returned had been extensively renovated after its years as a barracks, hospital, and then abandoned hulk. The basic structure, however, had remained sound over the years. When Johnson had moved in in 1851 the house represented an abode as fine as any of the other Greeneville gentry. The house stood directly upon the street, without a front yard, after the Northern Irish fashion common to early Greeneville. Its floor plan was the familiar one inherited from western Virginia—a front-to-back hall nearly eight feet wide, with a large room on either side, to the left the parlor, to the right Johnson's bedroom. On the rear ell was another bedroom and the dining room. The grade falls away rapidly from the house, and below the main level there was a kitchen and probably a servant's room; communication between kitchen and dining room was by an outdoor stairway that led to the main veranda.

In its high, narrow proportions, unbroken roof line, and absence of any portico, it was a house that can be found repeated in Greeneville and in any of the adjoining towns of eastern Tennessee. As was the custom, the dark ferrous red-colored bricks were left unpainted, although the mortar joints were penciled with white painted strips; the roof was covered by dressed oak shingles, and the exterior wood trim was painted a creamy yellow (white was a color used sparingly because of the high price of white lead).

Since the Johnsons had not lived in their house on any regular basis for nearly eighteen years, the modifications Johnson made to the house when they returned in 1869 made a fascinating commentary on the changing tastes wrought by two decades.

Closets were added for the first time, as were the diagonal corner cupboards. The original plain wood mantels were replaced with new mantels displaying the by-now familiar Greek Revival detailing. The most important structural change was the addition of a second story on the rear ell, which included the old veranda and added yet another, to make the conspicuous "double veranda." The new rooms were equipped with fireplaces, but, a sign of the times, they were bricked up as soon as they were built, since by now stoves, not open hearths, were used for heating. Oil lamps were installed throughout the house, and the floors were covered with mats and matting, except for the parlor, which was, of course, carpeted.

Johnson was too much a political war horse to leave politics alone altogether. "I intend to appropriate the remainder of my life, short as it may be, in the vindication of my character and that of my state," he announced shortly after he returned to Greeneville. More than anything else he longed to return to the U.S. Senate. "I had rather have the vindication of my state by electing me to my old seat in the Senate of the United States than to be monarch of the grandest empire on earth. . . . For this I live and will never die content without it!"

In pursuit of his goal, Johnson showed energy, political skill, and no little courage. Informed that a speech by him attacking his political adversary would be a signal for his assassination, Johnson mounted

Andrew Johnson's parlor still has its original furniture, most of it purchased in Washington at the end of his term. Among his souvenirs was a hand-carved ivory basket from Queen Emma of Hawaii (on the Paisley-shawl-covered table). The Steinway & Sons piano (below) cost $575 in 1869. Above it is a romantic painting of the Rocky Mountains that caught the President's fancy. The carpet, covered with geometric patterns, is red, green, and cream in color. On the table is the family Bible.

The basement kitchen has its original open fireplace and new cast-iron stove.

the soapbox before the Court House at Columbia and thundered in defiance, "These eyes have never yet beheld the man that this heart feared! I have said, and I repeat it now, Jesus Christ had his Judas, Caesar his Brutus, Charles I had his Cromwell, Washington had his Benedict Arnold, and I have my Edmond Cooper." It was perhaps the greatest anticlimax in the history of oratory, but the pistols that could be heard clicking to full cock in the swaying crowd were never fired. And in 1875 the state legislature, on the fifty-second ballot, elected Johnson to his old Senate seat, the only ex-President ever so to succeed.

He returned in triumph to Washington, D.C. and the scene of his earlier disgrace, when his fellow senators had all but found him guilty. As he entered the Senate chamber this time the whole Senate arose as one body in tribute to the Old Commoner. "I have no enemies to punish nor friends to reward," Johnson said. This, however, did not keep him from making one rousing attack on President Grant, but he concluded, as was his wont, with praise for the Constitution, "Let peace and union be restored to the land! May God bless this people and God save the Constitution!" It was, in effect, Johnson's final benediction. He suffered an apoplectic stroke and died July 31, 1875. He was buried by the Knights Templar, according to his wishes wrapped in the Stars and Stripes and with a copy of the Constitution set beneath his head. On his grave is carved the inscription, "His Faith in the People Never Wavered."

EIGHTEEN

Ulysses S. Grant

*He was made for great things, not little things.**

ARMS AND THE MAN have rarely found each other with more dramatic suddenness than in the career of Ulysses S. Grant In April 1860, Grant was a hard-bitten, disgruntled man who had failed as a soldier, farmer, and real-estate operator. As he walked off the river boat at Galena, Illinois, carrying two household chairs and followed by his diminutive, five-foot-tall wife, a former St. Louis belle named Julia Dent, and their four children, Grant himself would have predicted for himself a lackluster future at best.

The doubters would have included Grant's own family—his proud, querulous father and his two younger brothers, Simpson and Orville, whose leather-goods store at 120 Main Street in Galena was expected to furnish employment for Grant. The Grant brothers' terms were commensurate with their expectations: as bill collector and junior clerk, Grant, then thirty-eight, was to receive $800 a year. Of this $125 would have to go for Grant's first house in Galena, a plain, two-story brick cottage at 121 High Street, reached by a seemingly unending flight of 200 wooden stairs. Grant, a shabby, bearded figure in a patched and faded blue Army coat, could hope for an eventual partnership with his brothers, not much more, and perhaps not even that.

Less than two years later Grant was a brigadier general in the U.S. Army. Opposing him was his old West Point classmate and friend, Simon Bolivar Buckner, now brigadier general, Confederate States of America, in command of the Rebel stronghold at Fort Donelson. To Buckner, General Grant penned his historic message: "No terms except an unconditional and immediate surrender can be accepted. I propose to move immediately upon your works." Buckner was to protest that the terms were "ungenerous and unchivalrous," but surrender he did. The fall of Fort Donelson was the first great Union victory of the war; in Washington, Senators forgot their decorum, threw their hats and canes in the air; Congress enthusiastically voted Grant its heartfelt thanks; by the hundreds Northern citizens expressed their genuine gratitude in a more simple manner, by sending Grant box upon box of cigars. Even in the White House, the mood of gloom and oppression lifted from Lincoln: "Ever since that message to Buckner," Lincoln was later to remark, "I have felt that he was the man I could tie to, though I have never seen him."

Grant was the grandson of old Captain Noah Grant, who had fought the Revolution from Bunker Hill to Yorktown, then moved

Hiram Ulysses Grant (left) *with boyhood friend Harry Wilson.*

* Horace Porter, at the dedication of Grant's Tomb.

Grant's boyhood homes in Georgetown, Ohio, reflect the gradual rise of the family, who owned a tanning business. Grant, who was called "Useless" in these days, seemed interested only in horses and soon had a reputation for striking out on long trips on his own.

west to Ohio. Noah was prone to seek solutions in the bottle and paid scant heed, as Grant remarked, to "laying up stores on earth." Jesse Root Grant, Noah's son, was raised by strangers. He learned the tannery business from his brother and his brother's partner (the father of the abolitionist John Brown) in Deerfield, Ohio, until he could set up in business for himself. Jesse Grant married Hannah Simpson, quiet, austere, retiring and highly religious, in June 1821, and at Point Pleasant, Clermont County, Ohio, on April 27, 1822, Hiram Ulysses Grant was born.

The next year the family moved to Georgetown, Ohio, and it was here that Ulysses, or "Lyss" as his mother called him, grew up. There was no one in all Georgetown better with horses than Grant as a boy, nor anyone less adept at horsetrading. With a wince, Grant in his *Memoirs* tells this story on himself: "When I got to Mr. Ralston's house, I said to him: 'Papa says I may offer you twenty dollars for the colt, but if you won't take that, I am to offer twenty-two and a half, and if you won't take that, to give you twenty-five.' It would not require a Connecticut man to guess the price finally agreed upon."

Such tales soon earned Grant the nickname of "Useless" Grant. He himself saw his name in a different light, and in time made himself the best traveled boy in town, with trips to Maysville, Kentucky, and Louisville, once driving a two-horse carriage alone back from Chillicothe, a journey of seventy miles. On his grandest journey, Grant traveled east, by way of Philadelphia and New York to West Point, to enroll as a cadet. His greatest fear, apart from the Military Academy's stiff entrance exams, was the humorous potential of his initials, H.U.G. Unknown to him, Providence in the shape of the nominating congressman, T. L. Harner, had intervened. The appointment read for Ulysses Simpson Grant. William Tecumseh Sherman was one of the first to see "U. S. Grant" listed on the cadet bulletin board, and christened Grant "Uncle Sam," or "Sam" as he was later to be known to all his West Point classmates.

"I never succeeded in getting squarely at either end of my class, in any one study, during four years," Grant wrote of his West Point years. He was easily the best horseman (he held a record for jumping), but the dragoons were the elite, and 2nd Lt. U. S. Grant, twenty-first in a class of thirty-nine, drew the 4th Infantry. At Jefferson Barracks, St. Louis, the young officer was hazed by his dandified commanding officer, Captain Robert Buchanan, who endlessly fined Grant for being late to mess ("Another bottle of wine, Sir!" was Buchanan's penalty). But Grant did manage to meet and court the sister of his best West Point friend, Fred T. Dent. And when the 4th Infantry was ordered south to prepare for trouble in Texas, Grant realized that his attraction to the brunette beauty Julia Dent, a spirited horse-fancier like himself, was deeper than mere infatuation. "One of my superstitions," Grant tells us in his *Memoirs,* "had always been when I started to go anywhere, or to do anything, not to turn back, or stop until the thing intended was accomplished." It was the spirit that was later to run Lee to earth at Appomattox; in May 1844, it got Grant a wife, although the marriage had to wait until the end of the Mexican War, finally taking place in the Dents' town house in St. Louis on April 22, 1848.

Julia Dent unquestionably loved her shy, brooding lieutenant, as much as Grant adored his high-spirited Southern wife, cheerfully overlooking her cast left eye. But, still and all, it was a strange mar-

The Grant family. Back row, General Grant and Frederick Dent Grant; front row, Mrs. Grant, Ulysses S. Grant, Jr., Jesse R. Grant, and Nellie Grant.

riage. The Dents were a well-to-do Maryland family with a large estate, White Haven, outside St. Louis, and thirty slaves, including Julia's own three household servants. Grant came back from the Mexican War, having fought in every battle but Buena Vista, breveted captain for gallantry. But what goods he had laid up on earth were all intangibles; he had taken the measure of his fellow officers, and learned that even Robert E. Lee was not "immortal." He had demonstrated bravery, riding Indian fashion through the sniper fire of Monterey. At West Point, General Winfield Scott had been his ideal ("With his commanding figure, his quite colossal size and showy uniform, I thought him the finest specimen of manhood my eyes had ever beheld"); in the Mexican War, Grant also served under Zachary Taylor, and Grant liked what he saw: "General Taylor never wore uniform, but dressed himself entirely for comfort. He moved about the field in which he was operating to see through his own eyes the situation. . . . He was very much given to sit his horse side-ways—with both feet on one side—particularly in battle. . . . Both [Scott and Taylor] were great and successful soldiers. Both were pleasant to serve under—Taylor was pleasant to serve with."

Grant's army career after the Mexican War was the kind to drive a young officer to drink; in Grant's case, it did. The young newly-weds lived first at the barracks at Sackett's Harbor, then at 253 East Fort Street, where Julia made life homey with her new carpets and hand-painted china. Then in 1852, the regiment was ordered to the West Coast. One third of the detachment were lost crossing the Isthmus of Panama. After the troops' arrival in San Francisco, a wide-open town full of gold-rush Forty-Niners, Grant settled in to dreary barracks duty far from wife and family, first at Fort Vancouver, then in 1853 at Fort Humbolt (where he unsuccessfully tried potato farm-

Hardscrabble was ironic name Grant gave the house he built on his wife's dowry land near St. Louis in 1855 after he resigned his commission in U.S. Army.

ing to pad out his captain's salary). In Fort Humbolt he met his earlier nemesis once again; his commanding officer was Lieutenant Colonel Robert Buchanan, the arrogant officer who had made Grant's life hell in Jefferson Barracks. Threatened with a court-martial if he did not stop drinking and told to give up the bottle or his commission, Grant is supposed to have said he would do both. "Whoever hears of me in ten years," he wrote from the West Coast "will hear of a well-to-do old Missouri farmer!"

In New York on his way home, Grant was so broke that he had to borrow a few dollars from his old classmate Simon Bolivar Buckner to pay his hotel bill. And back at the Dents' White Haven estate, Grant was treated by Judge Dent, or "Colonel" as he was called by courtesy, as a failure. To restore his sense of independence Julia suggested he clear and farm the sixty acres Colonel Dent had given her as a dowry; Grant set about gladly building by hand their own log-cabin farm according to Julia's sketches. In a moment of grim irony, he called it Hardscrabble.*

This proved an appropriate name. For three years Grant labored to provide a living for his growing family, sometimes hauling wood ten miles for four dollars a cord, often sick with what was called, after the unpopular President, "Tyler's grippe" but which was probably malaria. Occasionally some of Grant's old fellow officers would run across him sitting at St. Louis' Planters Hotel. "Why, Grant," exclaimed General William S. Harney, "what in blazes are you doing?" Grant, wearing his old blue army overcoat, battered hat and heavy boots, replied laconically, "Well, General, I am hauling wood." The answer was so obvious, the accent so droll that the general and his staff roared with laughter; it is fair to assume Grant writhed inwardly. An old acquaintance has left this vignette: "I can see him now, sitting in an arm-chair, smoking an El Sol cigar and waiting with an air of extreme patience and resignation. But waiting for what? Did he himself know?"

The answer is, assuredly not. But when Lincoln issued his first call for volunteers after the fall of Fort Sumter, all that was lethargic, aimless, and directionless about Grant fell away. Instinctively the fellow citizens of Galena, Illinois, turned to this dark-bearded ex-army officer for guidance, electing him chairman of the meeting held at the court house to raise volunteers. "I am in for the war," Grant said grimly, "and shall stay until this wicked rebellion is crushed at the cannon's mouth." Ulysses was at last launched forth upon his destiny. As Grant himself recounts, "I never went into our leather store after that meeting, to put up a package or do other business."

The deafening roar of musketry, of shot and shell, and the screams of casualties, mounting to totals unknown in the history of modern war, shrouded in a halo of battle smoke the names of Fort Donelson, Vicksburg, Shiloh, and with them the name of their relentless victor, Unconditional-Surrender Grant. "I propose to fight it out on this line if it takes all summer," Grant told Secretary of War Stanton as the Union armies moved in on Richmond. "If I knew what brand of whisky he drinks," Lincoln remarked, "I would send a barrel or so to some other generals." Finally at Appomattox Court House, "the thing intended was accomplished."

Grant hurried directly back from Lee's surrender to City Point,

---

* The house, which has been moved several times, is now on the Anheuser-Busch estate outside St. Louis. It is not open to the public.

Grant's Galena house was the town's most distinguished hillside mansion. Built of brick in 1857, it has a small colonnaded entry and large bracketed eaves, both stylistic marks of period just before the Civil War. The dining room has Grant's White House china as well as fruits that Mrs. Grant preserved in wax, a hobby fashionable at the time.

the Union headquarters on the James River, where Julia Grant had shared army life with him, and then to Washington for the victory celebration. Lincoln and Grant had grown close during the final war years, but not so Mrs. Grant and Mrs. Lincoln. Indeed Mary Todd Lincoln had temper tantrums of jealous rage when she heard that the President had so much as even seen Mrs. Grant alone. When Lincoln invited the Grants to attend the play at Ford's Theater on the night of April fourteenth, Mrs. Grant refused. Grant, who had already verbally assented, was forced to beg off lamely that he wanted to go visit his own children in Burlington, New Jersey. Thus Grant was at Philadelphia's Broad Street Station that night when the news was telegraphed that Lincoln had been shot. By a fluke of petty feminine jealousy, Grant had been spared from the assassination that in all likelihood would have been his fate as well as Lincoln's.

Grant was not a political man; he had voted only once, for Buchanan. His only bid for political office had come after Fort Donelson, when he told a delegation of fellow townsmen, "I should like to be the mayor of Galena . . . to build new sidewalks from my house to the depot." But as General of the Armies and the most popular Union general alive, Grant's future in politics was inevitable. On his travels Grant received medals, horses, jeweled swords; soldiers and citizens alike turned out to cheer. No less than three houses in various parts of the country were offered him. The one the Grants chose to return to first was in Galena. On their arrival banners were strung across Main Street reading *HAIL TO THE CHIEF WHO IN TRIUMPH ADVANCES,* and, recalling his wish, another, *GENERAL, THE SIDEWALK IS BUILT.* In Galena's Main Street where a crowd of 10,000 greeted Grant as a hero, the General made a brief speech in the De Soto Hotel before being driven up the hill to see his new home, a handsome brick residence, newly furnished, for which the people of Galena had subscribed $16,000. As Grant walked out on the front porch with his wife after inspecting the house, tears were seen trickling down his bearded cheeks.

The Galena house had been built in 1857 by Jackson Davis, a leading citizen during Galena's boom days as a shipping center, before the Illinois Central's line made the rival city of Dubuque the leading terminal and freight center. Later occupants kept the Grant house almost as a relic; as a result it is today a nearly mint-perfect example of post-Civil War taste in interior furnishings, which include dishes from Grant's two terms in the White House and even, under a glass bell jar, fruits preserved in wax by Mrs. Grant herself.

Warm as their homecoming was, the Grants soon decided to move east. Their first choice was the house in Philadelphia which members of the Union Club had bought and furnished for $30,000. When this proved too far removed from Washington, the magnet which inevitably drew General Grant, the family moved into quarters at 205 I Street, on "Minnesota Row," for Christmas of 1865. This Washington residence was a handsome house, formerly occupied by Vice-President Breckinridge, two doors from one previously owned by Stephen A. Douglas. It was also vastly beyond Grant's means, and in March he was presented with $100,000 from a group of New Yorkers to pay off the mortgage. When it was found that Grant's library—such as it was—consisted almost entirely of patent-office reports, fifty "solid men of Boston" presented him with a library, bound in red calf, which cost $75,000.

General Grant was working quietly in his office in Army Headquarters in Washington in 1868 when Secretary of War Stanton rushed across the street from the War Department. "General," he cried, "I have come to tell you that you have been nominated by the Republican Party for President of the United States." Grant received the words without emotion. Adam Badeau, who was present, reported, "There was no shade of exultation or agitation on his face, not a flush on his cheek nor a flash in his eye." Only in one phrase, in his formal acceptance to the Republican Convention, did Grant find words with a touch of destiny. In a fiery plea for an end to animosities and a beginning to reconstruction, he said, "Let us have peace."

The South had been brought to prostration by the Civil War; the North had both prospered and expanded. Austerity was a thing of the past, and Grant's years marked an outburst of extravagance, crude business morality, and, in rich bumperfuls, an exultation in the first vast outpourings of the new machine age—crude, gaudy and garish. The Grants, with their twenty-five- and thirty-course official dinners, were as much a part of this as the gaudy redecoration of the White House (the first since Monroe's time). Furnishings tell much of the same story as clothing, whether the $4000 worth of Brussels lace used to gown Grant's beloved daughter Nellie for her White House wedding to Fanny Kemble's nephew, the handsome Britisher Algernon Sartoris, or the gown of one senator's wife, as observed by *Harper's*: "The first skirt is blue with over-dress of French blue, with a vest of Mexican blue. The fringe is knotted in a narrow hem on each skirt . . . all mingled in the most delightful confusion."

High Victorian taste called for such "delightful confusion" until even nutpicks came in half a dozen shapes and sizes. Vacation life carried its own relaxed rituals. In the Grants' case, the summer

President Grant was the first President to have a Summer White House. His favorite area was the New Jersey seashore; so unprecedented was this vacation move that questions were raised as to whether laws signed by Grant there were legal. Below is his favorite house at Long Branch, which was described as a "mixture of English villa and Swiss chalet." When ships at sea rendered honors, Grant's youngest son, Jesse (right), often ran to fire off the President's own private saluting cannon in reply.

Former President Grant's residence, 3 East Sixty-sixth Street, New York City, was ornately furnished with souvenirs and mementos from his round-the-world trip. The jars and black lacquered furniture in the back parlor (above) were a personal gift from Japan's Mikado.

White House was at Long Branch, New Jersey, a two-and-a-half-story "cottage," ringed round with a two-story porch, which one New York *Tribune* reporter appropriately described as a "mixture of English villa and Swiss chalet." Here Julia Grant liked to rock on the front veranda, wearing her favorite sunbonnet, and, although by then forty-six years old, once on a dare from her son vaulted the rail with a flourish of striped petticoats. The President was more sedate, sporting broadcloth and a tall hat, which he tipped decorously to ladies parading by the piazza, but he was happiest driving his buggy twenty miles a day along the ocean front. Ships ran in close to shore to salute the President; the Grants gravely returned the honor by running up a flag, or asking their son Jesse to fire off their private saluting cannon.

"I believe I am lazy and don't get credit for it," Grant wrote. "The fact is circumstances have thrown me into an occupation uncongenial to me." With great relief the Grants finally left the White House. At loose ends, they decided to travel around the world, Julia declaring she was one Penelope who would follow her Ulysses, not stay at home to weave. For the next three years the nation was treated to a vivid account of one of the most triumphal tours ever known as the Grants had honor upon honor heaped upon them on their travels round the world.

Back in Galena at their long journey's end, Grant wearied of leisure and became eager to resume his old place in the White House. But the public had grown indifferent to echoes of past martial splendor and cynically recalled Grant's corrupt government. Instead the G.O.P. nomination on June 1, 1880, went to young, blond-bearded James A. Garfield, and Grant remarked bitterly, "My friends have not been honest with me. I can't afford to be defeated. They should not have placed me in nomination unless they felt perfectly sure of my success." But in time he became more philosophical. To his daughter Nellie, he wrote "Had I been nominated there would have been the most violent campaign ever known in our country made against me. This I have avoided."

Life began anew for the Grants in New York, where a fund of $95,000 had been raised by Hamilton Fish, Joseph Drexel, George W. Childs, and J. P. Morgan to buy a town house at 3 East 66th Street (since torn down). It was turned into a treasure chest of Grant's mementoes. Persian and Turkish rugs and Bengal tiger skins were used to set off the gold-lacquer cabinet from the Mikado, whose personal black lacquer furniture was now resting in the Grant sitting room. All about were teakwood cabinets, malachite and enamels from Russia, jeweled caskets with scrolls symbolizing the freedom of cities round the world, medals, swords, and such homely reminders as the fifteen buttons Julia had cut from the General's coat after as many battles. The Grants could count their blessings; including the Long Branch cottage, Grant held $200,000 in real estate; his trust funds brought him $15,000 a year.

Then, in May 1884, disaster struck. The brokerage firm in which his son was a partner turned out to be a wholesale swindling operation. So completely was Grant's fortune swept away that when the scandal broke Grant had only $80 in his pocket and $130 in house money left. He borrowed heavily from William H. Vanderbilt, turned the money over to pay off the firm's debts. For himself he rejected all offers of help, including one from General William Tecumseh Sherman and another from President Chester A. Arthur. Having discovered that his writing could bring him money after his first two articles in the *Century Magazine,* Grant signed a contract with Samuel L. Clemens (better known as Mark Twain) for two volumes of his *Memoirs* for $25,000 in cash and 20 per cent of the royalties. Grant, then in his New York house, settled down manfully in the third floor library, with its bay window fronting on the street, working in a knitted cap (to ward off neuralgia) and large spectacles with hard-rubber rims. "Why, I am positively enjoying the work," he wrote. "I am keeping at it every day and night, and Sundays."

But soon a second affliction came to test his Job-like patience. While nibbling a peach, he discovered an acute pain in his throat. It persisted, and was soon diagnosed as cancer. Then began the race between death and the completion of the *Memoirs.* The cancer spread rapidly. On June 16, 1885, Grant boarded Vanderbilt's private railroad car for his last trip up the Hudson past West Point, en route to Saratoga. There he was installed in a small cottage owned by A. J. Drexel near Mount McGregor's Balmoral Hotel. By this time he could no longer speak, but his humor grimly stayed with him. "A verb is anything that signifies to be; to do; or to suffer. I signify all three," he scribbled as a message to his doctor.

Specially pleasing to Grant during his last pain-filled days was the steady stream of visitors, many of them old comrades-in-arms and, even more touching, some of his old Johnny Reb opponents, including Simon Bolivar Buckner. On July 16, Grant concluded his monumental task, two volumes of 1231 pages and 295,000 words. "There is nothing more I should do to it now, and therefore I am not likely to be more ready to go than at this moment," he wrote. Seven days later, at eight minutes after eight on the morning of July 23, 1885, Fred, the family's Negro servant, stopped the clock in Grant's small bedroom of the Drexel cottage. For the General, it was over.

Julia Dent Grant was a diminutive St. Louis belle who, despite a cast in one eye, held Grant's deep affection. She lived on after him until 1902.

NINETEEN

Rutherford Birchard Hayes

N O PRESIDENT before, and certainly none since, has found himself in quite the same predicament that beset Rutherford Birchard Hayes. On March 1, 1877, just three days before the date set for the inauguration, he stood on the platform of the Columbus, Ohio, railroad station, joking good-humoredly that "perhaps" he would "be back immediately." This was literally a possibility. For the first time, a special "electoral commission," had been formed to go over challenged electoral certificates. The examination had been completed, but the House of Representatives was in the grip of a seemingly unending filibuster.

It was not until after ten o'clock on the evening of March 1, while Governor Hayes, his family, and friends were en route to Washington that the House filibuster at last broke; it was 4:10 A.M. of March 2 before the president of the Senate finally announced that, by one vote out of the 389 cast, Rutherford B. Hayes of Ohio had defeated the Democratic governor of New York, Samuel J. Tilden.

The close electoral vote and the widespread charges of bribery and corruption cast a shadow on Hayes' presidency from the start. (Democrats referred to Hayes as Ruther*fraud* B. Hayes.) And the new President, by moving to conciliate the South and removing occupation troops from South Carolina and Louisiana, became nearly as unpopular with his own Republican party. Within six weeks it could be said that Hayes was without a party. When Hayes insisted that the traditional spoils system that had plagued Presidents from Jackson onward must undergo a change that was "thorough, radical, and complete," congressional ire knew no bounds.

In fact, Hayes was rescuing the G.O.P. from "Grantism"; he was also giving the Republican Party a new lease and a new mandate, that of becoming the party of responsibility and reform. In time, his efforts caused public opinion to veer toward him. By the end of his term, the man who had started out as "His Fraudulency" would be introduced to a Harvard audience by Oliver Wendell Holmes as "His Honesty, The President."

No small part in building up the President was played by his admirable, strait-laced wife, Lucy Webb Hayes, the first college-educated First Lady (Cincinnati Wesleyan Women's College) and a birthright prohibitionist. She was known far and wide as "Lemonade Lucy" for her refusal to serve liquor, let alone countenance card-playing, dancing, or cigar-smoking. But in an age then basking in the high noon of Victorian respectability, the near-ideal family life of the Hayes, with their hymn-singing and sentimental occasions (on her silver anniversary, Lucy Hayes insisted on being married all over again in her original flowered satin wedding gown), brought approval.

Rutherford B. Hayes' birthplace in Delaware, Ohio, was a brick structure, with wooden addition built after 1820. "Cabinet Wareroom" sign calls attention to building's later use for furniture display.

Spiegel Grove was largely rebuilt in 1880, when the older brick section was doubled in height and width. The central hall rises four stories through the house and terminates in the cupola. In this great, rambling house, there are no fewer than twenty bedrooms.

She became as popular in her day and way as was Dolley Madison in hers.

In his turbulent early days in the White House, perhaps Hayes found sustenance to surmount his particular problems in his own tradition as a Yankee from the West. Vermont and its individualistic standards were a part of his birthright, although he was actually born on October 4, 1822, in Delaware, Ohio, the posthumous son of a Vermonter, Rutherford Hayes, of Brattleboro, and Sophia Birchard, daughter of a Chillicothe, Ohio doctor.

Sardis Birchard, a hard-bitten Vermonter, became guardian of young "Ruddy" Hayes and his sister. Birchard saw that the young man had a good education, first at the Academy in Norwalk, Ohio, then at the private school of Isaac Webb in Middletown, Connecticut. Young Hayes dreamed of Yale, but family finances and his mother's wishes prevailed, and he graduated from Kenyon College with top honors and was class valedictorian (1842). His mother hoped her strong Methodism would lead him toward the pulpit, but Hayes decided, instead, on the law. He read for a year and a half in Columbus, Ohio, then went east to Harvard Law School (Class of 1845).

Hayes first hung out his shingle in Lower Sandusky (later Fremont), Ohio, a small settlement dominated by his Uncle Sardis Birchard. As he was himself to admit, it was a mistake: "the waste of those five precious years at Sandusky!" In 1850 he moved to Cincinnati, a larger arena for his talents. After his marriage in 1852 Hayes bought a narrow, three-story brick house at 383 Sixth Street. It was a happy time. "These ties, these affections—nothing in life to equal them!" he confided in his diary. But with the outbreak of the Civil War, Hayes made his position clear: "I would prefer to go into it if I knew that I was to die or be killed in the course of it than live through and after it without taking any part in it."

135 RUTHERFORD BIRCHARD HAYES

Family portrait of the Hayes family grouped on the porch of Spiegel Grove in 1887 shows, left to right, Birchard A. Hayes, Mary Sherman Hayes, the former President, Scott R. Hayes, Rutherford P. Hayes, the President's wife, Fanny Hayes, and Webb C. Hayes.

Hayes, who began the war as a major in the 23d Ohio Volunteers, and emerged as brevet major general, was not a skilled or brilliant officer, but he was popular with his men and unquestionably brave. Sergeant William McKinley, also destined for the White House, noted of his commanding officer, "His whole nature seemed to change when in battle. From the sunny, agreeable, the kind, the generous, the gentle gentleman . . . he was, when the battle was once on . . . intense and ferocious."

Tales of his heroism were spread back to Ohio by the troops in their letters home. But when Hayes was asked to stand for Congress, he wrote, "An officer fit for duty who at this crisis would abandon his post to electioneer for a seat in Congress ought to be scalped." These were the proper sentiments to Ohio ears, and even *in absentia,* Hayes was sent to Congress, where he became a "Radical," voting for reconstruction and Johnson's impeachment. Back home he was twice elected governor of Ohio, beaten for Congress in 1872, and re-elected governor of Ohio for the third time in 1875.

Hayes had felt his 1872 defeat for Congress painfully, and in May 1873, he took his family to make their permanent home in the house of his Uncle Sardis at Spiegel Grove in Fremont. The twenty-five acres of virgin timber had been bought by Sardis Birchard in 1845; Sardis had long been entranced by the eerie stillness and peace of the deep woods reflected in the clear pools of water like a mirror. *Spiegel* is the German word for mirror, and it took Sardis Birchard's fancy to name his estate after a German fairy tale. But not until 1859 was ground broken for the original house, a two-and-a-half-story gabled brick structure built by D. L. June, a prominent local contractor.

As soon as the Hayes family moved in, Rutherford B. Hayes built two frame additions to house a new kitchen, office, and library to accommodate his growing collection of books. The very next year, Sardis Birchard died, willing the house to Hayes. But it was not until

1880, when President Hayes, who vowed to serve but one term in the White House, was preparing to return to Fremont, that the extensive alterations we see in the present Spiegel Grove were made.

The mansion today represents the heyday of Victorianism. And, in this case, *grew* is the operative word, for Hayes' first move was to duplicate the original building and also make it twice as high; the result is the otherwise inexplicable double-gabled front façade along which stretches the broad (fourteen-foot-wide) eighty-foot porch or veranda. In 1889 further extensive modifications were made, with the result that only two rooms of the original house still remain—the red parlor on the first floor and the ancestral room directly above, which had served as Uncle Sardis' bedroom.

The final mansion that emerged was grandiose in scale; the central area was opened up through four stories to a balanced cupola, and the hall was dressed up with white walnut paneling. The immense brown-and-gold drawing room reflects the elegance of the White House's East Room. Behind it is a narrow library decorated with portraits of the Presidents of the United States. To the rear of this is a state dining room, again clearly copied after its prototype in the Executive Mansion. On the second floor is a maze of bedrooms and guest rooms, twenty in all.

The library, which was enlarged to include 6000 volumes of Americana bought from Cincinnati publisher Robert Clarke, included the works of Ralph Waldo Emerson, "my ancient favorite," as Hayes called him in corresponding with his youthful friend, William Howard Taft, as well as Hawthorne, Scott, Lincoln, and William Dean Howells, and Byron and Browning. The wealth of this library was to form the backbone of the present Hayes Memorial Library and Museum when it was opened on May 30, 1916, and to form the nucleus for the Memorial Library's present collection of over 30,000 volumes and manuscript division with over 400,000 items of Americana.

1876 had been the centenary of the founding of the Republic, and Hayes had a lively sense of history. He was proud that one of the main drives of Spiegel Grove to the south of the house was the old Sandusky-Scioto Indian trail. He was also not without sentimentality. In 1877, President Hayes began the custom of christening oaks after his friends. In addition, he planted slips from other trees: the Napoleon willow from one at Saint Helena, and the Washington willow from the grave at Mount Vernon, two oaks from acorns from Hartford's Charter Oak. Many are still alive, now grown to girths of four and five feet.

Hayes was determined to be of service to the community after his term as President, and he succeeded nobly, being commander-in-chief of the Loyal Legion, a member of the Odd Fellows Lodge and the G.A.R.; he interested himself in prison reform, manual training, and Negro education. He keenly felt the loss of his wife, who died in June 1889. When he felt his own death approaching, he insisted that he return to their home, saying, "I'd rather die in Spiegel Grove than anywhere else." At his wintry funeral in January 1893, one of the conspicuous mourners was President Grover Cleveland, a Democrat, who told his wife, "He was coming to see me, but he is dead now and I will go to him." From the highest member of the opposition it was a handsome tribute to the Republican who has come down in history as "The Spokesman of Reunion."

Original bedroom in house built by Hayes' Uncle Sardis Birchard in 1859 was left unchanged when house was rebuilt in 1880. Painting over the fireplace is of Mrs. Hayes' mother, Marie Cook Webb.

TWENTY

James Abram Garfield

N O MAN ever started so low that accomplished so much in all our history—not Franklin or Lincoln even." Such, at least, was the considered opinion of Rutherford B. Hayes of his fellow Ohioan, James A. Garfield. History, however, remembers Garfield as the President who was shot twice in the back by a deranged office-seeker, Charles J. Guiteau, less than four months after he took office as President of the United States in 1881.

Garfield's rise to prominence started at the lowest level possible; his father Abram, a migrant New Englander, died when James was two from a combination of the "ague" and the exhaustion of combating a forest fire roaring through the bark-girdled trees that threatened his log cabin. This left the courageous frontier mother, Eliza Ballou Garfield, all alone to raise her "four young saplings" in the small log cabin at Orange, in Cuyahoga County, Ohio. Young James Garfield, precocious by nature (he learned his alphabet and simple reading by the age of three), learned to do a man's work by the time he was ten, worked as a bargeman, farmer, and carpenter. But for all his rustic clothes, patched pants, and hickory-straw hat, he consistently led his class, first at Geauga Academy; later at Western Reserve Eclectic Institute (Hiram College); and finally at Williams College (1856), where in praise of his college's president he was inspired to give that famous definition of good education: "The ideal college is Mark Hopkins on one end of the log and a student on the other."

With a physique made powerful by haying, harvesting, and driving mules along canal towpaths, young Garfield became a big, six-foot, blond-bearded man who was also a gifted speaker; a member of the Disciples of Christ, he served as a lay minister; had he remained in New England, he would have been a preacher. Instead, he went back to Hiram College to teach Latin and Greek, and, in time, to marry his onetime classmate Lucretia Rudolph.

When the Civil War broke out, Garfield helped raise the 42d Ohio Volunteer Infantry, including in its ranks many of his former Hiram students; at thirty he was the youngest brigadier in the Union Army, a hero of Shiloh and Chickamauga, and, in 1863, a member of Congress. Visiting New York when the word came that Lincoln had been assassinated, the yellow-bearded veteran emerged as the man to rally the populace. From the steps of the Sub-Treasury, Garfield orated in words never forgotten by those who heard them: "Clouds and darkness are around Him; His pavilion is dark waters and thick clouds; justice and judgment are the habitation of His throne; mercy and truth shall go before His face! Fellow citizens, God reigns and the Government at Washington still lives!"

Garfield, born in Orange, Ohio, was the last of the log-cabin Presidents. His father died fighting a forest fire here, leaving a widowed mother to raise her "four young saplings" in this small log cabin.

James A. Garfield was so precocious that he learned to read at three. As young man, he graduated from Williams College. His wife, Lucretia Rudolph, was classmate at institute later called Hiram College. Garfield's ancestors came to Massachusetts with Winthrop; his wife was descended from Gen. Nathanael Greene, but in Ohio young couple had to make their own way.

Nine times Garfield presented himself to the Ohio electorate; nine times he was returned to the House of Representatives. With Maine's James G. Blaine, he became the recognized leader in the House. With his career prospering in the nation's capital, Garfield, in the fall of 1876, decided that it was high time he owned a place "where my boys can learn to work and where I can get some exercise, where I can touch the earth and get some strength from it."

The farm that James A. Garfield bought at $115 an acre for his wife, aged mother, and family of four sons and a daughter* was at Mentor, twenty-three miles east of Cleveland. It had on it an unpretentious farmhouse built by James Dickey, an early settler in the old Western Reserve. Dickey's small house overlooking Lake Erie was the nucleus of the later twenty-six-room mansion which Garfield built and called Lawnfield. Over four years, with later additions, it reached the dimensions of a full-rigged Victorian house, with gables, bay windows, balconies, carriage porch, and verandas.

In 1880, an uproarious Republican Convention sighted Garfield, there as campaign manager for Ohio's favorite son, John Sherman, as presidential timber in his own right. Opposing the 306 "Stalwarts," who voted throughout for a third term for Grant, Garfield represented the "Half-Breeds." Leaders of the "Stalwarts" was New York's Roscoe Conkling, once ticked off by James G. Blaine for his "grandiloquent swell, his majestic, supereminent, overpowering, turkey gobbler strut." But when Garfield walked onto the platform as Conkling was in full tide of his oration, the young Ohioan received such

* James R. Garfield, who became Secretary of the Interior, 1907–9; Henry A., later president of Williams College; Irvin M., to become a Boston lawyer, and Abram G., a future Cleveland architect; the daughter, who became Mary Garfield Stanley-Brown, lived until December 30, 1947.

Lawnfield, Garfield's house in Mentor, Ohio (above), grew from small farmhouse to 26-room mansion by 1880. Photograph (below) shows Queen Anne–style summer house at Long Branch, New Jersey, where Garfield died after having been shot by a deranged office seeker.

an overpowering burst of welcoming cheers that Conkling, furious, was forced to pause. Later Conkling sent over a newspaper with a mocking note scribbled in the margin, "I congratulate you on being the dark horse!" It was meant in jest, but on the thirty-fourth ballot, Conkling's sarcasm became reality. In the melee, Garfield sat perspiring and limp. "Get me out of here," he gasped to his seatmate, and was barely able to make his way outside the convention hall to a public hack, and even then the top of the carriage was torn away by the mass of enthusiastic, yelling delegates.

Following the custom of the time, Garfield refused to travel during the campaign. At Mentor, Ohio, a small frame house, still there to be seen, was set up on the front lawn; equipped with telegraph wires, it served as Garfield's campaign headquarters for the press and politicians. Garfield regularly gave simple chats from the Lawnfield porch, speeches both graceful and tactful, which delighted the delegations of voters shipped there regularly by the Republican Party. But if Garfield was often guarded, his backers were no such thing. Orated Republican Robert Ingersoll: "The Democratic Party is a party of famine; it is a good friend of the early frosts; it believes in the Colorado beetle and the weevil."

As the returns came in, it seemed at first as if the Democrats—beetles, weevils, and all—would win. In the final totals, however, Garfield and Arthur won by a scant 10,000 votes, or .08 per cent more than the votes cast for the Democrats' General Winfield Scott Hancock. In electoral votes the outcome was decisive: 214 to 155.

Rarely has a President had such good will from the people as flowed toward Garfield as he stood on the steps of the Capitol beside Rutherford B. Hayes on Inauguration Day, March 4, 1881. The picture of robust health, the bearded Garfield first kissed the Bible, and then, in a gesture that captured the imagination and hearts of the inaugural throng, he turned next to kiss his aged mother, Eliza Ballou Garfield, the frontier woman who had lived to see her son triumphantly rise from log cabin to White House.

But as Ralph Waldo Emerson once commented: "The President pays dear for his White House." A mild man, good fellow, lover of poetry and literature, James A. Garfield was appalled at the jostling horde of office-seekers that besieged him in the White House. "My God!" he said bitterly, "What is there in this place that a man should ever want to get into it?" A party fight between the "Half-Breeds," led by James G. Blaine, and the "Stalwarts," still smoldering from their convention defeat, made life even more difficult.

On July 2, 1881, Garfield was looking forward to his Twenty-fifth Reunion at Williams College as a happy vacation, and was in such good form that he took a dare from one of his sons and leaped over his own bed in the White House. At the old Baltimore & Potomac station in Washington later that day the new President was still in fine spirits, unaware that a darker destiny awaited him. Two flashes of a revolver suddenly stabbed out and knocked him forward to the floor; to the stunned throng his assassin screamed, "I am a Stalwart! Arthur is now President!"

For more than eleven weeks Garfield was cared for, first in the White House, then at the New Jersey summer resort, Elberon, by the first White House lady doctor, Dr. Susan Add Edson, a leading homeopathic physician, before his life finally ebbed away on September 19, 1881. He was only forty-nine years old. Today, the hat he was wearing when he was shot, along with his familiar lunch basket, the Bible on which he took his oath, the manuscript of his inaugural address, and a set of the monogrammed Haviland china used by the Garfields in the White House, as well as Mrs. Garfield's gowns and much of the President's library, are still to be found in the rambling mansion at Mentor, Ohio, a small village, not unlike its New England prototypes, which preserves with reverence the relics of the twentieth President's brief fame and tragic death.

Sketches made during Garfield's 1880 campaign show (top), Garfield's own study, (below) politicians thronging the hallway.

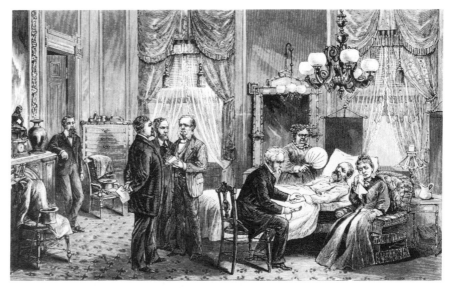

Garfield's death, September 19, 1881, in the vacation house at Long Branch, New Jersey.

TWENTY-ONE
Chester A. Arthur

ONE HUMID DAY in August 1903, a band of dignitaries that included Secretary of the Navy William E. Chandler and Robert Todd Lincoln, gathered on a lonely road in North Fairfield, Vermont, to dedicate the newly polished Barre granite monument to Chester Alan Arthur. All that remained by then of the small farmhouse and birthplace of Vermont's first native-born President was a cellar hole and a clump of willows. Today a replica of Chester A. Arthur's birthplace stands in its place, a fitting reminder of Arthur's humble beginnings.

Arthur, like John Tyler, was known as "His Accidency." A handsome, six-foot-two, polished gentleman from New York's best clubs he had been nominated Vice-President on the Republican ticket with James Garfield mainly as a sop to G.O.P. regulars. The ticket won, but Garfield was assassinated within months after taking office.

One of Arthur's political followers summed up even his own party's reaction when he cried, "Chet Arthur, President of the United States! Good God!" The country battened down for a rule of bossism, corruption, and pork-barrel politics. The country could not have been more wrong. For though Arthur ranks as an average President at most, he was honest, able and capable of standing up even to the most powerful of bosses.

His father, the Reverend William Arthur, was born in Ballymina, County Antrim, Ireland in 1796, possessed a degree from Queens College, Belfast, and after his arrival in New England had been converted to the Baptist ministry at the age of thirty-one. Arthur's mother was Malvina Stone, born in Waterville, Vermont, in 1802, the daughter of a New Hampshire pioneer. Young Arthur got much of his early education in Union Village (now Greenwich), New York, where he attended the small academy run by James I. Lourie, a graduate of Union College. Young Chester is supposed to have carved his initials in the attic beams (the old Academy is now the Home for Aged Women on Academy Street). Contemporaries recalled,"When Chester was a boy, you might see him in the village street after a shower, watching boys building mud dams across the rivulet in the roadway. Pretty soon he would be ordering this one to bring stones, another sticks, and others sods and mud to finish the dam; and they

Arthur was born in a small farmhouse in North Fairfield, Vermont, the son of a Baptist minister, and became perhaps our most elegant President, known as "Prince Arthur." Old photograph shows the abandoned birthplace and (below) the replica built on the site.

Arthur was considered a machine politician and the tool of Boss Conkling, but once in office he won approval for attacking the spoils system and such pork-barrel bills as the River and Harbor Bill from Harper's Weekly, *which captioned this cartoon: "President Arthur, hit him again! Don't let the vulture become our national bird."*

would do all his bidding without question. But he took good care not to get any dirt on his hands."

In Greenwich, Chester also had his first political scuffle. The "ashpole" was erected in the village, Polk's standard (by contrast with Jackson's old hickory). When the opposition attempted to rush the ashpole, they were held at bay by the ardent Polk supporters, among them young Arthur. The parsonage where the Arthurs lived still stands, although twice removed, and is now on Woodlawn Avenue.

When the family moved to Schenectady, Arthur was able to enter Union College himself, teaching school between years to finance himself, and graduating Phi Beta Kappa in 1848. He taught school in North Pownal, Vermont, where three years later James A. Garfield, his future running mate, taught penmanship. Having read law, Arthur at the age of twenty-three finally abandoned schoolteaching, went to New York to join the firm of Culver and Parker, and, if possible, make a fortune. He succeeded. In New York, Arthur also met and married Ellen Lewis Herndon, a Virginia beauty and daughter of the U.S. naval hero. Their house at 123 Lexington Avenue soon became a center for musicales; it had a sumptuous library of more than 1000 volumes including Scott, Thackery, and Burns—Arthur's favorites— and an even more sumptuous cuisine.

Arthur seems to have entered politics as a lucrative hobby. During the early Civil War he was appointed quartermaster general, assigned to outfit New York's quota of troops, the largest from any state in the union. That Arthur did this effectively and without a hint of scandal is much to his credit, and it was remembered, along with Arthur's services to the G.O.P., in 1871 when President Grant made Arthur collector of the Port of New York, a post worth $40,000 a year and the cornerstone in Boss Conkling's Republican machine.

A man in such a position seemed to professional politicians the least likely to promote anything like the "snivel service" favored by Garfield's and Arthur's predecessor, Rutherford B. Hayes. And yet, once in office, this is precisely the position Arthur took. In so doing he struck the first important blow at the flyblown spoils system that had been the operative principle of government ever since Jackson. It was a position that won Arthur few friends; the rumor that he was bossism's friend died slowly. And when Arthur tried his own hand at being a boss by naming his candidate for governor of New York, the hypersensitive electorate rebelled, elected instead an unknown mayor from Buffalo, Grover Cleveland.

Unhappily for Arthur, he is little remembered for his origins and early struggles (largely unknown even in his own time), or for his brave moves toward good government (largely frustrated), but for the figure of elegance that he cut—he was shaved and even pedicured by his butler, ordered some twenty-five coats from his New York tailor at a time—and his efforts to refurbish the White House with the exotic *art nouveau* decorations of Louis Comfort Tiffany.

Arthur died twenty months after leaving office, thus fulfilling his own prediction that he would never have lived through a second term. He was buried at Albany's Rural Cemetery beside his wife, who preceded him by six years. A decade after his death a bronze statue was erected to Arthur in New York's Madison Square, its gaze, appropriately enough, directed at the site of the old Union League Club.

Grover Cleveland

We love him most for the enemies he has made.*

NOT SINCE bachelor James Buchanan had departed in 1861 for the rural delights of Wheatland had the Democratic Party had the pleasure of having one of its own in the White House. But in 1884 it looked as if the Democrats' hour, awaited for twenty-three long years, was about to strike. Leading the G.O.P. ticket was the by now somewhat tarnished "Plumed Knight," James G. Blaine ("monumental liar from the State of Maine"). This time the Democrats had, in Grover Cleveland, a man virtually unknown but above reproach—or so it seemed.

And then on July 21, 1884, came a bombshell. The scandal-loving Buffalo *Evening Telegraph* published the story that Grover Cleveland, ten years before, had fathered an illegitimate son by pretty thirty-six-year-old Maria Halpin, a widow from Pennsylvania with more than one suitor at the time. Faced with almost certain defeat, Cleveland had just one comment to his friends, "Tell the truth."

It was a manly gesture, and although Cleveland was never to hear the last of it, an appealing one that gained him the support of such divines as Boston's great Unitarian minister Dr. James Freeman Clarke and Brooklyn's renowned Henry Ward Beecher. When scandalmongers brought Cleveland a packet of letters purporting to divulge similar evidence of Blaine's private life, Cleveland paid the price, then asked, "Are all the papers here?" Assured they were, he shredded the letters, had them burned in the fireplace, and remarked, "The other side can have a monopoly of all the dirt in this campaign."

But even such refreshing high-mindedness might not have earned Cleveland the victory had not a Blaine supporter, the Reverend Samuel D. Burchard of Manhattan's Murray Hill Presbyterian Church, made passing reference to the Democrats as "the party of Rum, Romanism and Rebellion." It was an alliterative insult reckoned to offend voters by the thousands, and it was to help to defeat Blaine. When Cleveland won by 219-to-182 electoral votes, he strode onto the Washington scene a formidable figure to behold (five feet eleven inches tall, 240 pounds), but an unknown on the national scene.

Cleveland was simple, straightforward, a man of common sense, masculine, a plodder by nature, but unbudgeable in his sense of duty. Such sentiments are at home in a parsonage, and it was in the Old Manse or parsonage of the First Presbyterian Church in Caldwell, New Jersey, that Cleveland was born on March 18, 1837, the fifth child of the Reverend Richard Falley Cleveland and Ann Neal, a Baltimore girl and daughter of one of Maryland's leading book pub-

The Presbyterian parsonage in which Cleveland was born in 1837 in Caldwell, New Jersey, was known as The Old Manse and was built in 1832. Cleveland left here when he was three, moving to a succession of parsonages as he grew up. Known for his independence and honesty, he was elected Mayor of Buffalo, Governor of New York, and President for two terms.

* General Edward S. Bragg, seconding Cleveland's nomination, July 9, 1884

Westland, as Cleveland renamed his Princeton home, had been built in 1854 and was patterned on Morven, the colonial governor's mansion in Princeton, built in 1702. To this house the Princeton College band came after football games to serenade the President. Cleveland's study was at the right.

lishers. The newly born in his quaint wooden cradle was christened Stephen Grover in honor of Caldwell's previous minister.

Grover Cleveland (the Stephen was dropped by his parents early in life) was sixteen when his father died in the small town of Holland Patent, New York, to which the Cleveland family had just moved from Fayetteville, New York. With younger brothers and a mother to support, Cleveland abandoned his hopes for Cornell, taught and was bookkeeper for the New York Institute for the Blind, finally accepted an offer from his mother's uncle, Lewis F. Allen, a stock farmer and one of the best-known men in Buffalo, to come and live with him.

Soon Cleveland set up bachelor quarters on his own in a cockloft of the old Southern Hotel and began his apprenticeship in the law with Rogers, Bowen and Rogers. Cleveland paid a substitute to serve in his place in the Civil War, a common practice, but one held against him politically later. His reason was that he was needed to support his mother and under-age brothers and sisters. At the age of forty-four, he was tapped by the Democrats, who wanted to "cater to the better class," and won election as mayor in 1881, governor in 1882, and President in 1884.

The Cleveland family, after the former President had moved to Princeton, New Jersey, are assembled on the porch of Westland. From left to right, Esther, Francis Grover, Mrs. Cleveland, Ruth, Richard Folsom and Grover Cleveland. Mrs. Cleveland as a widow remarried, lived until 1947.

145 GROVER CLEVELAND

Kitchen in Caldwell's Old Manse has equipment of the early 1830s, along with such souvenirs of Cleveland's fishing enthusiasm as his old fishing basket.

Cleveland reached the White House at the end of his meteoric rise just short of his forty-eighth birthday, still a bachelor and still never having owned a house. Two years later all this changed with dramatic suddenness as Cleveland announced his betrothal to Frances Folsom, a young beauty of twenty-four who had been the daughter of his Buffalo law partner Oscar Folsom, and who had been his ward since her father's death when she was eleven. The first wedding of a President in the White House took place in the quiet Blue Room and it brought out all the prurient curiosity of the press—"ghoulishness," Cleveland called it.

At the end of his first term, Cleveland was all too pleased to desert the harsh, glaring limelight of the Executive Mansion. After the scandal of the campaign, he no longer felt at home in Buffalo. He bought a house at 816 Madison Avenue in New York,* an unremarkable red brick town house tastefully furnished inside with oak paneling, cheerful rugs, and an exquisite life-sized marble bust of Mrs. Cleveland. Here, on October 3, 1891, was born Ruth, first of the five Cleveland children. Cleveland, who had reservations concerning his own parentage of Maria Halpin's son, was overjoyed, and wrote to a friend as one "who has just entered the real world, and sees in a small child more of value than I have ever called my own before, who puts aside as hardly worth a thought, all that has gone before—fame, honor, place, everything."

From 1891 until 1904 the Clevelands summered on Buzzards Bay, Cape Cod, in a roomy two-story clapboard cottage that they called Gray Gables. It was situated on Monument Point, between Cedar Pond Creek and Uncle Bill's Cove. Here at last Cleveland could give vent to his passion for fishing, hushing his boat companion, Richard Watson Gilder, editor of the *Century*, by saying, "If you want to catch fish, attend strictly to business."

In 1892, Cleveland was again nominated on the Democratic ticket. As a running mate this time he had Adlai E. Stevenson, a name to echo loud and long in distant future American presidential campaigns. Supporters of the Cleveland–Stevenson ticket whooped it up by singing:

> *Grover! Grover! four more years of Grover!*
> *Out they go, in we go; then we'll be in clover!*

Against Harrison, Cleveland won even more handsomely than he had over Blaine.

In many ways the second term proved much more difficult than the first. Faced with a money crisis, the President stood for hard money; confronted with the Pullman strike, he used troops to restore order. The nation thrilled when his daughter Esther became the first President's child to be born in the White House. But the Clevelands were made miserable by cruel and unfounded rumors that their children were imbeciles, that the President was becoming a drunkard. "I don't know in the shuffle what will become of me," Cleveland wrote his old friend, Richard Watson Gilder, "but I think perhaps I ought to look after it a little."

Both Cleveland and his wife had decided independently that after the White House their home should be the elm-shaded college town of Princeton, New Jersey. The Princeton undergraduates had

* In 1892 the Clevelands moved to 12 West 51st Street.

hailed Cleveland on his visit to Princeton with a huge banner, GROVER, SEND YOUR BOYS TO PRINCETON. Then too the Clevelands had made the acquaintance of Andrew F. West, a classics professor at Princeton, and through him developed a warm affection for the distinguished faculty.

On Christmas Eve, 1896, the Clevelands got their nicest present, a letter from Charles Francis Adams saying that the house they had their eye on was theirs for $30,915. "The title," Adams wrote lightheartedly, "is absolutely clear back to William Penn. If he did anything out of the way in getting it, the Indian who once owned it has a case against your ownership." This large house, called Westland (in honor of Professor West), was to be Grover Cleveland's home until his death on June 4, 1908. It had been built in 1854 by Commodore Robert Field Stockton for his daughter when she married William Dod, first Episcopal rector of Trinity Church in Princeton, and was patterned on Morven, the colonial governor's official mansion in Princeton, built in 1701. It was thus a replica of a classic Georgian colonial house, with twin parlors on either side, high roofs, and handsome marble mantelpieces. True to Victorian custom, the Clevelands added on more and more rooms to the rear.* One of the ex-President's first moves was to install a billiard room, and soon a small group of cronies, called the Poverty Club, were gathered round to play cards at ten- and twenty-five-cent limits. "My father used to say that it was wicked to go fishing on Sunday," Cleveland joked, "but he never said anything about draw poker."

Cleveland proved a welcome celebrity to the undergraduates, who soon took to serenading him on his birthday. Regularly victory parades after football games would end up at the Cleveland mansion, and the hale ex-President would appear on the balcony to lead the cheers in person. Cleveland also proved he could be a good friend to a young faculty member. When one newcomer, John Finley, failed to find suitable housing, Cleveland built him a stucco-covered house on the corner of Westland, a fine, conventional structure, but one that at first collected water in the basement. When Finley hesitantly pointed this out, the jovial ex-President replied, "Well, my dear fellow, what did you expect—champagne?" Finley later reciprocated this handsome favor by finding Cleveland a new summer house after the death in 1904 of young Ruth Cleveland at Gray Gables. This new vacation lodge was Intermont, near Tamworth, New Hampshire, within sight of Mount Chocorua and Mount Passaconaway, not far from the fine fishing at Lake Ossipee and Winnepesaukee.

Having asserted probity in both his private and official life, Cleveland lived to see himself widely respected as his waning years set in. After his first term, he had jocularly asked, "What shall be done with our ex-Presidents?" and added, " 'Take them out and shoot them' is worthy of attention. One thing I cling to with especial pleasure—the memory, or rather the contemplation of the course of the last administration and the assurance that after all we were able to do something for our country. And with this comes the thought of the devotion and affection of the men, good and true, who stood about us, and I ask myself, 'Is not this after all enough for one life?' "

Grey Gables, on Monument Point, Buzzards Bay, Cape Cod, Massachusetts, was Cleveland's summer home between 1891 and 1904. The two-story clapboard cottage is approximately the same age as Joseph Kennedy's gabled cottage at Hyannis Port. But, whereas the Kennedys are enthusiastic sailors, Cleveland preferred to fish, telling his friends, "If you want to catch fish, attend strictly to business."

---

* So extensive did these additional rooms become that later the rear of the house was detached, moved to the back of the lot, where it remains today as a self-contained and relatively large house in its own right.

TWENTY-THREE

Benjamin Harrison

Benjamin Harrison, last of the bearded Union generals, was himself the grandson of a President, William Henry Harrison. His wife, Caroline Scott Harrison, was a college professor's daughter, and one of the founders and first president general of the Daughters of the American Revolution.

YOUR GRANDMOTHER who thinks of everything and everybody insists that I shall send the old crib. . . . It is so richetty I am afraid it won't stand the journey." So John Scott Harrison, son of the ninth U.S. President, wrote in 1858 to his own son, Benjamin Harrison, destined to be the twenty-third President. The crib in question, still to be seen at Benjamin Harrison's home at 1230 North Delaware Street in Indianapolis, is in many senses symbolic of the American family that in terms of honors and service ranks second only to the New England Adamses. For it was in this crib that Benjamin Harrison, grandson of "Old Tippecanoe" Harrison and great-grandson and namesake of the Signer of the Declaration of Independence, was placed after his birth on August 20, 1833. On its arrival in Indianapolis, Benjamin Harrison duly recorded the expenditure of $2.50 for new mattress and repairs, had it ready for the arrival of his second child, Mary (called Mamey) in April.

Benjamin Harrison, last of the Union generals to become President and, what perhaps amounts to the same thing, last of the bearded Presidents, resolutely declared, "I want it understood that I am the grandson of nobody. I believe that every man should stand on his own merits." And yet his ancestry was too obvious a political asset to be overlooked, either by his Democratic opponents, or by his supporters.

In a real sense, however, Benjamin Harrison was right to keep his heritage as a private source of strength but refuse to take it into the market place. Proof that famous sires do not necessarily produce great offspring was to be seen all too clearly in the lackluster career of his own father, John Scott Harrison, who failed at farming on the brick homestead built for him by William Henry Harrison a few miles from the ninth President's Big House at North Bend, and who accomplished little of note during his two terms in the U.S. Congress.

Yet life at The Point, as the Harrison house was called because the 600-acre farm was on land lying between the Ohio and the Big Miami, was wholesome. Staunch Presbyterians, the Harrisons "all assembled in the parlor and sung hymns from four o'clock until bedtime" (as Benjamin's sister recalled). Education was taken seriously. Not only were lady tutors taken on to teach the children, but attendance at the nearby log-cabin school was strictly enforced. Benjamin, a chubby towhead, not only managed to rise at four or five in the morning to do his chores, but half-ran to school to get there early enough to play ballpen, three-corner-cat, or town-ball. He was an excellent scholar, and the family scrimped to send him to Farmer's College at College Hill, where he became a prize student of the celebrated Edinburgh Master, Dr. Robert Hamilton Bishop.

The Point, a 600-acre farm near Gen. William Henry Harrison's Big House at North Bend, Ohio, was Benjamin Harrison's pious, strict boyhood home.

Harrison's Indianapolis home was the 16-room house on North Delaware Street. Built in 1874, it cost exactly $21,123.10. When he was nominated for President in 1888, neighbors crowded to his house, later demolished the picket fence for souvenirs.

After the death of Benjamin's mother in 1850, the seventeen-year-old transferred to Miami University, Oxford, Ohio, then known as "The Yale of the West." Here he courted the vivacious, talented, and artistic Caroline Lavinia Scott, daughter of a Miami professor who had founded "Carrie" Scott's alma mater, Oxford Female Institute. The two were not married until Benjamin had read law for two years in Cincinnati and gotten his start in Indianapolis.

The succession of Indianapolis houses in which Benjamin and Carrie Harrison lived was an index of Harrison's determined rise in the world. Their first rented house was a one-story frame house with open shed behind, where Mrs. Harrison could cook in summer. Before leaving for his law office, Harrison chopped the day's supply of wood and would fill the water buckets when he came home for lunch—at the time, Harrison was court crier at $2.50 a day. Their second house, at North New Jersey Street, had two stories and an attic, as well as a richly carpentered front porch. Following Harrison's election as reporter to the supreme court on the Republican ticket, the family moved into their third residence, an even more sumptuous house at the corner of North Street and North Alabama, one on which Harrison continued to make payments throuogut his service in the Grand Army of the Republic.

When Harrison's standard-bearer, Abraham Lincoln, stopped in Indianapolis on his way to the White House in 1861, the young lawyer-politician noted grimly, "It seemed to me hardly a gay crowd, and he not to be a glad man." One day shortly afterward Indiana Governor Oliver Perry Morton took Harrison and a friend aside, said solemnly, "Gentlemen, there is absolutely no response to Mr. Lincoln's last call for troops."

As a Harrison, Benjamin knew where his duty lay. On the way down the state capitol steps he enlisted his former law partner as his first recruit, stopped off to buy a military cap and hire a fife player, and went to work to raise a company for the newly formed Indiana 70th Volunteer Infantry Regiment. Harrison's diligent proselytizing and patriotic fervor got results. The regiment was oversubscribed with volunteers; when it left, Harrison rode at its head as colonel. It probably was one of the blessings of war that Harrison's men were given nothing for two years but guard duty along the Louisville & Nashville Railroad before being sent into action. But faced with a charge across an open field and up a hill at point-blank range in the face of Confederate batteries at Resaca, the Indiana Hoosiers won even Sherman's praise. At Peach Tree Creek in Georgia, Harrison won his lone brigadier's star with cold steel.

When Harrison was discharged from the Army on August 7, 1863, he was only thirty-two, but he emerged a vastly more mature man and a bond was forged with his men that never broke. To his regiment he said, as the 70th Indiana disbanded, "Do you remember the enclosure, my Comrades, at the foot of the hill at Resaca, up which we made that fearful charge? How we gathered their torn blankets around them, and then tenderly composed their limbs for the last sleep, casting branches of evergreen in their graves! They lie there still, and along by the wayside lie others. . . . I almost feel that I would rather lie within that little mount at the foot of the hill, than to have had no participation in this struggle."

At home, Harrison's fine legal mind, retentive memory, and mastery of detail made for him an outstanding legal career. Shortly

Harrison's Indianapolis home gained a large veranda after his return from the White House, when Harrison experimented with installing electricity. The guest room (opposite, top) has a "half tester top bed" used in the 1870s and old Empire bookcase from the Harrison home in North Bend, Ohio. The master bedroom (below) has the massive, hand-carved bed in which President Benjamin Harrison died. Beside the mantel is an exercise machine which Harrison used to keep fit. The cradle was used by all six of William Henry Harrison's children (including the father of Benjamin Harrison) at North Bend. The front parlor (opposite) retains the sparkle and glitter of the house as it was redecorated in 1896 for Harrison's second marriage. It has an Aubusson rug, gold lacquered mirrors, and cut-crystal chandeliers. The ostrich feather fan on display at right was sent by Mrs. Ulysses S. Grant to Mrs. Harrison from Vienna in 1890.

after the war his income had already reached $10,000, and in 1867 he bought a double lot, with 150-foot frontage, 200 feet deep on North Delaware Street. Seven years later he began to build the red brick edifice that still stands there as his shrine and memorial.

The sixteen-room North Delaware Street house, by Harrison's own meticulous accounting, cost exactly $21,123.10. Echoing a tradition that goes back to the Harrison family's James River plantation house of Berkeley, it had twin parlors and a library that was Harrison's particular pride with its handsome, massive bookcase, made by a poor German cabinetmaker in appreciation for Harrison's legal services (Harrison had appealed the German immigrant's case to the Supreme Court, finally won it). Surrounded by elms and oaks, with a strawberry patch and grape arbors, the house epitomized security, prosperity, and permanence. It was also to serve as a backdrop for Harrison's most stirring political triumphs and defeats.

Although Harrison failed to be elected governor in 1876, the year after the house was completed, he won election to the U.S. Senate from here in 1881. Following his failure in 1887 to win re-election (by one vote in the legislative assembly), Harrison in 1888 made his famous speech at the Detroit Rink: "I am a dead statesman, but I am a living and rejuvenated Republican." It was a phrase that keynoted his campaign for the presidency.

Harrison, the compromise candidate, was nominated on the eighth ballot. He and his well-wishers waited out the nomination in his law office in the Wright Block, East Market Street, Indianapolis.

When the news arrived, one effusive lady flung her arms around Harrison, gave the scholarly gentleman a resounding smack. Harrison was barely able to hurry home before a crowd of jubilant neighbors had assembled. Standing erect and pleased on the small front stoop, he gave the first of his many "neighborly chats," producing such a wave of enthusiasm that impatient souvenir hunters demolished the picket fence before the house. In the excitement, it seemed to bother General Harrison not at all. "When a man receives the approbation of his neighbors," he said with tears in his eyes, "he is indeed blessed."

As a campaigner, Harrison was content to speak from his own front porch. As he explained to Whitelaw Reid, "I have a great risk of meeting a fool at home, but the candidate who travels cannot escape him." Against such homey surroundings, even Harrison's somewhat chilly manner seemed to disappear and his succinct phraseology carried his message clearly and well via the telegraph wires to newspapers across the country. His belief in a high tariff—"An American market for Americans"—was popular in a campaign that became "Beef" Cleveland *versus* "Brains" Harrison, and Harrison was victorious.

It is Harrison's tragedy that his defeat at the end of his first term came from the "bosses" within his own Republican Party, including his Secretary of State, James G. Blaine, more than from any fresh argument enunciated by Grover Cleveland. Harrison decided to go to the polls for vindication. When Mrs. Harrison protested, "Why, General? Why when it has been so hard for you here?" the President replied, "If Blaine and some of those who I have thought were my

Harrison's law office furniture (opposite) *is placed on the second floor. The novel desk opens into two parts, with the right side used for filing. Above it is the emblem of the Grand Army of the Republic. The portrait is of Harrison's law partner.*

Harrison's library (below) *was the room in which he formally accepted the nomination and where campaign strategy was laid out. The massive, hand-carved bookcase at right was a gift from a grateful German immigrant client. The jars and ornate humidifier before the fireplace, at left, were gifts from the Hungarian Ambassador, while the Bible came from the "Tippecanoe Club" of Marion County, Ohio. The entrance hall* (above) *is also full of mementos, including an 1800 Maryland clock, a staircase newel post decorated with a fire-hose nozzle from a Volunteer Fire Brigade, and an extraordinary steer-horn chair, covered in leopard skins and identified with a gold plaque carrying Harrison's name in diamonds, that came, naturally, from a rich Texas cattle king.*

political friends had not turned upon me, as they have done, I should retire from office with no thought of allowing my name to be used in the nominations. But no Harrison has ever run from a fight, Caroline, and there is going to be a fight!"

The President's summoning up his fighting ancestry at this critical moment was honorable but, as it proved, foolhardy. This Mrs. Harrison was never to know; she died October 19, 1892, a few weeks before Grover Cleveland was swept back triumphantly into office. But the President's appeal to the "Harrison in him" could not have failed to strike in her a sympathetic note. The nation was now more than a hundred years old and with territorial expansion had come a quickening sense of patriotism resting on a living heritage. Caroline Scott Harrison herself had begun collecting the historic plate and silverware of the White House and proposed that the White House should have a historical art wing completed for its centennial in 1892. She was also one of the founders and first president general of the Daughters of the American Revolution, a patriotic woman's organization that recalled to old-family Americans that a firm tradition united them despite the dreadful blood-letting of the Civil War.

Harrison's own sense of patriotism found its outlet in his collected essays, *This Country of Ours,* which was long read in American classrooms and had a wide influence in South America as well. In many ways, the warm sympathy shown the recent widower and ex-President by his townsmen in Indianapolis proved a solace. And in 1896, he married his deceased wife's niece, Mary Scott Lord Dimmick, who had served as his secretary while in the White House.

For the new bride, the house on North Delaware Street was renovated, and electricity, much to Harrison's consternation, was substituted for gas. About this time also the porch with its Ionic columns was added. Much of the original furniture was stored in the ballroom on the third floor, where it was at the time the house was turned over to the Arthur Jordan Foundation by the second Mrs. Harrison in 1937. While Benjamin Harrison remained alive, the house provided a rich background for the Harrisons' social activities. The former President returned to the practice of law with great success and distinction, leaving an estate of $400,000 at the time of his death of pneumonia on March 13, 1901. The second Mrs. Harrison survived him by forty-seven years.

A final anecdote illuminates the length as well as the brevity of our history. William Henry Harrison, whose house provided Benjamin Harrison's birthplace, was himself born in 1773, before Lexington and Concord. His grandson not only lived to see the twentieth century, but in a curious way served as an inspiration for the man who was to become the nation's thirty-first President, Herbert Hoover. Hoover recalled in *Collier's* in 1951 how ex-President Benjamin Harrison once attended a Stanford University baseball game, brushing by the ticket-taker without paying his twenty-five-cent entrance fee. As student manager of the ball team, Hoover approached the ex-President, "my first contact with a great public man. . . . I collected the money. Mr. Harrison was cheerful about it and also bought an advance ticket to next week's game. He would not take 50 cents' change for a dollar. But I insisted that we were not a charitable institution and that he must take it. Justice must occasionally be done even to ex-Presidents and I here record that he took two more tickets. Upon this solution, he became even more cheerful."

TWENTY-FIVE

William McKinley

McKinley was born above this small store in 1843 on the main street of Niles, Ohio, a manufacturing town and center for pig-iron smelting. To insure that their nine children would have a good education, McKinley's parents moved to Poland, Ohio, to benefit from its superior academy. McKinley himself volunteered for Civil War service at the age of eighteen.

"The currents of destiny are flowing through the hearts of the American people."

WILLIAM McKINLEY was the last of the Civil War veterans to attain the White House. Among the most high-minded of men, McKinley derived his standards from the small businessman class which was paving the way for the industrial revolution. His grandfather, a Revolutionary War veteran, had been an iron founder who followed the ore to the Susquehanna Valley; his father, William, Sr., had run charcoal-smelting furnaces in Ohio. The future President, the seventh of nine children, was born in the small pig-iron manufacturing town of Niles, Ohio, on January 28, 1843. When he was a boy, his father moved the family to Poland, Ohio, so that the children could benefit from the superior education of the local academy. From there young Will managed just one year at Allegheny College, in Meadville, Pennsylvania, before his father died, forcing him to drop out and turn to schoolteaching.

Lincoln's call for volunteers thus found the eighteen-year-old schoolteacher and postal clerk at loose ends. With his cousin, Will McKinley "in cold blood" decided to sign up in the Ohio 23d Volunteer Infantry. He proved a fearless soldier. A devout Methodist, he firmly believed he was safeguarded by his pledge to his mother to return unharmed. Armored with this sublime assurance, McKinley survived all that the "Secheers" could throw at him, winning General Rutherford B. Hayes' praise as "one of the bravest and finest officers in the army." He returned home a strapping young major who neither swore, smoked, nor drank but who carried with him the friendship of every man and officer with whom he had served. For a career, he decided on the law, and took his law degree at Albany Law School. He then settled down in the small, then-booming town of Canton, Ohio, moving into a small frame house on the corner of Shorb and Tuscarawas streets with his elder sister, a schoolteacher.

William McKinley had a combination of mildness and near-angelic sweetness, which was not unmixed with a precise and calculated awareness of the effect this would have on his listeners. Years later, when he was in the White House, one irate congressman burst into the President's office, emerged coddled and mollified after a brief exposure to the McKinley treatment, vowing, "I don't know a blamed word he said, but it's all right, boys." In politics, McKinley was a natural-born winner.

On the front porch of their Canton, Ohio, home, Mc-Kinley liked to pause for his after-dinner cigar where he would not bother his wife, an invalid who spent most of her time crocheting and knitting by the bay window of the parlor. McKinley's spotless record and angelic temperament made it almost impossible for even his enemies to bear a grudge for long.

Starting as city attorney, where he warred against the saloons, he moved to Congress in 1877 at thirty-two, and in a normally Democratic area, swung Stark County again and again into the Republican column. Six times McKinley was returned to Congress before he was elected to serve two terms as governor of Ohio. As the Republican Convention of 1896 approached he seemed to the Cleveland industrialist Marcus Alonzo Hanna the God-given instrument to defeat William Jennings Bryan.

But there was one shadow in his personal life, the grave illness of his wife. The Major had married Ida Saxton, the fragile, petite daughter of Canton's leading banker (at the time they met she was cashier in her father's bank, thus she was the first career woman to become First Lady). The impeccable young couple honeymooned in New York, then settled in the white frame house on North Market Street given Ida McKinley by her father as a wedding present. Their first child, dark-haired Katie, whose portrait the McKinleys kept with them ever after, died at the age of two. A second daughter, lived only five months. These tragedies, combined with phlebitis and deep depressions, changed Mrs. McKinley into a feeble, self-centered, nervous invalid, subject to frequent and increasingly violent epileptic attacks for the rest of her life.

McKinley became her nurse, throwing a napkin over her face to hide her convulsions when they began, endlessly ministering to her, and enduring stuffy rooms because of her proneness to colds. McKinley took his daily constitutional on the porch outside her room. There he had his daily cigar, a taste that seemed to have come with politics, although for years he substituted chewing the stub of his imported Garcías, since Mrs. McKinley found the smell of a good cigar offensive.

As a lawyer-politician, McKinley had risen to Congress and the governor's office, but he had not become rich. In 1876, he sold the house on North Market Street, and began twenty years of living in transient quarters in Washington and Ohio. In 1896, however, McKinley, then at the end of his second term as governor, decided it was time to put down roots again. Sentimentally he and Mrs. McKinley journeyed back to Canton. To their great delight, they found their old North Market Street house was for rent and decided to move back in again (they bought it outright for $14,500 in July 1899). The governor and his wife owned little furniture—an old lounge that was recovered in leather and placed in the library, two small rocking chairs, but little else. For advice they turned to Mrs. Myron T. Herrick, their wealthy friend from Cleveland, who ordered the carpets, bought the elaborate, claw-footed table of Ohio woods that McKinley had so extravagantly admired at the Chicago World's Fair in 1893. The seven double blankets, "good and wide," came wholesale from Marshall Field's in Chicago, the china from Colonel John N. Taylor of the East Liverpool potteries. Up on the wall went paintings of their lost daughter Katie and McKinley's favorite horse, Midnight.

To celebrate their silver wedding anniversary she sent out formal cards of invitation that covered all of Ohio; McKinley ordered $400 worth of refreshments. The guests came to Canton by the trainload, tramping for six hours up the carpet laid from curb to front porch and through the house banked with flowers and filled with the music of the eight-piece orchestra. Strained and graying, Ida McKinley determinedly lasted through the ordeal to prove that she would be no drawback to her husband's White House hopes.

At the 1896 Republican Convention in St. Louis, the first mention of McKinley's name set off a demonstration. In his Canton library, hundreds of miles away, McKinley was able to pick up the private telephone, hear the convention roar coming over the leased wires "like a storm at sea with wild, fitful shrieks of wind." McKinley's triumph on the first ballot set off saluting cannons and fire bells in Canton and by nightfall McKinley had spoken to 50,000 of the citizens who poured into Canton from surrounding towns.

The G.O.P. strategy, as outlined by Mark Hanna, called for a stay-at-home campaign, patterned on those of Hayes and Garfield. Postal Telegraph and Western Union lines were set up on the second floor, a private telephone was installed in the library. For special guests the table was set for twelve each day, while the press, bar-

McKinley's assassination in 1901 caused nation-wide mourning, but McKinley's Canton home from which he had made his famous front-porch campaigns was forgotten; by 1934 it was abandoned and about to collapse.

The McKinley house on Canton's North Market Street was given to them as a wedding present in 1871. Later sold, it was rebought in 1899. An invalid, Mrs. McKinley preferred to stay indoors, surrounded by souvenirs of her husband's career and lost daughter, Katie.

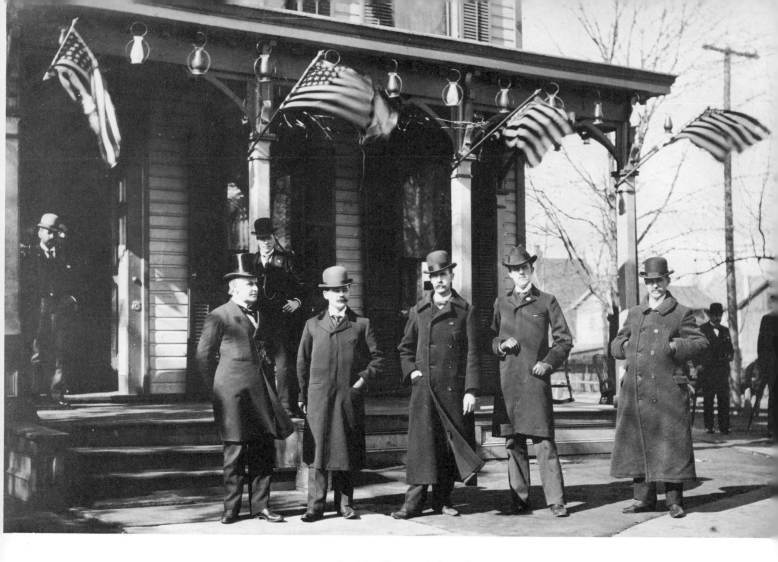

*During McKinley's 1896 and 1900 campaigns, Canton,
Ohio, was a pilgrimage goal for thousands of staunch
Republican supporters. McKinley was never too busy
to don his silk hat and pose with visiting politicians
and delegations. Snorted Theodore Roosevelt, "They
are advertising him like some patent medicine."*

racked in Canton's hotels, lounged on the wicker porch furniture. The
press of people reached unbelievable levels.

By election eve, the white iron fence, grape arbor and rose bushes
had been demolished by souvenir hunters; even the posts supporting
the porch had been pushed in by the weight of numbers. Millions
were spent on the campaign, and McKinley won by 271 votes to 176
for Bryan.

In 1900, McKinley was back in Canton, countering William
Jennings Bryan's challenge with the prestige of McKinley prosperity
("the full dinner pail"). To his aid came the fast-rising governor of
New York, Theodore Roosevelt. The McKinley-Roosevelt ticket, was
triumphant.

His second term assured, McKinley and his wife decided in the
summer of 1901 to take a three-month respite from the hectic Washington life. They returned to Canton and enjoyed the most idyllic
sojourn they had known in years. The North Market Street house
had received $3000 in improvements; a pillared porte-cochere had
been added to the driveway on the north side and that end of the
porch expanded to include an octagonal gazebo overlooking the
lawn and garden. As an added delight, Myron T. Herrick's automobile and driver were put at their disposal, and they thrilled at the
adventure of touring the country roads in a "horseless buggy."

The only event scheduled to interrupt their idyl was the opening, in 1901, of the Pan-American Exposition in Buffalo. McKinley

would not have missed it for worlds. "Expositions are the timekeepers of progress," he exclaimed. When his private secretary advised against mingling with the crowds, McKinley mildly protested, "I have no enemies. Why should I fear?" McKinley even insisted that he shake hands with at least a few of the visitors.

McKinley had no way of knowing that among the crowd would be Leon Czolgosz, a native-born anarchist, who had already bought a .32 Iver-Johnson pistol. At 4:07 P.M. on September 6, Czolgosz approached President McKinley, just then emerging from the Exposition's Temple of Music. The President reached out his hand in greeting; Czolgosz brushed it aside, fired two shots point-blank. As the President sagged into the arms of bystanders, he murmured, "Don't let them hurt him. Go easy with him, boys." Then speaking to his secretary, he whispered, "My wife—be careful, Cortelyou, how you tell her—oh, be careful!"

Eight days later President McKinley lost his battle for life, his lips forming the words of his favorite hymn, "Nearer My God to Thee." The press reported his final words: "Goodbye all. It is God's will. His will, not ours, be done." His passing left a strange, awesome silence in the room. Dr. Roswell Park, who was attending him, said in later years, "Up to this time, I'd never really believed that a man could be a good Christian and a good politician." It was a statement that McKinley himself might well have chosen for his own epitaph.

TWENTY-SIX

Theodore Roosevelt

"In life, as in a football game, the principle to follow is: hit the line hard; don't foul and don't shirk, but hit the line hard."

DEE-LIGHTED! Bully! By Jove, I *am* glad to see you!" It was pure elixir that Theodore Roosevelt exuded. The reaction of the cartoonist Homer Davenport was typical. On his way back to the Oyster Bay railway station from a meeting with Theodore Roosevelt, Davenport suddenly found the phrase that summed up his feelings; he drew a cartoon of Uncle Sam placing his hand on the shoulder of TR and saying, "He's good enough for me." It was a caption that reflected the sentiments of hundreds of thousands of Americans who elected him President by the greatest majority received by any candidate up to his time.

Most Americans know that Theodore Roosevelt was an undersized, thin-legged, asthmatic child who by dint of pure will forced himself to attain hardy manhood. "When I was twenty-one," he was later to write, "I promised myself that I would live my life up to the hilt until I was sixty, and would be prepared for anything that happened after that." Young Roosevelt's struggle to find his health is half of his thrilling life story; the second half flows logically from the first.

He was born on October 27, 1858, the son of Theodore Roosevelt, Sr., a sixth-generation American of Dutch descent and a well-to-do glass importer, and Martha Bullock, a Southern belle from Atlanta, Georgia. The house where the future President was born is at 28 East 20th Street, New York. Today it is surrounded by glowering lofts and dingy business buildings. In its heyday, however, it was in a prosperous neighborhood, with a view over the back garden to the Goelet mansion on 19th Street. It's entry is a stoop (as it was called in the Dutch fashion) over an "English" kitchen-basement. On the first floor was the front parlor and the dark, windowless inner parlor and library, lighted by a gas chandelier decorated with great quantities of cut glass (a bow in the direction of French Second Empire style that in the 1850s was just coming into vogue). To the rear was the dining room which occupied the full width of the house. Service from the kitchen below was by dumbwaiter to the small side pantry.

It was a dark and cheerless environment, with horsehair-covered furniture that scratched the children's legs, glass-covered bookcases, and an air of gloomy respectability. On the second and third floors were three bedrooms leading off from each landing; the servants' rooms were on the fourth floor. The delight of the children was the

Theodore Roosevelt's birthplace, at 28 East Twentieth Street, New York City, was built in 1848 and was one of the first of Manhattan's brownstone-faced town houses. Today it has been restored as a national historic site.

President Theodore Roosevelt, photographed in the library of Sagamore Hill, is sitting at the desk where he conducted the nation's business and in his spare time wrote most of his thirty books and over three thousand articles. Official messages came over the nickel-plated telephone at his left.

wide, airy porches across the back of this house and the one next door, owned by Uncle Robert Roosevelt. There, at least, the children could play in the sun. It was on the third-floor porch, reached by steps through the tall windows from "Thee's" room, that young Roosevelt's celebrated gymnasium was built.

Roosevelt was a sickly and scrawny twelve when his father spoke to him seriously: "Theodore, you have the brains, but brains are of comparatively little use without the body; you have got to make your body work, and it lies with you to do it. It is hard drudgery to make one's body, but I know you will do it." Soon John Wood, a local gymnast, had installed parallel bars and weight-lifting pulleys on the back porch and there Theodore relentlessly practiced by the hour to develop his arms and chest.

Roosevelt's gasping attacks of asthma in childhood developed in him a voracious love for fresh air and outdoor living. To provide it the family went to Madison, New Jersey, or to the Adirondacks in the summers. When he was fifteen they moved to 6 West 57th Street, where young Roosevelt could be near Central Park, and the next year Theodore Roosevelt, Sr., took a summer house at Oyster Bay on Long Island, the summer-resort area that for three generations became the most beloved spot on earth for the Roosevelt clan.

As a sickly boy, tutored at home, young Roosevelt developed a passion for zoology and books (even in later life he would devour them at the rate of three a day). Strong enough to go to Harvard, he decided to major in science, keeping in trim by rowing and boxing at Cambridge. His myopia, however, made staring through the microscope a torture; anyway, it was the outdoor aspects of bird and game life that fascinated him (and as a boy had made him an amateur taxidermist). In his last two college years he turned to history and literature, graduating Phi Beta Kappa, and starting his first book, a history of the War of 1812, while a senior.

The death of his father, "the best man I ever knew," during his sophomore year heavily influenced young Roosevelt's future plan of action. Theodore Roosevelt, Sr., just before his death had been appointed Collector of the Port of New York by President Rutherford B. Hayes, replacing Chester A. Arthur. Politics were thus in the family. So was money; young Roosevelt inherited some $125,000. Upon graduation in 1880 he married Alice Hathaway Lee of Boston, attended Columbia Law School briefly, and finally decided to run for the New York state assembly from the silk-stocking 21st Assembly District. He was elected three times in succession, but this early career came to an abrupt halt when on the same day, February 14, 1884, first his mother, and then his wife, died. All that was left of his marriage was his newborn daughter, Alice. Reeling under the double blow, Roosevelt placed his child in the care of his sister and went west. There he hoped to overcome his despondency by plunging into a vigorous outdoor life. The West, just nine years after Custer's Last Stand, was still, as Roosevelt put it, "all daring and courage, all iron endurance of mis-

The front parlor of the Roosevelt town house where Theodore Roosevelt was born and spent his boyhood was considered by the children to be "a room of much splendor." It was open only for formal calls and on Sunday, when the gleaming crystal chandelier and blue satin hangings by the window made it seem specially elegant. The tea set belonged to T.R.'s mother.

fortune." Roosevelt was no tenderfoot, but the drastic winters of 1886 and 1887 all but wiped out his cattle venture, along with $50,000. In 1886 Roosevelt came back to New York to run in "a perfectly hopeless contest," the New York mayoralty. He lost, but as he said, "Anyway, I had a bully time!"

Two months before his first marriage, Roosevelt had begun buying property at Oyster Bay, acquiring in time 155 hilltop acres on Cove Neck for a total cost of $30,000. In 1880 he had commissioned the architectural firm of Lamb and Rich (later Rich and Lorenzo), at 486 Broadway, to design the house he intended to name Leeholm in honor of his bride. In 1882, he signed a contract with John A. Wood and Son, carpenters, of Lawrence, Long Island, for $16,975 to begin work.

Writing 30 years later, and after he had gained an acquaintance of the more classic architecture of McKim, Mead, and White while redesigning the White House (a name Roosevelt made official in place of the older Executive Mansion), he wrote of his 23-room Oyster Bay mansion, "I did not know enough to be sure what I wished in outside matters. But I had perfectly definite views what I wished in inside matters, what I desired to live in and with; I arranged all this, so as to get what I desired in so far as my money permitted; and then Rich put on the outside cover with but little help from me. I wished a big piazza where we could sit in rocking-chairs and look at the sunset; a library with a shallow bay window looking south, the parlor or drawing-room occupying all the western end of the lower floor . . . big

The tone was set at Sagamore Hill by Theodore Roosevelt's many hunting trophies. At left is a dinner gong made of elephant tusks; center is the head of a water buffalo shot by Roosevelt on an African safari; at right, a view of the butler's pantry. To staff Sagamore Hill, ten servants were required, yet their total wages came to only $210 a month.

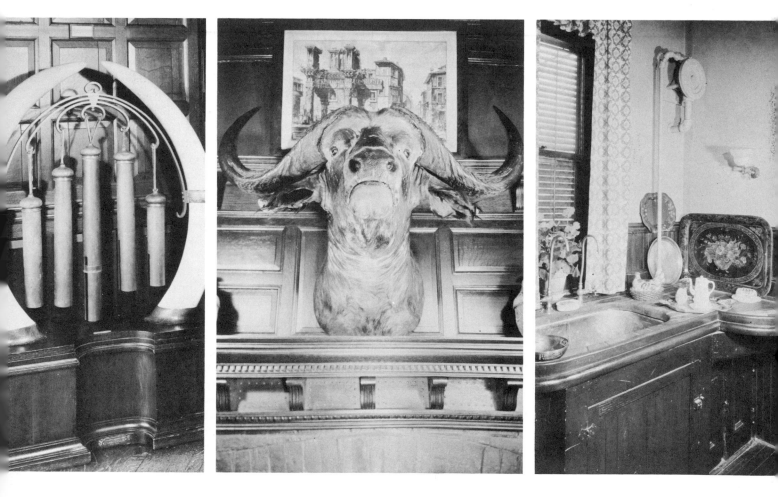

Sagamore Hill in its heyday was a rambling, Queen Anne structure, with ample verandas and broad awnings, built as a summer resort "cottage" in the 1880s. Within, the living spaces bore the unmistakable stamp of Teddy Roosevelt, with the library hung with hunting trophies and lined with books. Samurai sword and dagger were presents from the Emperor of Japan following Roosevelt's mediation which resulted in the Treaty of Portsmouth and peace between Russia and Japan.

fireplaces for logs. . . . I had to live inside and not outside the house; and while I should have liked to 'express myself' in both, as I had to choose, I chose the former."

Roosevelt renamed his new house for the Indian chief Sagamore Mohannis, who two centuries before had signed the land away to a white settler. Built on an exposed site overlooking Oyster Bay, "Sagamore Hill" would be exposed to full gale and hurricane winds, and the architects built solidly if not with great distinction. The foundations are twenty inches thick and the rafters, joists, and roof boards in proportion. In the prevailing Queen Anne style, the house used red brick for the first story, wood for the second. It was painted a deep mustard, with green trim. There were gables, dormers, a spacious veranda, colored-glass windows, a modish porte-cochere. Roosevelt was adamant about fireplaces; there were to be four on the first floor and four on the second, with a dumbwaiter hoist to bring up the wood. But even with the addition of two hot-air furnaces going full blast in the cellar, winds found their secret entries and swept through the house with such chilling effect that the family dubbed Sagamore Hill "The Birdcage."

Soon Sagamore Hill was introduced to its new mistress, Edith Kermit Carow, three years Roosevelt's junior, a favorite friend of his younger sister, and an old friend of the Roosevelt family from childhood days at Oyster Bay. On her very first visit, she discovered that Sagamore Hill had its own peculiar flavor, halfway between a baronial hall and a natural-history museum. When Edith Roosevelt took over her new summer house as a bride, it was already stuffed with trophies testifying to her husband's fifteen-year-long battle for physical strength; over the hall fireplace was a buffalo head from Little Cannonball Creek in Dakota, on the wall an elk from the Wyoming Bighorns, and, in the upstairs "Gun Room," the beginning of his massive collection of rifles and shotguns.

Theodore Roosevelt became in time the father of four boys and

two girls. "For unflagging interest and enjoyment," he wrote in his *Autobiography,* "a household of children, if things go reasonably well, certainly makes all other forms of success and achievement lose their importance by comparison." Perhaps because there was much of the unquenchable boy about Roosevelt himself, he was an uninhibited playmate for the children. He invented games for them, including the famous point-to-point obstacle race that took the Roosevelt children through brush and briar, over haystacks, and ended with all of them rolling down the precipitous 150-foot high Cooper's Bluff. He taught his children to be fearless riders. Bringing home a new Flobert rifle to his son, Ted, Jr., too late to test it on the home rifle butts, TR crept upstairs with his son, and, after swearing the boy to secrecy, fired a trial shot into the ceiling!

The one calming influence in this family of unquenchable gaiety was his wife Edith. Famous in the family is the day that Roosevelt climbed the sixty-foot windmill to free one of the wind paddles, in the process picked up an ugly scalp wound. Entering the front door, bleeding profusely, he was met by his wife's unabashed look. "Theodore," she drawled in a bored voice, "I wish you'd do your bleeding in the bathroom. You're spoiling every rug in the house!"

As Roosevelt in public life mounted the ladder from Police Commissioner to Assistant Secretary of the Navy, Rough Rider, Governor, Vice-President, and finally, with the assassination of McKinley, to the presidency itself, Sagamore Hill was a meeting place for the actors, authors, prize fighters, painters, historians, and practical politicians attracted by Roosevelt's magnetism and at last an extension of the Executive Branch itself, the Summer White House. To cope with her household, Mrs. Roosevelt had the use of a full staff: a farmer, gardener, coachman, cook, and a waitress, nurse, maid, chambermaid, laundress, and furnaceman. For this retinue she had to pay only $210 a month! In 1890, her meat bill ran between $29 and $119 a month, grocery staples (bought at Park & Tilford's in New

Theodore Roosevelt loved to romp with his children, often becoming as enthusiastic about their games as the youngsters themselves.

York) came to $35. Even the coal and wood for the drafty halls of Sagamore Hill came to only $300 a year.

As the years went by, Roosevelt realized that he needed something more formal and spacious for receiving guests than Mrs. Roosevelt's parlor. Twenty years after the house was built, Roosevelt commissioned his old friend, C. Grant La Farge (son of the famed painter John La Farge) to design the north hall—or Trophy Room, as it came to be called after its completion in 1907. This large ceremonial space—it measures thirty feet by forty feet and rises a story and a half—was done in luminous, soft red-browns, with paneling of Philippine mahogany, classic black-walnut columns at the side, and ceiling of American swamp cypress and hazel.

Furnished with throws of leopard skins and hung with elk, moose, and buffalo heads, it is a treasure trove of souvenirs. The elephant tusks came from Emperor Menelik of Abyssinia; the two Samurai swords (later to be tenderly oiled by visiting Admiral Togo) were the gift of the Emperor of Japan; Roosevelt's Rough Rider hat and binoculars hang from an elkhorn where he placed them when he returned from Cuba. It was a room that saw visiting ambassadors, costume balls, and, for hours on end, the figure of Theodore Roosevelt sitting by the fire absorbed in reading while Mrs. Roosevelt sat sewing until suddenly he would slap his book, and explode, "I wrote that twenty five years ago and those swine are saying that I've just cooked up the issue for political purposes!"

The room that saw most of Roosevelt, however, was his study, a combined library, office, and inner sanctum where he wrote most of his 30 books, 3000 articles, and a vast number of the 150,000 letters by him still known to exist. It was in this snug library that Roosevelt cornered, first, Japan's Baron Kaneko and then, a month later, Russia's cynical Serge Witte, to lay the groundwork for the Treaty of Portsmouth that ended the Russo-Japanese war and won for Theodore Roosevelt the Nobel Peace Prize.

Much of Roosevelt's public life passed outside the walls of Sagamore Hill. But here his memorable activities make their physical presence felt. For here lived a man who could activate a fleet, lead a charge, build a canal. He was a man who brought crowds to their feet cheering in Chicago in 1912 when he cried in his high-pitched, staccato voice, "We stand at Armageddon and we battle for the Lord . . ." With one quip, "I feel as fit as a bull moose," he gave his own National Progressive Party its nickname, "The Bull-Moose Party." When shot in the chest (his speech and glasses case, now on display at his birthplace, deflected the bullet), he cheerily remarked, "It takes more than that to kill a Bull Moose," and went on, bleeding profusely, to deliver an hour-and-a-half speech. "I am always willing to pay the piper," he once wrote his old friend Henry Cabot Lodge, "when I have had a good dance; and every now and then I like to drink the wine of life with brandy in it."

When war was declared against Germany, Roosevelt promptly offered to raise two divisions but his offer was turned down by President Wilson. But Roosevelt proudly reported that all four of his sons and one son-in-law were on their way to the front. "I rage at my impotence to be of substantial service to all of you at the front," he wrote them. At night he tossed restlessly worrying about their safety, and with reason. Kermit and Archibald Roosevelt were wounded (both later died in service in World War II), and his son-in-law was gassed. The most daring of them all, Quentin, was shot down and killed flying over Cambrai. A half-hour after the news arrived, ex-President Roosevelt walked out of the house and handed a brief statement to the reporters on the veranda of Sagamore Hill: "Quentin's mother and I are very glad that he got to the front and had a chance to render some service to his country, and show the stuff that was in him before his fate befell him." Later Roosevelt wrote of his son's death in action. "Only those are fit to live who do not fear to die; and none are fit to die who have shrunk from the joy of life and the duty of life. Both life and death are part of the same Great Adventure." It was one family's loss, but a whole nation mourned.

The deeply sorrowing ex-President wrote his sister, "Corinne, I have only one fight left in me, and I think I should reserve my strength in case I am needed in 1920." But Theodore Roosevelt had already passed by nearly three months his own stated life expectancy of sixty years. On the evening of January 5, 1919, before going upstairs to bed, he said to his wife, "I wonder if you will ever know how I love Sagamore Hill." By morning he had died.

Mrs. Roosevelt lived on another twenty-nine years. After her death at eighty-seven on September 30, 1948, Sagamore Hill, and later Theodore Roosevelt's birthplace at 28 East 20th Street, were taken over by the Theodore Roosevelt Association. In 1962, Congress voted unanimously to establish the two residences as National Historic Sites. "As one stands here," Secretary of the Interior Stewart L. Udall said on a visit to Sagamore Hill at the time, "one gets the feeling that at any moment he may walk in the door—with great gusto." It is this awareness of the living presence of a vital, life-loving man that has brought Americans in increasing thousands to Sagamore Hill, to the house and grave of one of the greatest of all our American Presidents.

The family picture, taken in 1903, at Sagamore Hill, shows, left to right, Quentin, President Roosevelt; T.R., Jr.; Archibald, Alice, Kermit, Mrs. Roosevelt, and Ethel.

TWENTY-SEVEN

William Howard Taft

E HAVE BEEN wanderers on the face of the earth," wrote the jovial Yale professor of law to his wife on July 12, 1921. "It will be good to be anchored in a city we like." The professor, as any Yale man could have told at a glance, was William Howard Taft, who, at the age of sixty-three, was at last sailing into the berth he had so long desired and which had for so long eluded him, that of Chief Justice of the United States.

The law had been bred into Will Taft. His father, Alphonso Taft, a Vermonter who had gone to Yale, then headed west to Cincinnati, had himself sat on the bench, been twice a member of General Grant's cabinet (as Secretary of War and Attorney General), minister to Vienna and St. Petersburg; he had also seen to it that all his five sons by his two wives were educated in the law. William Howard Taft, the eldest of the second marriage, had prepared at Yale (1878) and Cincinnati Law School (1880). After graduation, he became assistant city prosecuting attorney, then swiftly rose to become the U.S. Solicitor General in Washington at thirty-three, then a U.S.

William Howard Taft's birthplace atop Cincinnati's Mount Auburn was built about 1850. It was a substantial brick house, with Victorian scroll-trimmed eaves and topped by a New England captain's walk. This picture, taken about 1870, shows young Will Taft standing in the yard while his younger brother perches on the gate post at left for the momentous occasion.

Circuit Judge at the age of thirty-five. Twice he turned down an offer of a seat on the Supreme Court tendered by Theodore Roosevelt. Then, at a small White House dinner in January 1908, the tempter knocked again.

From his easy chair, President Theodore Roosevelt threw back his head, closed his eyes, and intoned, "I am the seventh son of a seventh daughter. I have clairvoyant powers. I see a man standing before me weighing three hundred and fifty pounds. There is something hanging over his head. I cannot make out what it is; it is hanging by a slender thread. At one time it looks like the Presidency—then again it looks like the Chief Justiceship." "Make it the Chief Justiceship," replied Taft abruptly. "No!" cried Mrs. Taft. "Make it the Presidency!"

The presidency it was, for TR had the power and popularity to name his successor. Taft served unhappily as President and was later named Chief Justice by President Harding, who admired Taft's "progressively conservative and conservatively progressive attitude." Taft left no doubt which august position he preferred; in 1925 he said, "The truth is that in my present life I don't remember that I ever was President." It was a contented man who spoke, a man who had attained an ambition even beyond the White House, that of becoming the supreme magistrate of the nation.

No family in recent times has been more identified with Ohio politics and with Cincinnati than the Tafts, a tradition that carries down to the present day. Taft's eldest son, Robert Alphonso Taft, was U.S. Senator from Ohio 1938–1953, becoming to his party "Mr Republican"; Taft's second son, Charles Phelps Taft, was a former mayor of Cincinnati. (His daughter became dean and acting president of Bryn Mawr.) And yet there was much truth in Taft's letter to his wife that they had been indeed "wanderers on the face of the earth."

He was born, "a fat and smiling boy," on September 15, 1857, in a hillside house on Mount Auburn, one of Cincinnati's seven hills. Alphonso Taft's second wife, Louisa Maria Torrey, had come from Millbury, Massachusetts just four years earlier. To furnish the house the bride had splurged with $300 worth of furniture: a parlor table with black marble top ($65), a gothic chair with "figurell plush" ($15), a "whatnot" ($25).

Taft's later biographer, Henry F. Pringle, was to write, "Taft was not quickly stimulated by the aesthetic things of life. Music bored although it sometimes soothed him. He cared almost as little for art." Taft could be moved by nature, the gulls over the St. Lawrence River at dawn, the early morning view of Manila Bay, but Aesthetics and Will Taft rarely spoke. But he enjoyed sports. He was a good baseball player though slow around the bases, and liked swimming in the old canal. He was also fond of dancing and, most of all food; by the time he graduated from Yale he weighed 243 pounds, and though his weight soared above to 340, in later years, even with the sternest of regimes he never weighed less than he did in college. But, as Taft early learned, all the world loves a fat man. When in his college years he ponderously played the female lead in *Sleeping Beauty* at the Unity Club in Cincinnati, he convulsed the spectators—and got a humorous valentine from nearly every girl in the audience. The girl he eventually picked, Helen ("Nellie") Herron, was high-spirited, highly musical (she later founded the Cincinnati Symphony Orchestra), and, what Will Taft may not have known, had once spent a night at the

Taft and Mrs. Taft (Helen Herron) summered at Murray Bay, Pointe au Pic, Canada, from 1892 onward, and the campsite, overlooking the St. Lawrence River, was an assembly point for all the Tafts until it burned in the 1950s. This picture shows Taft after he had completed his term as President and was about to assume the robes of Chief Justice of the United States.

In 1886, Taft took his bride to "The Quarry," on East McMillan Street in Cincinnati, a shingled, Queen Anne–style house which became the birthplace of Senator Robert Alphonso Taft in 1889. The Taft children were entranced with the fire-engine house across the street.

White House as the guest of another Ohio President and her father's law partner, Rutherford B. Hayes; she had come back to Cincinnati vowing, "I will never be satisfied with anything less than a man destined to be President of the United States."

The Will Tafts moved after their marriage on June 19, 1886, first to a modest house on McMillan Street. When Taft was appointed U.S. Solicitor General in 1890, the family moved to a small house at 5 Dupont Circle, opposite the park, in Washington, paying $100 a month rent from his $7000 salary. Perhaps the closest thing to a permanent home the Will Tafts had was the rambling shingled cottage at Murray Bay, just outside Quebec. This cozy Canadian camp, set on a rocky highland surrounded by pines and looking out over the St. Lawrence, was first rented in 1892 and then enthusiastically bought by Taft. His appointment as U.S. circuit judge (the same position held by his father) brought Taft back to Cincinnati in 1892, but eight years later came a bolt from the blue that upset all domestic plans. At the request of President McKinley, Taft was asked to resign from the bench and form an administration to run the Philippine Islands newly won from Spain.

Taft quickly found that his opponent in the Philippines was not the Filipinos but General Arthur MacArthur, commanding the occupation troops. To Taft the Filipinos were "my little brown brothers;" to General MacArthur they were "natives" at best, and his troopers sang:

> He may be a brother to William H. Taft
> But he ain't no friend of mine.

Civil Governor Taft, a ballooning figure in his white tropical suits, drew no color lines; he affirmed, "We hold the Philippines for the benefit of the Filipinos, and we are not entitled to pass a single act or to approve a single measure that has not that as its chief purpose." Towering over the small-statured Filipinos, Taft, who treated them as equals, became a revered figure. He yielded to their own natural likes and customs and allowed cock-fighting to become legalized. His pro-

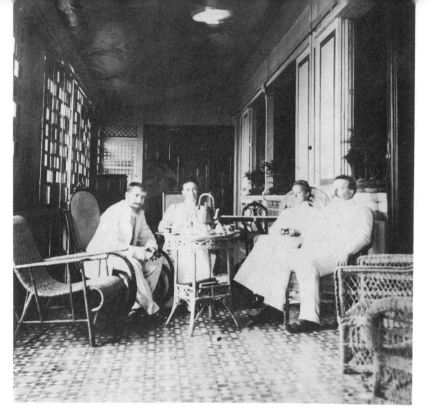

Malacanan Palace in Manila was Taft's official residence as the first Civil Governor of the Philippines between 1901 and 1904. The oval drive before the residence (above) was a setting for band concerts which Mrs. Taft so enjoyed that she sponsored a band shell on the Potomac in Washington when she became First Lady. His offices were in the left wing (below). The picture shows Mrs. Taft, second from left, and Governor Taft, right, having coffee with an aide and Mrs. Taft's sister, Maria Herron, during a moment of informal relaxation in the palace.

posal that a new conservatory of music be named for the martyred national patriot José Rizal increased their affection for him. On his own initiative, he traveled to Rome, negotiated the sale of the 400,000 choice agricultural acres held by the Spanish Friars for $7,200,000 with Pope Leo XIII, started a network of good roads, and set up a modern school system.

Aware that he was the successor to the Spanish governors, and that etiquette of a high level was required, he first installed Mrs. Taft and their three children in a spacious Spanish house on the Calle Reale, in Malate, a Manila suburb, and only reluctantly moved into the ornate but gloomy Malacañan Palace when his appointment as civil governor was made official. The Tafts had many servants—an American governess, Chinese house servants, Filipino stable boys and a dashing *cochero* to drive the children in their two-wheeled *calesa*. In the evening they religiously donned evening dress, played bridge avidly. For comfort, Governor Taft imported an outsized tub, so commodious that after his departure ten little Filipino boys could happily splash in it at one and the same time.

Indeed, the only battle Taft lost in the Philippines was on the scales; a sample lunch menu included "crabs or small lobsters or shrimp, beefsteak, cheese and salad, banana fritters or griddle cakes and fruit." In an effort to keep his weight down (it reached 326 by the time he left), he took to horseback riding. After one trip, Taft cabled Secretary of War Elihu Root: STOOD TRIP WELL. RODE HORSEBACK TWENTY-FIVE MILES TO FIVE THOUSAND FEET ELEVATION. Back came Root's famous reply: REFERENCE TO YOUR TELEGRAM. . . . HOW IS THE HORSE?

Summoned back to Washington at the end of 1903 to become Secretary of War, the Tafts lived at 1603 K Street. When they moved into the White House on March 4, 1909, they took with them, besides another outsized bathtub, the Oriental tapestries and teakwood furniture they had acquired in the Philippines and Japan. Another carryover was the famed White House cow, named Pauline Wayne; in

Taft's home was 1603 K Street, N.W., Washington, from the time he was made Roosevelt's Secretary of War until he entered the White House in 1909. The Tafts made the interiors interesting by installing the Oriental furniture they had bought in Manila and Japan.

President Taft weighed 340 pounds and exercised valiantly on the golf course to lose weight.

the Philippines Taft had imported a cow as a source of milk for the children, and the custom caught on with the family. President Taft kept up his horseback riding, became the first President to play golf and the first to own an automobile—in fact, Taft bought four automobiles, all of them White Steamers. "Well, children," he would boom as they dashed across the countryside, "enjoy all of this you can, for in four more years you may have to begin to walk again."

The election of 1912, when the Republican ranks were split by the Bull Moose Party, left no doubt that the Tafts would, indeed, have to "begin to walk." The question was *where*? The answer came with an offer from Taft's alma mater. Yale's President Arthur Twining Hadley offered Taft the venerable Kent Professorship of Law. Taft was delighted to be "out of the maelstrom of politics" and seized the offer of "a dignified retirement . . . which would approve itself to the general sense of propriety of the country."

"Men of Yale," he told the welcoming committee of students in New Haven, "as I hear your cheers and songs I feel young again, as if I had shed some of my years. All this may seem egotistical to you, but I come here wanting to help what little I can the young men who are going out into the nation. . . . If I can do this I shall thank God for the opportunity." As Taft finished, cheers floated over the campus, and at the strains of *Bright College Years* every hat was snatched off, including that of the ex-President.

During the eight years the former President lived in New Haven, he moved four times (not counting a leave of absence when the Tafts moved to 2029 Connecticut Avenue, Washington, where Taft served as co-chairman of the National War Labor Board). Their first New Haven house was Hillcrest, a turreted, pseudo-Romanesque mansion at 367 Prospect Street, which they rented from 1913 to 1918. They next moved to 70 Grove Street (since destroyed) in 1919, and then to a house at 113 Whitney Avenue, directly opposite the New Haven County Historical Society, which they bought for about $24,000 in 1920. The next year they moved on again to 60 York Avenue. They sold their Whitney Avenue house for $25,000 in 1921 after the news came to Taft at Murray Bay that President Harding had named him Chief Justice of the United States.

Taft left fond memories at New Haven, along with innumerable delightful anecdotes of his tenure there. By far the most conspicuous things about Taft were his girth and his chuckle. The fact of the matter was that when Taft sat in a normal-sized chair, he tended to get stuck. Once while sitting in a small theater with his three brothers, he commented to one of them, "Horace, if this theater burns, it has got to burn around me." His own Ford sedan had to be built with a specially wide door, and Yale still cherishes the gargantuan chairs made to make him comfortable, as well as the anecdote of the time he got the train to stop at Hicksville, a water-tank whistle stop, by telegraphing the conductor, STOP AT HICKSVILLE. LARGE PARTY WAITING TO CATCH TRAIN.

Taft, who had been able to save $100,000 while in the White House, paid $75,000 for his white brick house at Wyoming Avenue and Twenty-third Street in Washington. Built in the dignified neo-classic Georgian design so well adapted to Washington's over-all style, the Taft residence was roomy and dignified. It had three pleasant guest rooms on the second floor for visitors; the third floor was taken over entirely by the Chief Justice's library, reached by a newly in-

Hillcrest, 367 Prospect Street, New Haven, Connecticut, was Taft's residence from 1913, when he returned to Yale to lecture on law, to 1918. Such turreted, pseudo-Romanesque mansions, built in the 1880s and 1890s, fulfilled a yearning for propriety and respectability in Great Britain as in the United States.

stalled elevator. The Chief Justice, who took to walking the three miles to the courtrooms in the Capitol to keep down his weight, soon became a familiar Washington sight, a fine and portly, mustachioed presence that seemed to invite confidence. The story is well known of the house painter who dropped his brush from the scaffolding, glanced down at Taft passing beneath, and shouted, "Hey, mister, hand me that brush." The Chief Justice cheerfully obliged. On the Supreme Court bench Taft was sound, conservative, hard-working (he arose at 5:15 A.M., worked through until 10 P.M.), if not particularly spectacular. Most obviously of all, he was contented and in love with his work. "Next to my wife and children," he confessed, "the Court is the nearest thing to my heart."

He died March 8, 1930, and was buried at his request in the National Cemetery, the first American to hold both the office of President and that of Chief Justice, and the first to choose Arlington as his last resting place. Mrs. Taft died on May 22, 1943, leaving behind her one of the most beautiful gifts ever conceived by a First Lady, the thousands of flowering Japanese cherry trees, donated by Tokyo's Mayor Yukio Ozaki, which each spring turn the Potomac Park into a fragrant wreath for the delight of thousands of her countrymen.

TWENTY-EIGHT

Woodrow Wilson

THOMAS WOODROW WILSON, or "Tommy" as he was known until young manhood, was born December 28, 1856, in Staunton, Virginia, in an imposing white Presbyterian parsonage, a building whose two-story-high portico echoed Jefferson's own first Monticello. When Wilson was barely a year old, the family moved to Augusta, Georgia, where the Reverend Joseph Ruggles Wilson installed his family, including Tommy's two older sisters, in the brick parsonage that was to provide Wilson with his earliest memories. Among these were his recollections of the Civil War, a nightmare of incomprehensible shadows. Dimly Tommy knew that two of his uncles were generals in the Union Army; at home he watched ragged Confederate troops march by the house. Later, peeping out from the second-story blinds, he watched Union troops drive away with Jefferson Davis a prisoner in a carriage at the war's end.

As a boy, Wilson had to wear glasses and was dull in his studies. Like any normal boy he played hooky on occasion, once in play shot his cousin Jessie with a bow and arrow, ran into the house conscience-stricken, crying, "I am a murderer; it was no accident!" He was a fair baseball player, a first-rate soft-shoe dancer (much later, in utter secret, he used to practice his steps in the White House), started his own "Liftfoot Club" in the Wilsons' barn under a glowing red picture of Satan (and wrote its constitution, including complicated rules of procedure). Asked what he would like to be, he replied, "Senator from Virginia."

When Tommy was fourteen, the family moved again, this time to Columbia, the capital of South Carolina. Here Wilson saw more souvenirs of war—the mile-long, three-block-wide, burned-out business area left from Sherman's wartime march—and heard the young seminarians whom his father taught at the Presbyterian Theological Seminary talk heatedly of their disenfranchisement and the rule of the Carpetbaggers in terms of the eternal principles of moral law. Both made vivid impressions. Years later when as President Woodrow Wilson he was to journey to Paris for the Peace Conference, he refused to tour the battlefronts first; he knew, rightly, that the sight would turn him vengeful and bitter. In Columbia, the Reverend Dr. Wilson built his first house, a pleasing combination of Victorian and classic, with bow windows, arched windows and blinds, and a decorative trellised porch. It was a house that not only asserted the high social status of the Presbyterian elite but prompted in young Tommy an interest in architecture which he never lost.

Three years later, the Wilsons were on the move again, this time to Wilmington, North Carolina. It was another rise in the world—the pastor's salary was $4000. The church was rectangular with a modish

President Woodrow Wilson knew the sunniest days of his White House career when he married his second wife, the charming Edith Bolling Galt, in December, 1915. The outbreak of World War I, his own illness and exhaustion, and his losing fight for the League of Nations left Wilson an ailing and broken man.

Wilson was born in 1856 in the Presbyterian manse in Staunton, Virginia, in a building whose two-story portico recalls Jefferson's first Monticello; in the nursery is still to be seen the crib in which Wilson slept. Now a memorial to Wilson, the manse, built in 1846, has an imposing garden entrance (below).

high Gothic ceiling supported by six dark oak columns, and had a gallery in the rear for dark-skinned Christians. The pastor's manse was on Third Street, a wide and elm-shaded main street, with stately pillars marking the ante-bellum mansions, mansard roofs for the more recently prosperous, and gabled roofs for the most newly rich of all.

For a future scholar of high repute, Woodrow Wilson was still doing remarkably poorly. "Stand-offish," like his English-bred Presbyterian mother, Janet ("Jessie") Woodrow, diffident, thin-skinned, and idealistic, he tried Davidson College, only to have his eyes and stomach both give out. After a year of reading Greek at home, visiting the wharves three blocks away, and dreaming of running off to sea, he went to Princeton, his father's alma mater. A member of the Class of 1879, Wilson proved a good debater and was managing editor of the *Princetonian.* Still at loose ends after graduation, he decided on law, went to the University of Virginia, and then set up practice with a classmate in Atlanta, Georgia. When he discovered that "law and justice have little to do with one another," he decided to study history and politics at Johns Hopkins. There he met his first stiff challenge in the person of Professor Herbert B. Adams, a German-trained New Englander, who set him to find out how government is actually conducted, not how writers say it is. Wilson derived from this primary research his first book, *Constitutional Government,* a Ph.D., and a brilliant reputation in the academic world. He also now had job prospects bright enough to marry Ellen Axson, a Presbyterian minister's daughter he had known as a child in Augusta and had met again at church in East Rome, Georgia, while he was a struggling lawyer. A charming person of good sense, sweet temper, and highly developed artistic abilities (she had studied in New York's Art Students League), "Nell" Wilson proved both a balance wheel and incentive to Woodrow Wilson, as he now styled himself.

As a young professor, Woodrow Wilson moved up the ladder quickly. He was Bryn Mawr's first Professor of History, but found teaching young ladies uninspiring. At Wesleyan, he helped coach the football team to victory, cheering vociferously in boots and slicker during bad weather. In 1890 he was invited to return to Princeton, and soon became the most popular lecturer on campus, famed for his brilliant exposition, remarkable speaking voice and clear-cut moral dictums. In 1902 at the age of forty-six he was named president of Princeton University, breaking a long tradition that the president must be a Presbyterian divine.

On moving back to his old campus, Wilson had rented the house of Professor Hunt. But it had long been Wilson's dream to design a house of his own; his family, besides "Nell" Wilson, had grown by three daughters, Margaret (born 1886), Eleanor, called "Nellie," and in time to become the second wife of William McAdoo, and Jessie, who was to marry Francis B. Sayre in the White House. In addition, the Wilsons could count on visits from Mrs. Wilson's sister, Grandfather Wilson, and Wilson's widowed sister; average occupancy of the house was about ten. When Wilson, who could expect from $1500 to $4000 a year from his writings, bought the lot next to Professor Hunt's, the whole family started dreaming and planning their ideal home.

Wilson's daughter, Nellie, has written of her father's love of architecture. The plans he drew "were so nearly perfect that only a contractor was needed for the final detailed drawings." The style

Library Place, off Cleveland Lane, Princeton, New Jersey, was designed at the turn of the century by Wilson himself in the fashionable half-timbered Tudor style. "A deep, happy peace pervaded the house," his daughter Nellie recalled, "a sort of quiet rhythm that attracted and held people."

Wilson picked for Library Place was the half-timbered Tudor cottage style, an outgrowth of the early nineteenth-century Gothic Revival, with a masonry first story topped by an overhanging plaster-and-exposed-timber façade punctuated with windows of diamond-shaped, leaded panes. For a family whose favorite reading was Wordsworth, Shakespeare, and Browning, such a style, with its Elizabethan overtones, was filled with literary associations. Actually the façade, pleasant as it was, was mainly a stage set; the actual framing allowed great freedom of interior planning, and Wilson used it to advantage.

The principal room on the main floor was a large central hall, where the family gathered to read or sew about a huge open fireplace with a mantel decorated with the Apollo Belvedere and the Winged Victory of Samothrace. To the left was that survival from colonial and early-nineteenth-century times, the best parlor, or drawing room, small and furnished with Wilson's best satin-covered furniture; here fine books of poetry, including *The Hound of Heaven*, were scattered and here the velvet-covered family album of photographs was kept. Needless to say, children were not allowed to touch, or even enter unsupervised. Behind the parlor was Wilson's book-lined study and writing work room, hung with portraits of his parents and his heroes: Washington, Webster, Gladstone, Edmund Burke. The children would listen carefully for the sound of the rolltop closing. "It meant that he had finished and would soon come and play with us," Nellie recalled. "It was the most important moment of our day."

The large dining room opened directly off the main center room, and had long French doors leading into the garden. Meals were punctual, and Wilson warned his daughters to be ready in time by

Prospect House, the official residence of the President of Princeton, became the Wilson home in 1902, when Wilson was made head of Princeton at the age of forty-six. Wilson made sure that there was time for family gatherings about the fire. Photographed here, right to left, are Wilson's first wife, Ellen Louise Axon, and three daughters, Jessie, Eleanor, and Margaret.

telling them of Pat, who missed his train. "Ah, Pat," said his friend, "you don't run fast enough." "Sure, I ran fast enough," Pat answered, "but I didn't start soon enough!" Meals began with grace, and while eating the children were expected to listen, not talk. Since the children knew they were being trusted, Woodrow and "Nell" talked freely. The children, knowing who was stern master of the house, were sometimes provoked to glee when Wilson played the henpecked husband. "Oh, Woodrow," Mrs. Wilson would say after one of his rash statements, "you know you don't mean that." Their father would reply with utmost gravity, "Madam, I was venturing to think that I meant that until I was corrected."

The Wilson home radiated an extraordinary human warmth. Much of it was due to the self-sacrifice of the mother, who made the children's clothing herself, went without jewelry so that her husband could buy books. A deep harmony existed between husband and wife, and, of course, the children found Wilson's personality fascinating. "In all the years my father never disappointed me," Margaret Wilson once said. "He was the most interesting and delightful person!"

Wilson believed in dignity, but when Fräulein Boehm and Maggie Foley, the governess and nurse, were out of the way, Wilson could be full of fun. He was an inveterate punster ("Why did Robinson Crusoe?"), loved quoting limericks,* and threw himself wholeheartedly into charades; on one memorable occasion he put on his wife's hat, draped a feather boa and a long velvet curtain around himself, and with one hand held high, played the falsetto role of a high-society lady to the hilt.

Less of this lightheartedness was in evidence after the Wilsons moved into Prospect, the official residence of the President of Princeton on the college campus. He had galvanized Princeton into bringing its curriculum up to date, but he was soon in a row with his trustees over the new graduate school and his desire to abolish the college's aristocratic eating clubs. The squabbles were much publicized, and eventually caught the eye of the New Jersey political bosses. When Wilson won a promise of no interference from them, he ran for the governorship, winning, to their astonishment, in a landslide. He then promptly fought and defeated the Democratic Machine in New Jersey.

New Jersey had no official governor's mansion in Trenton, and the Wilsons were faced with shoehorning themselves into a suite at The Inn, on Princeton's Nassau Street. But in summer famine turned to feast as they moved to the mansion at Sea Girt on the New Jersey coast. This elephantine structure in the neoclassic style had been the state's contribution to the Chicago World's Fair of 1893. After the Fair it had been disassembled piece by piece and moved in sections to the seaside site. Nearby was the noisy railroad station and in front the National Guard Parade Grounds, where on Sunday the protesting Governor, in silk top hat, was expected to mount his charger and review the troops. The huge house creaked and groaned in the sea winds which set the chairs on the porch to rocking. But here the family enjoyed its first automobile, driven grimly by an old Irish chauffeur, and such exotic guests as Mrs. Mary Hulbert Peck, a

* For beauty I am not a star
  There are hundreds more handsome by far,
  But my face I didn't mind it,
  For I am behind it,
  It's the people in front that I jar.

As Governor of New Jersey, Wilson occupied the official summer residence, Shadow Lawn, in Sea Girt. His daughters thought "only a conflagration could have improved" the immense reception hall (above).

Shadow Lawn, at Sea Girt, was an elephantine building erected by the state of New Jersey at the Chicago World's Fair of 1893, then disassembled, and shipped to the seaside to become the official summer mansion. (Below) Wilson accepting the Democratic nomination.

friend Wilson had met in Bermuda, who daintily puffed away on her cigarette after dinner to the wide-eyed fascination and horror of the girls and Mrs. Wilson.

As the 1912 nominations approached, a good many visitors, were politicians. The key figure for Wilson was Willliam Jennings Bryan, the silver-tongued "Great Commoner," who had been himself three times candidate for President and remained the single most powerful force in the Democratic Party. The Republicans in Chicago had divided, with Taft heading the G.O.P. ticket and Theodore Roosevelt splitting off to found the National Progressive Party ("Good old Teddy," Wilson said with a smile, "what a help he is!"). As the Democrats gathered in Baltimore, a telephone booth was installed beneath the main stairs, with an extension in Wilson's bedroom. The convention battle was bitter, since, with a divided G.O.P., nomination was tantamount to election, and the Democrats had not won a presidential election in twenty years. Over the telephone, the Wilsons could hear Champ Clark's Democratic backers singing,

> Every time I come to town
> The boys start kicking my dawg aroun',
> I don't care if he *is* a houn',
> You gotta quit kickin' my dawg aroun'.

Mixed with it came the Tiger yells of Wilson's own Princeton supporters. The seesaw struggle dragged on for over a week; finally on the forty-sixth ballot the victory went to Wilson. As the band at Sea Girt, hidden out of sight, marched up to the Governor's summer mansion, thumping away at *The Conquering Hero Comes,* Wilson looked startled. Asked for a victory quote by the press, he in turn staggered the reporters by saying, "I can't effervesce in the face of responsibility." Wilson won the election easily. The Wilson family packed up their things at the house they had temporarily rented as a kind of refuge on Cleveland Lane, behind Grover Cleveland's house and gardens in Princeton, and in a blaze of publicity left for Washington.

The Woodrow Wilson who eight years later left the White House was a man broken in health and close to death. Behind him was the slogan, "Too proud to fight," and the chant "He kept us out of war" that paved the way for his re-election in 1916. The prevailing mood of postwar cynicism had only scorn now for "The war to make the

Woodrow Wilson's home after the presidency was at 2340 S Street, Washington, D.C. In the second-floor library, Wilson resumed his scholarly pursuits until his death in 1924. Upon Mrs. Wilson's death in 1961, the house was bequeathed to the National Trust.

world safe for Democracy." His loyal wife of twenty-nine happy years was dead, and there was now a second Mrs. Woodrow Wilson, the charming Edith Bolling Galt, whom he had married after sixteen months of widowhood in the White House.

At the end of his presidency, Woodrow and Edith Wilson moved to 2340 S Street, N.W., a comfortable three-story brick house with a view across the Potomac and a glimpse of both the Capitol dome and the White House portico. The furniture that for eight years had been in storage was brought down from Princeton. The aging, enfeebled Wilson was most touched to find that his staff had fixed up his own room on S Street with the easy chair, footrest, pillows, and tables just as they had been arranged in the White House. Also installed was a massive bed, measuring eight foot six inches by six foot two inches, a replica of the Lincoln bed which Wilson had used during his long illness.

Wilson built up his library, began work on his *The Philosophy of Politics,* even for a while formed a law firm. Seeing him driven in his car through the streets, pedestrians lifted their hats in respect to the white-haired, shrunken old man. A speech on Armistice Day, 1923, over the radio called out ten thousand sympathizers the next day. An appeal for funds for the Woodrow Wilson Foundation, chairmaned by Wilson's Assistant Secretary of the Navy, Franklin D. Roosevelt, brought in $800,000 from 120,000 donors. When Woodrow Wilson died, on February 3, 1924, crowds knelt outside on the wintry street. He was buried in the unfinished Washington Cathedral. Marking his grave is a mighty stone blade with cross-shaped hilt—appropriately it is a crusader's cross.

TWENTY-NINE

Warren Gamaliel Harding

"... Government is not of super-men, but of
normal men, very much like you and me. ..."*

BACK TO NORMALCY" was the slogan that in 1920
elected Warren G. Harding President. It was a slogan
sublimely welcome to a people exhausted by Wilson's
idealism, worried over industrial unrest and high prices, and eager to
get the 1920s under way. The Democratic ticket of Ohio Governor
James M. Cox and Franklin Delano Roosevelt went down to resounding defeat by a seven million majority.

Warren Harding was born November 2, 1865, on a small farm
(Blooming Grove), at Corsica, Morrow County, Ohio. He was the
first of eight children reared by George Tyron Harding, a farmer and
later homeopathic physician, and Phoebe Dickerson.

As a boy, Harding went to local schools, attended Ohio Central
College in Iberia, Ohio, an academy from which he graduated at sixteen. Easygoing by nature, he had had the run of a print shop when
he was six (his father was half-owner of the Caledonia *Argus*); later
he worked on a farm and then in a sawmill, made brooms, and was a
construction laborer. After Ohio Central College, the family moved
to Marion, Ohio (population 4000), and there Harding made a pass
at studying law, decided instead to become an insurance canvasser,
and at nineteen became a reporter on the Marion *Democratic Mirror*.
Perhaps patterning himself on his father, a short-term fifer in the
Civil War, Harding started up his own Citizens' Cornet Band of
Marion ("I played every instrument but the slide trombone and the
E-flat clarinet"), bought new uniforms on credit, and drilled the
group until they took third prize at the state fair.

Tall, handsome, and popular, Harding managed to borrow $300
to buy the four-page Marion *Star* (circulation 500), and soon started
things humming at the *Star's* office at 195 East Center St. With a
chaw of tobacco, W.G. was ready for a day's work. Small-town
journalism was his natural métier. In 1891 a new and invigorating
presence was felt at the *Star* with the appearance of Florence Kling de
Wolfe, daughter of the town's richest banker and a widow five years
older than Warren Harding, but a woman who was to make the *Star*
financially. "I went down there intending to help out for a few days,"
she later laughingly recalled, "and remained fourteen years." "Mrs.
Harding in those days ran the show," one *Star* newsboy† recalled.
"She was a woman of very narrow mentality and range of interest or

* Harding to his Marion, Ohio, neighbors after his nomination.
† His name: Norman Thomas, later longtime candidate for President on the
  Socialist ticket.

*Birthplace of Warren Harding, 1865, outside of Bloom-
ing Grove (formerly Corsica), Morrow County, Ohio.*

President Harding made an impressive figure with his rugged, masculine features, silver hair, and black eyebrows. Here he is seen with Mrs. Harding during the playing of the national anthem at the International Horse Show in Washington.

understanding, but a strong will and, within certain limits, of genuine kindliness. . . . Her husband was the front. . . . He was, as you know, very affable; very much a joiner and personally popular. He was a fine small-town or city booster and wrote editorials telling how Marion, Ohio, had more miles of Berea sandstone sidewalks than any town of its size in the United States. Nay, he ventured to say, in the whole world. This was his best line."

W.G. and his wife, whom he called "The Duchess," had started building their house at 380 Mount Vernon Avenue in 1890, the year before their marriage on July 8, 1891. It was a comfortable house, with its rotonda veranda, a tiled floor on the porch, and inside gas grates and a stained-glass window. Most important of all, it was substantial enough to impress Mrs. Harding's father, a Mennonite-reared, stubborn, narrow-minded banker who refused to speak to his daughter for years after her marriage to Harding.

What Ohio man isn't a politician at heart? Inevitably Warren Harding drifted into the state's number-one pastime, and under the

Warren G. Harding's home in Marion, Ohio, was the dream castle built by Harding and his bride-to-be in 1890 while they were still courting. The house, with its broad veranda and columns, reflects the revival of interest in Georgian architecture, here used as heavy-handed trim to the multi-gabled Queen Anne design. The broad porch became Harding's campaigning rostrum. Photograph (above) shows Harding and wife in 1920 immediately following his nomination for the Presidency on the Republican ticket.

The Harding house on Mt. Vernon Avenue, in Marion, Ohio, contains over two thousand mementos, gifts, and souvenirs of Harding's life in the four downstairs rooms of the former President's home. The rotunda porch still has its original wicker porch furniture, in the dining room is the buffet, ornamented with an extraordinary collection of vases, most of them presumably gifts, dining-room fireplace (opposite) is flanked by Warren Harding's golf clubs and cane collection; also in the Harding house are (bottom) Harding's chair, desk used in state legislature, silk hat, cane, favorite pipe, and brief case. The Harding home was opened to the public by the Harding Memorial Association in 1926.

sponsorship of Harry M. Daugherty, later to be known as "Boss of the Ohio Gang," Harding established himself as a fellow easy to get along with, a convivial drinker, good poker player, safe, conservative, and regular. From Marion, he went twice to the state capital as senator, and in 1904 he was elected lieutenant governor. In 1910 his bid for the governorship failed; but failure seemed to win Harding more friends than ever; everybody likes a good loser. In 1912 he was selected to put Taft's name in nomination; in 1914 he was elected to the U.S. Senate with a huge (102,000) plurality; in 1916 he was chosen keynoter for Charles Evans Hughes.

When 1920 rolled around, Harding's old political mentor, Harry Daugherty, put it up to him, "Ohio has always had a candidate. If she doesn't have one, the rest of the Union will think we have seceded." In a panic, Harding is reported to have replied, "You don't want me to give up the senatorship, do you? I haven't a ghost of a chance at the presidency." Daugherty thought otherwise.

In one of the most fantastic crystal-ball predictions in the history of politics, Daugherty told a reporter, "I don't expect Senator Harding to be nominated on the first, second or third ballots, but I think we can afford to take chances that, about eleven minutes after two, Friday morning of the convention, when ten or twenty weary men are sitting around a table, someone will say, 'Who will we nominate?' At that decisive time the friends of Harding will suggest him and can well afford to abide by the result."

And on Friday night, June 11, in the smoke-filled rooms of Chicago's Blackstone Hotel, precisely the scene Harry Daugherty had predicted was enacted. Harding accepted the nomination within minutes of the 2:11 A.M. deadline preordained by Boss Daugherty. The same day the convention delegates duly nominated Harding, then took the bit in their teeth to shout in Calvin Coolidge as the G.O.P. vice-presidential nominee.

Following the established tradition, Harding made his Marion home headquarters for the campaign, building a small office for the newsmen covering him. Soon the crowd began flocking to the Mecca of Marion. Harding loved to shake hands; "It's the most pleasant thing I do," he once confessed to his secretary. He advocated an

"America free, independent, and self-reliant, but offering friendship to the world." (*The New York Times* headlined it HARDING SCUTTLES THE LEAGUE.) But it soon was evident that Harding would win in a walk.

Warren G. Harding was the first salesman and the first newspaper editor to be elected President. His Cabinet included the best brains in the Republican Party, Mellon in the Treasury, Hoover for Commerce, Charles Evans Hughes for the State Department. Unhappily, the Cabinet also included Harding's cronies, with Harry Daugherty as Attorney General and Albert B. Fall as Secretary of the Interior. While Harding relaxed over poker, with cocktails before the sauerkraut and wienerwurst, and beer and Scotch (despite Prohibition) over the card tables with "The Duchess" acting as bartender, sinister rumors began to circulate about the "Ohio Gang."

As the late, great Washington newsman Richard Oulahan once pointed out, the President is often the worst-informed man in Washington; it is often to the interest of too many to keep information from him. Such was the case with Harding. He may well have had intimations of the brewing Teapot Dome scandal. In fact, neither the President nor Mrs. Harding was well. She suffered from a near-fatal kidney ailment; Harding himself had an acute cardiac condition. What was at first diagnosed as food poisoning from crabmeat (until it turned out that Harding had eaten none) brought the President to a near-collapse. And a few days later, in San Francisco's Palace Hotel, while Mrs. Harding was reading to him from a highly laudatory article in the *Saturday Evening Post*, Harding died suddenly of a brain clot on August 2, 1923.

Harding had what Mark Sullivan called "a fatal streak of softness." He could, given proper support and guidance, perform well, but such a trusting character as his is easy to bilk. Soon after his death there were scandals in the Alien Property Custodian's office and the Veterans' Bureau.

Upon Harding's death, a move was started to build a monument at Marion, a project to which countless schoolchildren across the nation contributed. The project, in the wake of the scandals soon exposed in Washington, lagged. The Harding Memorial was finally dedicated on July 4, 1927. On June 16, 1931, a solemn convocation was held, presided over by Chief Justice Hughes and attended by ex-President Coolidge. Said President Herbert Hoover of Warren G. Harding:

> His was a mind and character fitted for a task where the one transcendent need was the healing quality of gentleness and friendliness ...
>
> Here was a man whose soul was seared by a great disillusionment. We saw him gradually weaken, not only from physical exhaustion, but also from mental anxiety. Warren Harding had a dim realization that he had been betrayed by a few of the men whom he had believed were his devoted friends. That was the tragedy of Warren Harding.

Mrs. Warren Harding died a little more than a year later, on November 21, 1924. In her will she bequeathed the Harding home, its furnishings, and over 2000 mementoes, gifts, and souvenirs received by the Hardings to the Harding Memorial Association, which opened the four large rooms on the main floor to the public on February 8, 1926.

THIRTY

Calvin Coolidge

P LYMOUTH NOTCH, Vermont, a small hamlet on Route 100 in the south central part of the state, has been touched by history twice—once when gold was discovered there in 1855 (it petered out, providing just enough gold for a few wedding rings), and again on the night of August 2, 1923, when Calvin Coolidge was awakened in the middle of the night by a telegram announcing that President Warren Harding was dead, and that he, as Vice-President, had now become President of the United States. There at 2:47 A.M. in the sitting room of the Coolidge farmhouse, his oath of allegiance to the Constitution was administered by his father, Colonel John C. Coolidge, a notary public, by the light of the kerosene lamp, while his mother's Bible stood on the scalloped table beside them. "It seemed a simple and natural thing to do at the time," Coolidge wrote later. "But I can now realize something of the dramatic force of the event."

Five generations of Coolidges, dating back to Captain John Coolidge, a Revolutionary soldier and one of the town's first three selectmen elected in 1789, had lived in Plymouth Notch (population 432). Calvin Coolidge himself was born there on July 4, 1872, in a five-room, story-and-a-half cottage next to the general store owned by his father, a onetime carriagemaker who had become a prosperous farmer. Across the road, in what had been an inn in more prosperous time, lived his mother's parents; down the road some sixty-five rods lived his Coolidge grandparents. "They were a hardy self-contained people," Coolidge noted succinctly in his *Autobiography*.

The way of life known as a boy by Calvin Coolidge (he was christened John Calvin, but his first name was dropped in family usage) was, as he described it, a "hard but wholesome life, under which the people suffered many privations and enjoyed many advantages, without any clear realization of the existence of either one of them." Fortunately the house to which the Coolidge family moved in 1876, when Coolidge was four, has been preserved intact. It was a modest frame structure which Colonel John Coolidge bought for $375, soon afterward selling one of the barns for $100 ("My father was a good trader"). Bay windows were added to the sitting room and the piazza was built on the front; from Boston Colonel John brought back the black walnut horsehair furniture and piano which still grace the parlor.

In terms of amenities, the Coolidges were no better off than their neighbors. A privy, with the usual Sears Roebuck catalogue, was the only toilet until 1932; neither electricity, gas, nor telephone was installed until Calvin Coolidge himself built a modern six-room addition (since removed) to the house in 1931. Because Aurora Pierce, the

Coolidge's faithful housekeeper, lived in a manner unchanged in the old part of the house for forty-eight years, the old wood range was kept stove-blacked and rustless, the woodshed full (Aurora had stacked away twenty bushels of birch bark in the back room for lighting fires). She heated water for washing in the woodstove reservoir, washed by hand in the tin tub, kept the butter and milk cool in the cellar in earthenware crocks. From the decade after the Civil War, when Aurora Pierce was born (she hired out to the Coolidges in 1908) until she died in 1956, no changes were made in the old part of the house, or in her operation of it. It is easily the most authentic and completely furnished farmhouse of its period in the United States.

The heart of the farmhouse is, of course, the kitchen. On the walls are the pewter plates belonging to Coolidge's great-grandmother, Sally Thompson Coolidge, believed by the family to be part Indian. Between the windows are the mirror and shaving mugs used by Coolidge and his father for their morning shaves. By the sink are the dipper and washcloth (always hung up after use); beside it is the

Plymouth Notch, Vermont, is a small hamlet in the Green Mountains where the Coolidge family has lived since 1789. "It was here that I first saw the light of day," said Calvin Coolidge, "here I received my bride; here my dead lie pillowed on the loving breast of our everlasting hills."

woodbox—young Calvin's chore was to keep it filled. On the table the places were always set, with plates and cups bottom-up until after grace.

"Most of the visitors would sit in the kitchen with Father and Mother," Coolidge wrote in his *Autobiography,* "and the hardest thing in the world for me was to have to go through that kitchen door and greet the visitors. By fighting hard I used to manage to get through that kitchen door. I'm all right now with old friends, but every time I meet a stranger I have to stand by the old kitchen door a minute. It's hard."

His boyhood bashfulness stayed with Coolidge for life, giving his visage a stern, pinched look that could crinkle on occasion into a delighted grin, but rarely did. His classmates at Amherst (1895) grew to appreciate the dry wit of this pale, strait-laced redhead.

It was also his great good luck that a fellow Vermonter, Grace Goodhue, saw beneath his stubborn, laconic manner. The story of how Calvin Coolidge asked for Grace's hand from her bluff Lake Champlain-going father, Captain Goodhue, is classic.

"Up here on business?" Captain Goodhue asked the young lawyer.

"No. Up here to ask your permission to marry Grace."

"Does she know of it?" asked the astonished father.

"No, but she soon will," grimly answered Calvin.

The proposal, when it came, was hardly more romantic. "I am going to marry you," the future President blurted. Calvin Coolidge lacked all the graces; he skated awkwardly, danced abominably, even whistled poorly. What he did have was persistence. As he later said, "Persistence and determination alone are omnipotent. The slogan, 'Press On,' has solved and always will solve the problems of the human race." Persistence, in this case, won him a joyous, good-humored, extroverted girl who, as she said of herself, "was born with peace of mind."

The Coolidges' first home—one they kept for twenty-four years—was one half of the two-family house at 21 Massasoit Street in Northampton, Massachusetts, which they rented for $28 a month (the rent was raised to $40 when Coolidge became governor). It was a simple frame house with front porch, parlor, dining room, kitchen; upstairs were three bedrooms, a bath, and the attic. The furnishings were austere. Coolidge bought an oak bedroom set, installed the oak bookcase he had used at college. Captain Goodhue built them a couch, and there was a dependable Morris chair, Coolidge's favorite while smoking his cigar. When the local Norwood Hotel closed, the Coolidges bought the hotel linen and silverware, used them for years, defiantly exhibiting the hotel insignia.

Coolidge believed in commuting to Boston for politics, staying in a hotel room at the Adams House, coming back for week ends to Northampton, where Mrs. Coolidge was expected to look after their two sons, John and Calvin, Jr. Not until Coolidge had gone up through the ranks to lieutenant governor of Massachusetts in 1916 did he consent to Grace Coolidge's coming to Boston, and then they took up residence in *two* rooms in the Adams. It was while staying there in 1919 that Coolidge was catapulted to national fame. When the Boston police strike occurred, boys and hoodlums ran looting through the streets. As the streets of Boston were swept by anarchy, Governor Coolidge sent his famous message to the American Federa-

The Coolidge Homestead was bought by Calvin Coolidge's father for $375 in 1876. The bow window and porch were added soon afterward. The center rocking chair was one most used by President Coolidge.

The kitchen table (opposite, top) was kept set, with plates and glasses reversed. The cast-iron range and kitchen equipment are unchanged from the way Calvin Coolidge knew them in his boyhood, when this room was used both for cooking and for visitors.

tion of Labor's Samuel Gompers, "There is no right to strike against the public safety by anybody, anywhere, any time." And it was in the same modest hotel rooms in 1920 that Coolidge received word from the Republican National Convention in Chicago that he had lost the nomination for the presidency.

"Nominated for Vice-President," Coolidge told his wife as he laid down the telephone receiver.

"But you're not going to accept it, are you?" Grace Coolidge asked.

"I suppose I shall have to," Cal Coolidge replied.

Oddly enough, one of Grace Coolidge's fears when the Harding–Coolidge slate won in a landslide in 1920 was that the new Vice-President would leave her in Northampton. Coolidge relented, but he refused to take a house in Washington, not at the prices they were asking! Instead, the Vice-President took a small suite at the New Willard Hotel. A chance for much more handsome quarters was vetoed by Mrs. Harding. Senator Henderson's widow had offered her house as the official vice-presidential residence, provided the government would make an appropriation for upkeep. Mrs. Harding, according to Columbia President Nicholas Murray Butler, "burst into flame and almost shouted, 'Not a bit of it, not a bit of it. I am going to have that bill defeated. Do you think I am going to have those Coolidges living in a house like that? A hotel apartment is plenty good enough for them'." Needless to say, the bill failed.

Calvin Coolidge, a parliamentarian at heart, enjoyed presiding over the Senate, but in time he fretted at the enforced inactivity. He looked forward to summer recess when he could go back to Plymouth Notch, don his grandfather's blue frock, pitch hay, or, for more casual exercise, ride his favorite horse, "Captain," or go fishing with worms. It was after such a hot summer's day, helping his neighbor D. P. Brown finish haying, and after a good supper cooked by housekeeper Aurora Pierce, that Coolidge retired to the upstairs bedroom at nine o'clock on August 2, 1923.

Close to midnight, W. A. Perkins from Bridgewater, Vermont, roared into the yard in his 1918 Cole 8, bearing the telegram that announced Harding's death in distant San Francisco earlier that evening. Colonel John Coolidge in his nightshirt called up to his son that a telegram had arrived. "I noticed that his voice trembled," Coolidge later recalled. "As the only times I had observed that before was when death had visited our family, I knew something of the gravest nature had occurred. . . ." Although Coolidge was not by habit a religious man, after reading the telegram, both he and his wife knelt by the bed to pray, then dressed quickly and came down to give a statement to the reporters who by now had arrived by cars from the nearby towns.

Only after all the newspapermen (save Joseph H. Fountain of the Springfield, Vermont, *Reporter*) had left to file Coolidge's statement, did Congressman Porter Dale, who had driven up with Fountain, manage to make his point heard: "The United States has no President!"

"Father, are you still a notary?" asked Coolidge.

"Yes," replied the Colonel.

"Then I want you to administer the oath."

While the Colonel went into the kitchen to shave, Coolidge

The indoor privy, with its inevitable Montgomery Ward catalogue, was the only toilet facility until Coolidge modernized the Homestead in 1932.

These rooms recall the historic night of August 3, 1923. At midnight word had come to the Coolidge Homestead that Harding was dead and Coolidge was now the President. At 2:47 A.M. Coolidge took his oath of office, administered by his father, a notary public. He signed the oath on the parlor highboy desk (above), which has a picture of his mother on the wall beside it. The actual swearing-in ceremony took place beside the lamp-lit table (opposite). Afterward the new President retired to his upstairs bedroom and slept soundly through the rest of the night. His bed is covered with a quilt made by his sister, Abigail, at the age of thirteen.

walked across the road to call Attorney General Harry M. Daugherty to find the correct words of the presidential oath. Back at the house, Colonel John and Congressman Dale were looking up the same information in the Vermont Statutes. Coolidge had his secretary, Edwin Geiser, copy them on three strips of paper (cut to two-inch width to save paper!), then with his right hand raised, faced his father and repeated the oath in the same sitting room where in years past first his beloved mother, and then his younger sister Abigail, had passed away.

"Where succession to the highest office in the land is by inheritance or appointment," Coolidge later wrote, "no doubt there have been kings who have participated in the induction of their sons into their office, but in republics where the succession comes by an election I do not know of any case in history where a father has administered to his son the qualifying oath of office which made him the chief magistrate. . . ."

Following the ceremony, President Coolidge mounted the stairs and went sound to sleep. Before departing for Washington the next morning, he stopped at the hillside grave of his mother, who had died when he was thirteen. "It had been a comfort to me during my boyhood when I was troubled to be near her last resting place, even in the dead of night," he explained. "Some way, that morning, she seemed very near to me."

As President, Coolidge soon became identified with the financial boom of the Twenties (the "Coolidge Bonanza"). His stiff-backed Yankee probity set him apart from the scandals of the Harding administration, his eye for economy pared down the national budget ruthlessly, and his laconic rejoinders and dry wit were endlessly told by the press and his friends. Told by a gushing society hostess that she had bet she could get more than two words out of him at dinner, Coolidge replied, "You lose!" Asked by an admirer to give something, even a cigar band, as a souvenir of the visit, Cal Coolidge took a cigar, carefully removed the band, handed it over, and replaced the cigar. In later years, when a woman rushed up to congratulate him, gushing, "Oh, Mr. Coolidge, what a wonderful address! I stood up all through it!" Coolidge replied stolidly, "So did I!"

By comparison, Grace Coolidge glowed with warmth and a gentler wit. She played a role in bringing together the hero of the day, Colonel Charles A Lindbergh, and Anne Morrow. She also made a start at refurbishing the White House in period furniture, a task later to be taken up in earnest by the wife of the Thirty-fourth President. Coolidge's administration lacked all taint of petticoat government. "I have such faith in Mr. Coolidge's judgment," Grace Coolidge once said, "that if he told me I would die tomorrow at ten o'clock, I would believe him." In private sorrow, the two drew together at the time of the death of their son Calvin, Jr. (from an infected toe, the result of playing tennis without socks). But Coolidge did not even find it necessary to consult with her when he made his momentous and cryptic announcement: "I do not choose to run for President in nineteen twenty-eight."

"We draw our Presidents from the people, " Coolidge wrote in his *Autobiography*. "It is a wholesome thing for them to return to the people. I came from them. I wish to be one of them again." The old house at 21 Massasoit Street seemed small indeed after the White

The Coolidges' home, which they rented for twenty-four years, was half of the double-house at 21 Massasoit Street, Northampton, Massachusetts. The President returned here after the White House to find the rent had gone up from $28 to $40 a month.

Former President and Mrs. Coolidge photographed before their Northampton House, looking at copy of Calvin Coolidge's Autobiography, *in which he wrote, "We draw our Presidents from the people. It is a wholesome thing for them to return to the people. I came from them. I wish to be one of them again."*

House, yet the Coolidges welcomed it at first. But crowds of curious cruising slowly past the house in their automobiles soon made sitting on the porch a torture. In 1930 the Coolidges bought the well-secluded estate belonging to Smith College President Dr. Henry Noble Mac-Cracken called The Beeches. Costing some $45,000, it included a tennis court, small swimming pool, and a fine view of the Connecticut's "Ox Bow" bend.

Coolidge had the bitter experience of seeing his party blamed for the Depression, which came seven months after he left office. "We are in a new era to which I do not belong," he sadly told a friend, "and it would not be possible for me to adjust myself to it. . . ." Still he did manage to write newspaper articles and his *Autobiography*. Death, when it came on January 5, 1933, of a thrombosis, came quickly and silently. Mrs. Coolidge lived on until July 8, 1957, a warm grandmother, a staunch baseball fan, and a key organizer in her charity drives to aid deaf children. In the words of then-Senator John F. Kennedy, "She continued to epitomize the qualities of graciousness, charm and modesty which marked her as an ideal First Lady of the Land."

Both the ex-President and his wife were buried in the hillside cemetery in Plymouth Notch, beside their son, Calvin, Jr.

THIRTY-ONE

Herbert Hoover

HERBERT HOOVER'S beginnings were humble. He was born on the old frontier, during the administration of General Grant in the small settlement of West Branch, Iowa. As the son of a Quaker blacksmith, he had to start from the bottom. Yet, by the beginning of World War I, Hoover was the leading mining engineer in the world. He became so well known for his business and engineering acumen that in 1920 he was offered a $500,000 annual salary by the Guggenheim Brothers, only to turn it down for a $15,000-a-year post as Secretary of Commerce, first under Harding and then under Coolidge.

Yet Hoover's life is fraught with irony. The man who was praised for his humanitarian European relief projects became the President who presided over the financial crises of the Great Depression and lived to see his name (which once stood for efficient management) used as an epithet for the Depression shantytown "Hoovervilles." He has been fortunate enough to outlive these disasters too, and to regain in great measure his former stature. In recognition of his great abilities Hoover was called on, first by Truman, then by Eisenhower, to chairman the study group charged with drawing up plans to reorganize the Executive Branch. On his eighty-seventh birthday he invited reporters into his Waldorf Towers suite in Manhattan and, puffing on his pipe lit with kitchen matches, ruminated on the chances of nuclear war, on summit meetings, on Volume IV of his *Memoirs* (in progress).

Before ushering out the newspapermen, Hoover could not resist a friendly jab at the new President, John F. Kennedy, a man half his age. American youth has not grown "soft," Hoover said: "Too much attention is paid to what goes on in the cities. Out in the countryside, in the small towns, on the farms, Americans are just as patriotic as they ever were, ready to meet any emergency, any challenge." Former President Hoover knew whereof he spoke, for it was in just such grassroots "countryside" that he was born, on August 10, 1874, in a small, two-room wooden frame house, hard by the blacksmith shop of his father, Jesse Clark Hoover.

Tragedy came early to this small Quaker family; when Hoover was six his father died and when he was eight his mother also passed away. The three orphaned Hoover children were divided up among relatives, young Bertie, as he was called, going to live with his Uncle Allan Hoover on his farm outside West Branch. Hoover as a boy was dressed in homespun dyed with butternuts, picked strawberries all summer for five dollars, killed potato bugs for one cent a hundred to buy firecrackers, hunted prairie chickens with bow and arrow.

He was also an earnest and pious scholar. At fifteen, however, he had to stop school and go to work in the Oregon land-settlement

Hoover's birthplace was a plain house in the small Quaker settlement of West Branch, Iowa. He was orphaned at eight and raised by relatives nearby and in Oregon. Hoover was the first President to be born west of the Mississippi.

office of his uncle, Dr. Henry John Minthorn, as an office boy. At seventeen Hoover, who had taken some night-school courses, managed to enter Stanford, then beginning its first year.

At Stanford, Hoover worked his way running a laundry agency, peddling papers, doing odd typing. He also found time to manage the baseball team and to act as treasurer of the student government. In his senior year, he courted a freshman geology major with a "broad, grinnish smile," Lou Henry, born, as was Hoover, in Iowa, and daughter of the wealthiest banker in nearby Monterey, California.

As an undergraduate, Hoover had worked in the summers with his Stanford professor, Dr. John Branner, as a surveyor in the high Sierra Nevadas. After graduation, the best he could do was start off as a mucker working underground in a mine at Nevada City. He earned enough to make his way to San Francisco, where an interview with Louis Janin, then one of the biggest mine operators, started him off as a fledgling mining engineer. Five years out of college he was in western Australia, on Janin's recommendation, prospecting for London's Bewick, Moreing & Co. at the rich gold lodes of Coolgardie and Kalgoorlie. Humping over the arid landscape on a leg-biting Afghan camel, he proved his "nose for gold" by finding the Sons of Gwalie mine. His London firm bought controlling interest for $250,000, added the same amount in working capital, eventually took out $55,000,000 in gold.

At twenty-four, Hoover found out that he was to be transferred to Tientsin, China, at $20,000 a year. He cabled Lou Henry a marriage proposal, received her acceptance by return wire. China proved a turbulent, troubled background for early marriage. Hoover was sent prospecting as far as the Gobi Desert; at the end of their two-and-a-half years the young Hoover couple found themselves besieged by rampaging Chinese in the Boxer Rebellion. Hoover's hasty erection of barricades made of sugar sacks and bags of rice from the "godowns" or warehouses played a vital role in saving the European community. At twenty-seven he was ordered back to London, made a junior partner in Bewick, Moreing & Co., and placed in charge of some twenty mining ventures scattered around the world.

As a mining consultant, Hoover circled the globe five times. After such intensive travel both he and Lou Hoover felt the need for "moorings" in the United States. In 1902 they shared in building a small Monterey cottage, and in 1907 built their own six-room cottage on the Stanford campus. In fact, this was but token residence. For more than a decade their real home was London, then the mining capital of the world. At their flat at Hyde Park Gate their two sons were born, Herbert, Jr., on August 4, 1903, and Allan Henry, July 17, 1907. And in 1907 they moved to their own spacious house and garden, The Red House, on Campden Hill.

The outbreak of the first world war caught 150,000 Americans stranded abroad. Hoover was asked to head up the rescue operations. Then the fall of Belgium to the Kaiser's armies placed the entire civilian populace of Belgium in dire peril of starvation. As an American and thus a neutral, Hoover was asked to take on the Belgian Relief Committee. It meant dropping an income of $100,000 a year and probably passing up a chance at a vast wartime mining fortune, but Hoover agreed.

For Belgian Relief, Hoover made forty hazardous crossings of the North Sea's mine-infested waters. A curious by-product of one

The plain Quaker interiors of Hoover's birthplace testify to the extreme frugality of his early childhood. While living here, Hoover wore clothes of homespun dyed with butternuts. By the age of ten, he had read the Bible from cover to cover, and had begun his interest in geology by searching for agates and fossil coral in the railroad gravel bed.

such crossing was his discovery while reading a book by Cornell's Dr. Andrew D. White that historians lamented the lack of the "ephemera," the casual documentation so quickly destroyed and so necessary to evaluate a period. Hoover resolved to fill the gap for his own time. The result became Stanford's Hoover Library of War, Revolution and Peace, which today holds over three million invaluable documents of the twentieth century.

With the entry of the United States into the first world war, Hoover, back in Washington, convinced Wilson that "food is second only to military action in winning the war," and was appointed U.S. Food Administrator. After the war, he headed the American Relief Organization to feed famished victors as well as victims, and General Pershing remarked, "Mr Hoover is food regulator to the world!"

After the war, Hoover returned to California, freed of the burdens of responsibility. "A primary right of every American family," Hoover wrote in his *Memoirs*, "is the right to build a new house of its heart's desire at least once. Moreover, there is the instinct to own one's own house with one's own arrangement of gadgets, rooms and surroundings. It is also an instinct to have a spot to which the youngsters can come back. Mrs. Hoover had long dreamed of building a house upon a nearby campus hill [in Palo Alto] where the glorious views of the mountains and bay came into sight. It was to be a Hopi house—not Spanish—with flat roof, and all modern inside. . . . The house was all her own making, but the dreams which she built into it had a rude awakening."

The house was begun on June 1, 1919, on land leased from Stanford, the alma mater of both Mr. and Mrs. Hoover, and finished by November 1920. The house reflected the 1920 vogue for the mission style, which had the advantage of hearkening back to the earlier adobe-walled houses of the Spanish era, at the same time the deep verandas and patios allowed for outdoor living and comfortable "porch furniture" which marked the easy American acceptance of inside-outside living.

But, except for a few weeks in the summer, the Hoovers had little opportunity to use their new house. As early as 1907, he had confessed that he longed for some "executive position in which I can

The Hoover home on the Stanford University campus at Palo Alto, California, was designed under Mrs. Hoover's guidance in 1919. She was inspired by the cubical massing and flat roofs of primitive Hopi Indian adobe dwellings. A rare photograph taken in the Palo Alto home shows the Hoover family, including the two sons, Allan, and Herbert Hoover, Jr. The house is now the official residence of the president of Stanford University and is called the Lou Henry Hoover Home in honor of the late Mrs. Hoover, in whose name the former President gave the house to the university that was their common alma mater.

serve my country." This opportunity came first with war-relief work, then as Secretary of Commerce under Harding and Coolidge. In 1921 the Hoovers' real home became 2300 S Street in Washington and then, on March 4, 1929, the White House.

Hoover had been in office barely seven months before Black Friday, October 25, 1929, began the series of disasters for which his term is remembered. Herbert Hoover was a fine administrator, but anything remotely resembling a politician's flair was alien to his training as a mining engineer and international businessman. Hoover's way was to erect a wall of silence about the White House, where as "The Chief" he often worked through the night.

When the Hoovers left the White House, where they had been able to dine alone only three times in four years, they were at last able to relax at their Palo Alto house after almost nineteen years of public service, and motor about the country at will. Hoover was free to engage in his favorite sport, fishing, which, he claimed, served "to wash one's soul with pure air. And it is a discipline in the quality of men—for all men are equal before fish." The log cabins Hoover had built as a White House retreat on the Rapidan River were given by him to the Shenandoah National Park; and in 1934 the Hoovers moved to their suite in the Waldorf Towers in Manhatten, an apartment that became their permanent residence. Upon Mrs. Hoover's death on January 7, 1944, the Palo Alto house was given to Stanford University, where it now serves as the official residence of the president of the University.

While at Palo Alto, shortly after Franklin Delano Roosevelt was inaugurated, Hoover was asked by a small boy for three of his autographs. Perplexed, the ex-President asked, "Why three?" "Because," replied the boy, "when I swap, it takes two Herbert Hoovers to get one Babe Ruth." Hoover's deep reserve was never to pay off in the grandstands. Largely unknown was the fact that Hoover banked his salary, and in a gesture of munificence unknown since Washington, gave it to charity. And working in his favor was his early training. As Mrs. Hoover once explained, "He has deeply ingrained in him the Quaker feeling that nothing matters if you are 'right with God.'"

THIRTY-TWO

Franklin Delano Roosevelt

The only limit to our realization of tomorrow will be our doubts of today. Let us move forward with strong and active faith.*

THE GREAT formative influence on Franklin D. Roosevelt's early life was the manorial life lived along the Hudson and the standard of the Roosevelt family. The way of life he knew as a child began early in the 1800s, when a new mode of living beckoned to the wealthy merchants of Manhattan, that of becoming landed gentry with far-ranging summer homes overlooking the Hudson. There, so promised the famous American architect Andrew Jackson Downing, they would enjoy that "accessible seclusion that is one of the most captivating features in the life of the country gentleman whose lot is cast on the banks of the Hudson—the broad Hudson which forms the grand feature in all these varied landscapes—the Hudson always so full of life in its numberless bright sails and steamers. One might fancy himself one thousand miles from all the crowded and busy haunts of men."

Such large country estates were barely self-sustaining, rarely profitable; the money to finance them came from the banks, real estate offices, and trading centers of the city. In the case of the Delano family, who lived in the forty-room Algonac near Newburgh, the wealth came initially from the China trade; for the Roosevelt family at Hyde Park, the money stemmed from a New York sugar refinery, banking, and railroads. After James Roosevelt (born 1828), had married for the first time in 1853, it was only natural that he should go looking for an estate of his own, as had both his father and grandfather before him. The one he picked in 1867 was two miles south of the village of Hyde Park, with land running steeply through the wooded bank to the Hudson. There some forty years before had been built a clapboard house painted tan and brown, with typical Hudson River brackets running out under the eaves, a three-story tower, and a broad expanse of open veranda on the southeast side with a fine view down the broad river.

There was much to please James Roosevelt and his first wife, Rebecca Howland, and their infant son, James Roosevelt Roosevelt (called "Rosy"). First there was the flourishing Rose Garden, planted in 1830 and surrounded by a tall hemlock hedge, where Mrs. Roosevelt picked "thousands of roses before breakfast." There was room for horses, a prerequisite, for James Roosevelt was a great horse fancier and owner of "Gloster," first horse to better 2:20 for the mile. If the house seemed gloomy with its dark shadows, it was also cool. Soon

Fourth of July press conference in 1939 found F.D.R. trading quips with newspapermen at his Top Cottage on the Hyde Park estate.

---

* F. D. R.'s tribute to Thomas Jefferson written the night before his death.

Springwood, as the new owners christened their house, was handsomely filled with furniture bought abroad on their travels—a sideboard from Italy for the hall, a Dresden chandelier and mantel for the Music Room, Brussels carpets and "Turkey carpets" for the living room, oil cloth for the working areas of kitchen and pantry.

When Rebecca Roosevelt died suddenly of a heart attack on August 31, 1875, in the Roosevelt's Manhattan town house at 15 Washington Square, all life seemed to stop at Springwood. Then five years later, James Roosevelt, fifty-two, drove a new mistress up to Springwood, the dark, handsome Sara Delano, twenty-five, strong-willed and imperious daughter of a sea captain. She was to preside at Springwood for sixty-six years, until her death in 1941. A wedding meant another trip abroad and more purchases—a Smyrna carpet in Paris, silver and a Dutch sideboard for the dining room, a grandfather clock that still stands in the hall. Soon after the newlywed couple returned, Sara Delano Roosevelt, on January 30, 1882, presented "dear James" with a son, named Franklin (for his uncle) Delano (for Sara) Roosevelt. James Roosevelt proudly announced that the "bouncing boy . . . weighed ten pounds without his clothes;" to the mother, her first and, as it turned out, only child looked "plump, pink and nice."

As the sole child in the house (Franklin's half-brother, only one year younger than Sara Delano, had by then left and married), Franklin Roosevelt could hardly help but be spoiled. "Franklin," his mother would admonish, "where is your obedience?" "My 'bedience," the-two-year-old toddler would reply, "has gone upstairs for a walk." From his past-middle-aged father Franklin gained a love of outdoors —horseback riding, shooting, fishing, and, most of all, boating and sailing. The year after Franklin was born, James Roosevelt took the family to Campobello, a small island seventy miles northeast of Mount Desert, Maine; they so enjoyed the sailing and company (including the founder of Groton School, where Franklin's name was promptly enrolled) that James Roosevelt had a large, rambling house built on the four acres of land he purchased.

But it was Sara who read to young Franklin while he sorted out his stamps, found him late at night trying to read through the whole dictionary because there were "so many words he didn't know," who agonized through his first efforts, at the age of eleven, at becoming a taxidermist determined to mount one example of every bird on the place, and admired his boat models. James Roosevelt took a great interest in the local public school, stopping by regularly to overhear classroom recitations for twenty years, but Franklin, following the custom of the big-estate children, was tutored at home in the top story of the tower until he was ready for Groton.

At Groton and Harvard (1904), Franklin Roosevelt showed no great distinction. At college he belonged to the "Gold Coast" and the club world (Hasty Pudding, Fly); his one major effort was to become president of the college daily, the *Crimson,* and in this he succeeded. Against such a conventional background, his announcement from college to his mother, widowed three years before, that he was engaged to his fifth cousin, Anna Eleanor Roosevelt, came as a bolt from the blue. Sara Delano Roosevelt insisted her son take a Caribbean cruise "to think the engagement over." Franklin obliged but, as Eleanor proudly noted, "Franklin's feelings did not change." A visit by Elea-

Franklin Roosevelt's boyhood room has a brass bedstead in which his mother found him reading the dictionary because he found so many words he didn't know.

nor to Campobello somewhat softened Sara Delano to the inevitable. The wedding, held on St. Patrick's Day, 1905, was the peak of fashion; President Theodore Roosevelt came to give his niece away; the clergyman was Groton's own Reverend Endicott Peabody.

Roosevelt first turned to the law, attending Columbia Law School. But in the summer of 1910 Judge John E. Mack of Hyde Park "kidnaped" Franklin Roosevelt, took him to a policeman's picnic in Fairview. "On that joyous occasion of clams and sauerkraut and real beer," Roosevelt later recalled, "I made my first speech, and I've been apologizing ever since." In the fall he found himself nominated by Judge Park for state senator on the Democratic slate. Roosevelt turned his boyhood study on the ground floor into a political head-quarters, hired a red Maxwell from Mr. Hawkey, and toured every village and hamlet. To the surprise of the opposition's diehards in the traditionally Republican era, Roosevelt was elected, not once, but twice in a row.

For two years Franklin and Eleanor had been living in one of the twin brick-fronted townhouses at 47 and 49 East Sixty-fifth Street in New York which Sara Delano Roosevelt had bought and fixed up so that both the second-floor drawing rooms and the first-floor dining rooms could be made one by simply opening the double doors. After election, the young Roosevelts with their growing family (Anna Eleanor, 1906; James, 1907; Elliott, 1910) escaped and set up house-keeping in Albany, the state capital.

Franklin Roosevelt had been aboard the welcoming tug that greeted former President Theodore Roosevelt on his return from Africa in 1910 and witnessed the hysterical ovation Teddy received, a welcome that effectively opened TR's own comeback campaign that lead to the founding of the "Bull Moose" Party. At the 1912 Demo-cratic convention, Franklin himself voted loud and strong for Wilson, and in 1913 he was offered the position of Assistant Secretary of the Navy, the post that had been Teddy Roosevelt's under McKinley in 1897. For eight years, under Secretary of the Navy Josephus Daniels, Roosevelt established himself as a man "with a flashing mind," if not a politician. Or as one of his associates put it, "He acted as if he did not care anything about the political consequences."

With Franklin in Washington and doing brilliantly, he and Sara Delano Roosevelt decided it was time to overhaul the Hyde Park estate with a view to the future. In 1914, on the eve of the first world war, the architect Francis L. V. Hoppin (of Hoppin and Koen) was engaged to make an extensive alteration and addition, and Roosevelt himself began enthusiastically making wood models. The squat tower that had been Franklin's upstairs school and playroom was changed to make a complete third floor with bedrooms and

The Roosevelt Manhattan town house at 47-49 East 65th Street was actually a double house, shared by the widowed Sara Delano Roosevelt on one side and Franklin and Eleanor Roosevelt (left) on the other. The drawing rooms and dining rooms could be connected by opening the large double doors.

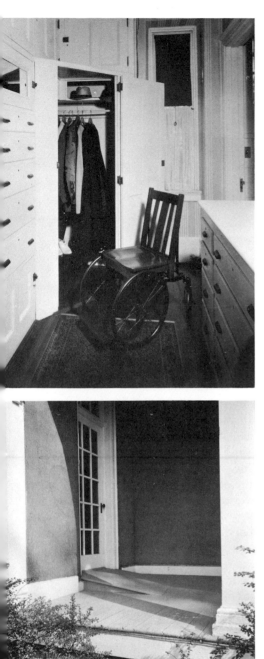

At Hyde Park, ramps (above) from the porch and extra handrails for the stairs were installed to assist Franklin Roosevelt after he was stricken with poliomyelitis in 1921. In the dressing room (top) beside his second floor bedroom are still to be seen his cape, suits, hat, and his private wheelchair.

nurseries; the old clapboards were replaced with brick and yellow stucco. On the exterior, the whole building was recast in the neoclassic mode that had swept into fashion with the Chicago World's Fair of 1893. Wings were added to the north and south and the front was extended to include the classically columned portico and sweeping balustraded terrace that were served as backdrop for so many historic occasions.

On the inside, much of the 1867 house that Sara Delano Roosevelt had known since she arrived as a bride in 1880 was unchanged. True, there were modernizations; where previously the house had only two bathrooms (one for the Roosevelts, one for servants), it now had seven. The most pronounced change was the addition of the large south wing. When Franklin had been abroad in 1903, he had visited the Roosevelts' friends in Grantham, England, Sir Hugh and Lady Cholmeley. "What a house!" he had written his mother. "The family must have thought me crazy to rubber so at the pictures & Library for it was *almost* my model library—with three distinct parts and yet all thoroughly liveable and satisfactory." It was this room Franklin took as a model for the new, oak-paneled south living room and library, with its two fireplaces over which hang the Gilbert Stuart portrait of his great-great-grandfather Isaac Roosevelt, the Revolutionary War patriot, and his great-grandfather, James, first of the family to settle in Duchess County, in 1819. Leading from this library was the open, screened porch looking out over the south lawn and replacing the deep-set old fashioned bracketed verandas.

On August 9, 1920 the new house was given its first test. A crowd of five thousand gathered before the front portico to hear Franklin D. Roosevelt officially accept his nomination as vice-presidential candidate on the Democratic ticket with James M. Cox. As the cheering throng trampled over the well-kept lawn, smashing the rose bushes, Sara Delano Roosevelt moved not a muscle. "I don't want my boy in politics," she said, "but if he is, I want him to win." In 1920 no one running on Woodrow Wilson's record had a chance, but the image of the broad-shouldered, handsome, Harvard politician from the Hyde Park Roosevelts remained vividly in the minds of Democratic politicians across the country.

Defeat seemed to roll easily off Roosevelt's back. At thirty-nine he was in his prime. He was an active lawyer again; he was forging ahead in business; the last two of his five children, Franklin D., born 1914, and John A., born 1916, were growing up. Vacation life at Campobello was full of fun and games. On August 10, 1921, Franklin, who had been sailing with the boys, put ashore to fight a forest fire; he stayed for a swim, returned home to race the boys the mile and a half from the landing, then read his mail in a wet bathing suit, before going for another quick dip in the icy Bay of Fundy. That night he went to bed with a fever. Unknown to any of them, Franklin Roosevelt had come down with poliomyelitis; he was never to walk again except with the aid of heavy leg braces, crutches, or a cane. When the full extent of his affliction became apparent, his mother urged him to retire to Hyde Park, take up the life of a cultured recluse. Her suggestion was opposed by Dr. George Draper (Franklin's doctor and Harvard friend), by Eleanor Roosevelt, by Louis McHenry Howe, a gnomelike former New York *Herald Tribune* Albany correspondent who since 1912 had been Franklin's chief political adviser and Gray Eminence. More important, it was opposed by Roosevelt himself.

The Roosevelt home at Hyde Park was remodeled in 1915, when the tower was removed and wings added to the building. At left is the library; at right F.D.R.'s office. The front portico was used on election eve, when the President would greet the victory parade of townspeople from the village of Hyde Park. The photograph below shows the scene on November 4, 1936. Surrounding the President are, left to right, his daughter Anna; mother; son John; F.D.R. himself; Eleanor Roosevelt; and Franklin D. Roosevelt, Jr., supporting his father.

He returned to Hyde Park to fight for his health. Evidence of his struggle is still apparent in the ramps for his wheel chair, the paved paths over which he was pushed, the strong handrails attached to the staircase which he walked, dragging one leg at a time until "the sweat would pour off his face, and he would tremble with exhaustion." Rings and parallel bars were put out on the south lawn, and for hours each day he would exercise. The quarter-mile gravel drive leading from the door, through the double rows of maples, to the brownstone gateposts over which he had so blithely ridden his pony, Debby, as a boy, was now set as a new challenge; each day he was to walk with crutches a little further. It was a terrific strain on his heart, but by the end of the summer, he could make good the full distance.

In May 1924, Franklin Roosevelt, his powerful hands grasping the lectern, rose in Madison Square Garden to nominate Governor Alfred E. Smith for the presidency, calling him "The Happy Warrior of the political battlefield." Smith's bid failed (the Democrats turned to John W. Davis), but even the Republican New York *Herald Tribune* admitted that Roosevelt, by his performance, was "the real hero of the Democratic convention." Afterward he went to Warm Springs, Georgia, to "swim to health," becoming so enthusiastic over the curative powers of the water therapy that in 1927 he donated two-thirds of his personal fortune to set up the nonprofit Georgia Warm Springs Foundation.

In 1928, Alfred E. Smith was nominated to run against Hoover, and Roosevelt was picked to run for governor of New York State. It was a year of Coolidge prosperity and a Republican sweep. "Well," said Al Smith, "the time just hasn't come yet when a man can say his beads in the White House." Roosevelt bucked the trend, carried New York by 25,000 votes, then won again in 1930, this time by a plurality of 735,000. In 1932, Roosevelt was offered the Democratic nomination and flew directly to Chicago to accept, thus dramatically

Springwood, the boyhood home of Franklin D. Roosevelt, was built about 1827. This photo shows the country estate manor as it appeared in 1882, the year F.D.R. was born there. The tower (left) was used as Franklin's schoolroom.

demonstrating that his disability would prove no handicap for a good campaigner. As he mounted the convention platform on the arm of his eldest son, James, he gave a mighty wave and beamed his famous smile at the cheering delegates. Over the radios of America a soon-to-be-familiar voice, aristocratic, mannered, beautifully timed and deeply convincing, promised aid to the "forgotten man" and "a New Deal for the American people." So began that extraordinary love affair between Roosevelt and the voters, which was to last until his death thirteen years later.

It was through the White House that the American public first got to know Hyde Park almost as intimately as their grandparents' house. F.D.R. rarely missed a chance to motor or take a train up to Hyde Park, parking his private railroad car on the special Hyde Park siding, where newspapermen covering the President grumpily lived out of Pullmans and dining cars. His small office off the terrace became the nerve center of the nation as the mansion at Hyde Park became the Summer White House; the dining room was regularly Election Eve headquarters as Roosevelt in shirtsleeves kept the tally. And then, as victory after victory mounted up, the torchlight parade of neighbors from the village would swing up the drive.

Roosevelt, with his wife and Sara Delano Roosevelt, would move out of the front door to greet them. F.D.R.'s remarks swept them into his own confidence and family associations. In 1944 he harked back, as he so often did, to his earliest political memories. "I remember," he said, "my first torchlight parade right here in 1892, Cleveland's election, and I was asleep, or supposedly asleep, right up in this window, a little room at the head of the stairs, and I was listening, and I didn't know what was the matter; a queer light outside the window, with people coming up on farm wagons; before the days of the automobile. It was Hyde Park, a large part of it, coming down here to have a Democratic celebration.

The library was modeled on one F.D.R. had seen in Grantham, England, in 1903. Portrait over the fireplace is Isaac Roosevelt, F.D.R.'s great-great-grandfather, painted by Gilbert Stuart. Franklin Roosevelt used to sit in leather chair at left of fireplace, where he could serve cocktails and, on Christmas Eve, read Dickens' Christmas Carol *to the family.*

The visit of King George and Queen Elizabeth of Great Britain was a festive occasion. Seated in the center is Sara Delano Roosevelt.

"And I got up and appeared down here in an old-fashioned nightgown of some kind, on this porch, and I was wrapped in an old buffalo robe that came out of a wagon, and I had a perfectly grand evening!"

It was a squire's life that was depicted in the flood of press reports, but, except among the even more wealthy, the Hyde Park way of life caused little resentment, only affection. Soon the country knew of F.D.R.'s dog, Fala, who arrived on April 7, 1940, of his Christmas-tree nursery at Val-Kill, of his bright blue Ford which he drove down to the railroad station. The nation heard, too, of his custom of sitting in his Governor's chair by the fireplace in the library, where he liked to serve the cocktails, and on Christmas Eve read Dickens' *Christmas Carol;* as his daughter recalled, "His facial expressions while imitating Mr. Scrooge were quite fearsome to the young!" When F.D.R. found that the family church, St James's, had been marked in gilt lettering, "Church of the President," under which some wag had chalked, "Formerly God's," he told the story on himself with great gusto, and the public chuckled with him.

Strangely enough, it was only when he came to public buildings that he managed to raise the hackles of the local citizenry. F.D.R. was a great believer in fieldstone and the early Hudson River styles of the original Dutch builders. "It is true," F.D.R. wrote, "that our modern life calls for conveniences unthought of in the Seventeenth-century New Amsterdam, but the charm of line, the judgment of location, the spirit of simplicity of the homes of our ancestors, are all a good influence on a civilization which to some of us seems to be reverting to the more humble and honest ideals." But if F.D.R. had his fieldstone way only with difficulty with public buildings, he had

President's Summer White House study at Hyde Park was room in which he planned early political campaigns. Here also F.D.R. and Churchill discussed the first atomic bomb project.

Top Cottage, which Franklin Roosevelt designed himself, was a small, cozy retreat on the estate where he liked to retire and "get away from the show."

a holiday drawing the plans himself for Top Cottage, the informal house of stone and clapboard with its deep, sloping eaves and own swimming pool on a hill across the state road from the old house.

It was to Top Cottage, "away from the show," that F.D.R. brought King George and Queen Elizabeth on the summer visit in 1939, introducing them to their great delight to American hot dogs and strawberry shortcake. The visit produced its moment of merriment back in the Hyde Park's east living room when the President offered the King a cocktail, saying with a twinkle, "My mother does not approve of cocktails and thinks you should have a cup of tea." Replied His Royal Highness, "Neither does my mother," and helped himself to a drink. But for Eleanor Roosevelt, the visit was a hostess's nightmare, as she confided cheerfully to the readers of her syndicated column, "My Day":

"At Hyde Park, the servants we brought from Washington suffered from a jinx which followed its course in three mishaps: My mother-in-law's serving table in the dining room has a center standard. Too many dishes were put on one side, and in the middle of the dinner, the table tipped over. No one could think for a minute because of the noise of breaking china.

"Later in the evening, with a tray full of glasses, water, ginger ale and bottles, one of our men going into the big library slipped and dropped the entire tray on the floor. And as a final catastrophe, on Sunday afternoon, my husband, moving backwards across the grass by the swimming pool, almost sat on another tray of glasses and pop bottles . . . ."

In 1939, Franklin Roosevelt decided to deed Hyde Park to the nation as a National Historic Site, and in May 1940 dedicated the Franklin D. Roosevelt Library adjacent to the house. The building to house the archives of his administration as well as his collection of naval art was developed from his own rough sketches, and executed, needless to say, in fieldstone. Almost immediately he began using his new office in the Roosevelt Library, bringing over each day another object from the old house, a rug that was a gift of the Shah of Iran at the Teheran conference, andirons that once belonged to John Adams, a Chippendale chair used by George Washington, and the copy of Washington's desk used by Woodrow Wilson on his four trips back and forth to Europe on the transport USS *Washington* at the time of the Versailles Peace Conference.

When F.D.R. heard that the Episcopal bishop of Washington hoped to have his tomb placed in the capital's Episcopal Cathedral, as Woodrow Wilson's had been, he snorted, "Why, the old body-snatcher!" and promptly wrote down the minutely detailed specifications for his own grave in the Rose Garden at Hyde Park: "A plain white monument—no carving or decoration. . . ." After his sudden death on April 12, 1945, at Warm Springs, Georgia, his body was lowered into the earth of his ancestral acres before representatives of the Armed Services and the massed Cadet Corps from West Point, across the Hudson. When the Roosevelt family waived their rights to life tenancy, the Secretary of the Interior accepted full title on November 21, 1945, and on the first anniversary of Franklin Delano Roosevelt's death, the house and library were opened to the public. Hyde Park is now a pilgrimage shrine for Americans second among Presidents' homes only to George Washington's Mount Vernon.

THIRTY-THREE

Harry S Truman

"I N ALL THE YEARS since I left the White House, I have wondered why so many people come from so far away and take so much trouble to look at the house where I live," Harry S Truman wrote in his autobiographical *Mr. Citizen,* adding wryly, "Perhaps it is because once a man has been President he becomes an object of curiosity like those other notorious Missouri characters, Mark Twain and Jesse James."

The town of Independence, in Jackson County (so named by Andy Jackson supporters to spite Henry Clay supporters, who had established Liberty in Clay County, farther north) has had its high moments in American history; it was the jumping-off point for the Conestoga wagons heading out along both the Sante Fe and Oregon trails; here the Mormon Joseph Smith set up his New Zion and remained until mobs and the state militia forced his band of religious enthusiasts westward in 1833. And, though Mark Twain had little to do with the town, Jesse James' gang did—there was a cell in the Independence jail where Frank James once was held.

But today such historic attractions pale to insignificance compared to the chance of seeing the Thirty-third President of the United States swing out through the iron gate in front of his house at 5:30 A.M., following a routine established decades ago on the farm, and set off on his brisk, 120-paces-a-minute early-morning constitutional. Or there's a chance of catching a glimpse of the former President getting his hair cut at Frank Spina's 10th Street Barbershop. Mr. Spina was in Truman's World War I outfit (Battery D, 129th Field Artillery, 35th Division), and as Harry Truman says, "Frank Spina knows just how I like my hair cut." But the surest place to find Harry Truman during working hours is in the $1,750,000 Harry S Truman Library, a magnificent edifice of Indiana limestone on the edge of town. There the former President has been known to take time off, show visitors around, even on occasion sit down and play a few chords of *The Missouri Waltz* on the piano when not busy dictating to his secretary, Miss Rose Conway.

Harry S Truman is by now thoroughly settled down again in the small-town ways of Independence, a town to which he came at the age of five in 1889 when it had a population of only 6000. Spring and summer he likes to sit on the back porch, getting caught up on the newspapers; in winter the living room serves the same purpose. The house has several TV sets and a radio, but they aren't used much; Mr. Truman prefers to read history and autobiographies, while Mrs. Truman ("Bess," as she was known to thousands during the Trumans' tenure of the White House) prefers detective stories. To do the cooking there is Vietta Garr, who sleeps out. Big occasions are when the Trumans' daughter Margaret, now Mrs. Clifton Daniel,

This plain, five-room frame house in Lamar, Ohio, was the birthplace of Harry S Truman in 1884. The tall pine planted to celebrate the event is still growing.

arrives with her *New York Times*-editor husband and their two sons, Clifton Truman, born June 5, 1957, and William Wallace, born May 19, 1959. The house on North Delaware now exudes the quiet peacefulness of senior citizens at home anywhere in the U.S.A.

Ex-President Truman still makes a clear distinction between the dignity of the presidential office he once held and plain old H.S.T. from Independence. "That may seem to some a fine distinction, but I am glad I made it," he has written. "Otherwise I might be suffering today from the same kind of 'importance' complex that some people have come down with." Pride in the office he once held and the desire to be plain himself often cause a conflict, but Harry Truman has resolved it to a degree through architecture; the Harry S Truman Library, with its massive archives, display of historic documents, and file of 3,500,000 presidential papers, represents his high office; the homey house on North Delaware represents his citadel as plain Mr. Citizen.

He was born on May 8, 1884, the son of John Anderson Truman, a mule trader by profession, and Martha Ellen Young, a Kentuckian like her husband, in a plain five-room frame house that his father had bought two years before for $685. His arrival was a signal event which his father celebrated by planting a pine tree at the side of the white cottage (it is still there) and nailing a horseshoe over the door for good luck. His birth also caused some controversy; one side of the family wanted him named Harrison Shippe Truman, the others wanted his middle name to be Solomon, in honor of his maternal grandfather and a onetime wagon-train master. The compromise at the christening: the future President was simply named Harry S Truman.

The Truman family was to move time after time throughout young Harry's childhood as the breadwinner's fortunes rose and fell. When Harry was a year old, they moved first to Harrisonville, where Harry recalls "chasing a frog around the backyard." Every time the frog jumped, Harry slapped his knees and roared with laughter, and Grandmother Young remarked, "It's very strange that a two-year-old has such a sense of humor." At three, Harry was put up with his grandparents at Grandview and at five he was moved into a $4000 house on Chrysler Street in Independence. Though the Trumans were Baptists, Mrs. Truman liked the pastor of the First Presbyterian Church and sent young Harry there to Sunday School. Among the pupils was a curly-haired five-year-old, Elizabeth Virginia Wallace— "Bess." It was a one-sided infatuation. It took young Harry five years to muster up courage to speak to her, twenty-eight more years before he proposed, and another two years before he married her.

Six years after the Trumans first arrived in Independence, the family moved to Waldo Street. "Peanuts" Truman, as the elder Truman was known, was tough and cocky, "a little and wiry man who joked a lot and knocked people's hats off when they weren't looking." "If my father's honor was impugned," Harry Truman has recalled, "he'd fight like a buzz saw." As a mule trader, he had a good eye, but he decided to plunge in grain futures, and at the age of fifty-one the elder Truman found himself wiped out. It was a blow from which John Truman never recovered. The family sold their house, eventually moved in with Grandfather Solomon Young on his 600-acre farm at Grandview, a suburb of Kansas City. For Harry Truman, just graduated from high school, the family's financial collapse meant the end of his plans for a college career. He moved into a boarding

Truman's 14-room house in Independence was built in 1865 and still retains its Victorian scrolled gables and bracketed veranda. Such commodious, if old-fashioned, houses have been termed by one architectural critic "Harry Truman Comfortables."

The William Chrisman High School ROTC marches by the Truman home on November 3, 1948. Although the flag is on the flagpole, the Trumans were not at home on this particular day.

house (another boarder in the same house was Arthur Eisenhower, elder brother of Dwight D. Eisenhower), worked as a bank clerk, a theater usher, played the piano at songfests, took time off to see President Theodore Roosevelt ("I was disappointed to find that he was no giant, but a little man in a long Prince Albert coat to make him look taller"), and put in time in the Missouri National Guard. In 1906 his father sent him an emergency call: come back to Grandview and help manage the 600-acre farm. Harry Truman did, for twelve years enduring the grueling dawn-to-dusk life of a dirt farmer.

Independence was twenty miles from the Grandview farm, but soon Harry Truman was making the trip, first on horseback or by buggy, later in a secondhand four-cylinder Stafford. His goal was still the curly-haired girl from Sunday School, Bess Wallace, who by now had proved herself a star athlete at Kansas City's Barstow School for Girls, where she was forward on the basketball team, played tennis, skated, and once even won the shot-put contest. By contrast with this active, vivacious young lady, Harry Truman, with the bifocals he had worn since he was eight and his taste for history, was old sobersides himself. But he was persistent, and soon the old-fashioned household at 219 North Delaware accepted him as Bess' leading suitor.

As World War I drew closer, Truman helped recruit the 2nd Missouri Field Artillery, found himself elected a first lieutenant when the battery was sworn into the Regular Army's 129th Field Artillery of the 35th Division. Sent to France, he was put in command of the trouble-making battery D, whose Fighting Irish from Kansas City had already

A festive day at Truman's home at 219 North Delaware Street in Independence was April 21, 1956, when Margaret Truman married Clifton Daniels, Jr., of The New York Times. This picture shows the bridal couple standing in the hall at the foot of the stairs.

The Trumans today have spruced up the living room, but much, including the sofa and coffee table, has remained the same over the years. Even in retirement, the former President remains a natty dresser and voracious reader.

worn out three commanding officers and liked to boast "We'd land somewhere, get into a fight, and then we'd go to Mass." Captain Harry Truman proved he had picked up enough mule-skinner vocabulary to stop a panic in the Dizzy D Battery when German guns bracketed it. U.S. Army Chaplain Curtis Tiernan, who was there, recalls gleefully, "He took the skin off the ears of those boys. It turned those boys right around." Battery D henceforward put in fine performances under fire in the Vosges, Meuse-Argonne, and St. Mihiel, and were shelling Metz when the Armistice came. "It was so quiet it made my head ache," Captain Truman later recalled. By the time he got back to Independence he was a major, and he proudly carried with him an engraved loving cup from the Fighting Irish of Dizzy D, a token of the men's affection paid for out of the kitty of the enlisted men's crap games.

Harry Truman and Bess Wallace had considered themselves engaged during the war (Truman had held off the marriage for fear he "might return a cripple"), and on June 28, 1919, they were married in the red-brick Trinity Episcopal Church in Independence. After a brief honeymoon in Chicago and Detroit the newlyweds returned to live at 219 North Delaware Street in Independence with Bess' mother, Madge Wallace, and her grandmother, Elizabeth Emery Gates. Except for the ten years Truman served as senator and his eighty-two-day period as Vice-President, when the Trumans lived in a small, $125-a-month apartment at Tilden Gardens, off Connecticut Avenue, N.W., the roomy house on North Delaware was to be Harry Truman's only home, and the one to which he returned after nearly eight years in the White House.

The Gates-Wallace house, set well back from the street and sur-

rounded by oaks, maples, lilac bushes, and shrubs, presents essentially the appearance it did when it was first built by George Porterfield Gates in 1865. George Gates (Bess' maternal grandfather) was head of the Waggoner-Gates Milling Company, a firm still in existence in Independence, with Mrs. Truman's brother Frank acting as its vice-president. The fourteen-room house Gates built contains seven bedrooms—six upstairs and one on the ground floor—a large, high-ceilinged parlor, a music room, and a dining room which has seated as many as thirty. The interior bears witness to the original owner's prosperity: there are three tiled fireplaces with marble mantels; much of the original walnut and mahogany furniture is still in use; several of the windows are "enriched" with colored glass borders. Typical of houses built before central heating became general, the main room on the ground floor can be closed off with double sliding doors in cold weather.

From the outside can be seen the mansard roof and dormer windows, a design imported from France in the 1850s, and at the time a blessing for the attic floors, usually reserved for servants. The other remarkable exterior feature—again typical of its period—is the massive porch, or veranda, which allowed a modified kind of outdoor living and later provided Mrs. Truman a pleasant setting for outside bridge games. The porch is ornamented with intricate jigsaw trim composed of repetitive units turned out by sawmills, which testify to a kind of exuberant delight with machine-made decoration that gives so much of American Victorian architecture its effervescence. The effect is somewhat heavy and fussy but highly decorative. To the rear of the lot stands the old coach house and hayloft, its hand-hewn walnut timbers still sturdy.

Harry Truman has respected the house in its entirety. Over the years, it has acquired only minor modernization, central heating, electricity, telephones (with an upstairs extension to allow for family conferences when Margaret calls) and radio, with only here and there a touch of later decades, an Oriental rug from the 1930s, low coffee tables from the 1940s. Built in a Civil War Victorian style which one critic called "Harry Truman Comfortable," the house has remained just that.

It was from the security of such rooms that Harry S Truman entered political life, often with his back against the wall, and so hard-pressed for finances that he had to borrow $3000 against his life insurance to finance his own 1940 re-election campaign for senator, then helplessly stood by during the same year while the mortgage was foreclosed on his eighty-eight-year-old mother's farm. Yet he managed to overcome an early postwar business failure as a haberdasher and rise successively from judge of Jackson County to senator to Vice-President to President, climaxing his political career with his upset campaign for reelection in 1948.

No American president ever revered his office more highly than did Harry Truman. As the end of his second term approached, he himself summed up his feelings about his service in these words, written in a note to his daughter, Margaret. "Your dad will never be reckoned among the great. But you can be sure he did his level best and gave all he had to his country. There is an epitaph in Boothill Cemetery in Tombstone, Arizona, which reads, 'Here lies Jack Williams; he done his damndest.' What more can a person do?"

Former President Truman, Citizen of the World, is also right at home back in Independence, Missouri. There he still rises before six in the morning and sets off for his brisk constitutional, keeping at the regulation army pace—120 steps to the minute.

THIRTY-FOUR
Dwight D. Eisenhower

ON A HOT JUNE day, President Dwight David Eisenhower stood in the warm Kansas sun across from his boyhood home on South Fourth Street in Abiline. Hard by was the church of the Brethren in Christ, the Mennonite sect to which his family had belonged. Nearby, too, were the railroad tracks that divide Abilene's "south side" from the better-off "north side." The President's pleasurable task on that warm June afternoon was to lay the cornerstone for the new $3,000,000 Eisenhower Museum and Library to house papers, films, and books relating to his administration, his war mementoes, and his academic degrees from around the world. With great naturalness and ease—he was, after all, back home—he let his mind dwell on his parents who had raised their six sons in the small white frame house still standing next door:

I want to call attention to the virtues of the times, to—at least as my brothers and I devoutly believe—the extraordinary virtues of our parents. First of all, they believed the admonition "the fear of God is the beginning of all wisdom." Their Bibles were a live and lusty influence in their lives. . . . And they were frugal, possibly of necessity, because I have found out in later years we were very poor, but the glory of America is that we didn't know it then. All that we knew was that our parents —of great courage—could say to us: Opportunity is all about you. Reach out and take it. . . . They were people of great courage, and I think they never stopped—they never had time—to hate or despise an enemy or those that used them spitefully. I don't think they ever loved the drought and the locusts that ruined their first business down in the little town of Hope, a few miles south of here—a drought and the locusts that really drove them to Texas. . . . But they accepted these trials and tribulations and with never a thought of failure. . . .

Those days were essentially simple ones. . . . Now we realize the world is a great interdependent, complex entity. . . . And yet, in spite of the difficulties of the problems we have, I ask you this one question: if each of us in his own mind would dwell more upon those simple virtues—integrity, courage, self-confidence and unshakeable belief in his Bible—would not some of these problems tend to simplify themselves? Would not we, after having done our very best with them, be content to leave the rest with the Almighty? I think it is possible that a contemplation, a study, a belief of those simple virtues would help us mightily.

Gabled frame house in Denison, Texas, has been repainted and refurbished since it was discovered to be the birthplace of Dwight D. Eisenhower. His parents had moved to Texas when the small store they had started in Hope, Kansas, failed.

The six Eisenhower brothers gathered for a reunion with their mother in their boyhood home in Abilene in 1926. At the time, Ike (on steps) was a lieutenant colonel attending General Staff School.

Such was the faith of Eisenhower's Mennonite parents, David Jacob Eisenhower and Ida Elizabeth Stover, and the President's tribute to them provides both creed and context for the deeply held beliefs of "Ike" Eisenhower, the most popular Soldier President since General Ulysses S. Grant. His faith is that of his forefathers, tested and retested over years of adversity, and handed down by his Virginia-born mother and Pennsylvania-bred father. They had met as students at Lane University in Lecompton, Kansas, a small United Brethren college. Married before graduation, they both left college, started married life running a small general store in Hope, Kansas. It failed, as Eisenhower noted, from "drought and the locusts." Pinched for money, David went south to Texas to work as a "wiper" on the Missouri–Kansas–Texas ("Katy") Railroad, first in Tyler, then in Denison, where he summoned his family to join him. There, on October 14, 1890, was born David Dwight Eisenhower (he later reversed the order of his Christian names) in a small white house near the tracks, the third of Ida Elizabeth's seven sons, of whom six were to grow to manhood.

Texas left no memories with Dwight Eisenhower for he was only one when his father left his job in the railroad shops, went north again to Abilene, Kansas. There his brother-in-law had a $50-a-month

Eisenhower home, at 201 South 4th Street, Abilene, Kansas, is today an historic shrine, next door to the $3,000,000 Eisenhower Museum.

job waiting as a mechanic-engineer in the new Belle Springs Creamery. The pay was not much, but the prospects were better. The Eisenhower family moved into a small house on South Second Street, and, in 1898, bought the house of their veterinarian uncle Abraham with its three acres and big barn on South Fourth Street. Here Mrs. Eisenhower was to live on until her death in 1946, four years after her husband's, when the house became a national shrine.

In 1958, when Ike came back for a visit to the South Fourth Street house, he sighed, "It's amazing! Every time you come back to it the rooms shrink." But he loved showing his wife Mamie the old dough tray and the old piano with its red-and-blue cover, pointing out, "My great grandfather wove that." Rubbing his hand on the darkly polished bannister leading to the upstairs rooms where the six brothers slept, he said with a grin of fond recollection, "Brother, the times I slid down that!"

There was a good deal more than the new air conditioning in the old house to remind President Eisenhower of the fast flow of years. In his youth, baths had been in a tin tub in the kitchen with water from the well, heated on the stove. Their one pot-bellied stove had heated the two downstairs rooms; hardly a waft of hot air ever seemed to ascend via the ceiling registers to the upper floors. There, when their father called out, "Boys!" at 5 A.M., the six youngsters scrambled to get on their clothes *under* the blankets. Their father worked from 6 A.M. until 6 P.M., for six, and sometimes, seven days a week. To keep order among her six scrapping sons, who would punch each other on the nose at the drop of a hat, the mother often had to resort to the maple switch. "He who conquers his temper is greater than he who taketh the city," she would sternly remind them, and, in later years, the public and press around the world would witness hot-tempered Ike's struggle to carry out her admonition.

Food in the Abilene home was simple, mostly "frugal dishes": puddin' meat, scrabble, corn-meal mush, with fresh vegetables from the garden, milk from the cow, eggs from the chicken pen. Clothes were handed down through five boys until the old brogans finally were fitted on Milton, the youngest. There was always time for Bible-reading around the table by the family, urged on by a mother who, as a girl, had memorized 1365 verses in six months. There was great group loyalty along with pugnaciousness, and Ike developed the fighting spirit that, except for a bad knee resulting from a hard tackle at West Point, might well have made Ike an All-American football player.

Dwight D. Eisenhower's decision to go to West Point (he also tried for Annapolis, passed, but at twenty was over-age to be a midshipman) was not too surprising from a combative boy who took on the north-side champion in a bare-fisted fight, held his own until after sundown. But after graduation as a member of the class of 1915, he faced long, bleak years of monotonous garrison duty. As a just-appointed first lieutenant at Fort Sam Houston, he married the Denver belle, Mamie Geneva Doud, on July 1, 1916. At the age of fifty-one, twenty-six years after graduation, Dwight D. Eisenhower was only a colonel. But with World War II, he caught the eye of General George C. Marshall, who put him in command of the North African invasion. Two years later "General Ike" was the Supreme Allied Commander on whom D-Day depended. After V-E and V-J Day, as a five-star general, Eisenhower was named president of Columbia University, then sent back to Europe as Supreme Commander of the Allied Powers in Europe.

In the years leading up to the White House, the Eisenhowers had never actually owned a house of their own. They had life tenancy on an apartment in Scotland's Culzean Castle. They had resided briefly in the twenty-one-room mansion of the president of Columbia, and had known the delights of an eighteenth-century château in the Forest of Marly near Versailles. But none of these was a real home, and in November 1950, the Eisenhowers at last found the dream location they wanted to make their own.

The place that caught their eyes and hearts was a 189-acre farm three miles south of Gettysburg, Pennsylvania. In World War I Eisenhower had been in command at nearby Camp Colt and learned to know the historic Civil War battlefield by heart. Then too, at Columbia he had become interested in land reclamation through one of his brothers. "When I die," he resolved, "I am going to leave a piece of ground better than I found it." The Gettysburg farm looked like the spot. The hundred-year-old, nine-room brick farmhouse was not much to brag about. But in November 1950, the Eisenhowers decided to buy, paying $24,000 for the farm and house. Another $16,000 went for the machinery and livestock, the foundation of Eisenhower's later venture into raising pure-bred Black Angus cattle.

It was five more years, and an estimated $100,000, before a new fourteen-room house could be built around the old. And yet another five years were to pass before Ike and Mamie were to drive up the snowy road on a wintry January night in 1961 to take possession of their house as private citizens after Ike's fifty years of public service. The Eisenhowers, however, were no strangers to their own house. It had been here that President Ike had slowly recuperated from his near-fatal heart attack, and here also that he had brought a whole parade of distinguished guests: Sir Winston Churchill, Earl Montgomery of Alamein, Nehru, Adenauer, and President de Gaulle, whose Gallic verdict had been, "Place, agreeable. Site, interesting. Host, charming."

The new house bore little resemblance to the old. On entering, one found a broad hallway running through to a spacious glassed-in porch that looked eastward out over Seminary Ridge, the Civil War site where General Pickett had launched the desperate attack that was to be the high-water mark of the Confederacy. This porch, with its couch, wicker easy chairs, and wrought-iron bridge table rapidly became the General's favorite room. To the left of the hall on entering was the formal living room, with its banana-yellow walls, pumpkin draperies, and avocado-gold rug all focusing on the handsome white marble fireplace that had been given the Eisenhowers on their thirty-eighth wedding anniversary by the White House staff.

This fireplace and mantel had been in the White House from 1854 to 1883, serving five presidents until it was removed by Chester A. Arthur when he auctioned off thirty cartloads of White House

The back of the Gettysburg farm has a glassed-in porch looking out over the lawn, with the barns in the distance (top).

A putting green banked with sand traps (below) *keeps General Eisenhower's golf game in trim. Behind are the big barns required for his cattle-raising operation. "When I die," Ike once said, "I am going to leave a piece of ground better than I found it." Gettysburg is the realization of that vow.*

furniture. Discovered in a Washington secondhand store, it is now one of the Eisenhower's proudest possessions, rich in history and sentiment. As Mrs. Eisenhower said, "This will remain here forever, a constant reminder of our friends."

To the right of the hall is the dining room, with gray walls and a raspberry red carpet; the dark mahogany table seats sixteen. Farther to the north is the kitchen, and beyond it is General Eisenhower's den, bare and masculine, with a red-and-brown hooked rug and the original oak beams and Dutch oven of the original house which he insisted be saved. A secretary's office, three baths, and a bedroom complete the ground floor. The second floor has six bedrooms, more baths, and a private sitting room for Mrs. Eisenhower. The top floor is given over to a studio for Ike's painting.

As a retired five-star general, Dwight Eisenhower still keeps a small military and personal staff. Sergeant John Moaney, his orderly since 1942, still rises to get him his early-morning breakfast—the early rising habits of Abilene are still with Ike. The chauffeur is still the dependable Sergeant Leonard Dry, Ike's official driver for two decades. At the red brick office at 300 Carlisle Street in Gettysburg, once the residence of the president of Gettysburg College, Eisenhower has gathered his old staff, his White House secretary Mrs. Ann C. Whitman and Mrs. Helen North (who served the General back in NATO days), his White House Army Aide Colonel Robert L. Schulz. Perhaps most pleasing of all is the presence of his son, Lieutenant Colonel John S. Eisenhower, an aide serving without pay, who has taken over an old schoolhouse, reputed to be the headquarters of General James Longstreet during the battle of Gettysburg, and converted it into a pleasing white brick home for himself, his wife, and four children near one corner of his father's farm.

The Gettysburg farm has been outfitted to please an active, extroverted man. Near the house is the immaculate practice putting green, a skeet-shooting range, and, behind the house, Ike's own brick cook shack with its gleaming electric range and rotisserie. But as the Eisenhowers have come to know, simple retirement is all but impossible for a man upon whom twice, as Supreme Commander in Europe and as President of the United States, the hopes of the free world have hinged. Letters still pour in at a rate of more than 2300 a week; there is a constant stream of visitors, ranging from old wartime comrades and Republican Party leaders to tourists who sometimes scale the locked gates, hoping for a glance of Ike and Mamie. In spare moments he pecks away at the mountainous task he has set himself, the multivolume memoirs of his administration. There is never enough time, or so it seems, even in retirement. But by eleven o'clock on most nights, the lights in the big rambling farmhouse are turned out, and then only Heidi, the Eisenhower's pet *Weimeraner,* is awake to bay the moon as it rises over the slumbering battlefield of Gettysburg.

Focus of the living room in the Gettysburg house is the white marble fireplace that was used in the White House between 1854 and 1873, until it was auctioned off by President Chester A. Arthur.

THIRTY-FIVE

John Fitzgerald Kennedy

*Ask not what your country can do for you—ask what you can do for your country.**

THE BLUE-AND-WHITE presidential flag strains at the flagpole halyards in the stiff Nantucket Sound breeze. Up from the private pier, where the sloop *Victura* and fifty-two-foot motor cruiser *Marlin* are moored, comes a light-blue electric golf cart loaded with members of the Kennedy clan and empty wicker picnic hampers. It is headed for the Kennedy Hyannis Port "Compound," a cluster of three large beach houses. To the right on Merchant Avenue, actually a narrow Cape Cod lane, stands the triple-gabled eighteen-room Big House, the residence of former Ambassador Joseph P. Kennedy; to the left is Attorney General Bobby Kennedy's twelve-room cottage, to the rear and farthest back from the sea is the eleven-room shingled summer White House, inconspicuous behind its low picket fence. Surrounding the compound is a formidable eight-foot cedar picket stockade, erected at the request of the U.S. Secret Service.

Curiously enough for a young family man with a private income of some $500,000 a year, this is John Fitzgerald Kennedy's only home, apart from the White House. The modest frame house at 83 Beale Street, Brookline, Massachusetts, in which he was born on May 29, 1917, has long since passed out of the family. The three-room Beacon Hill apartment at 122 Bowdoin Street that served as his official residence while campaigning three times for the House of Representatives and twice for the United States Senate has been rented again to strangers. Hickory Hill, the fifteen-room house (on a seven-acre estate) which had once been Civil War Headquarters for General George McClellan and which was the first home for John Kennedy after his marriage is now the home of his younger brother, Bobby. The snug Georgetown house with its double drawing room and good-sized rear garden, which Kennedy bought in 1957 for $78,000 and spent an estimated $20,000 renovating, was sold for a reported $105,000 a month after the Kennedys entered the White House. The 400-acre Virginia estate at Glen Ora is rented, not a permanent home. What permanent roots Kennedy has are sunk deep in the dunes of Cape Cod at Hyannis Port, the summer resort he has known with deep affection since he was eleven years old.

The 4.7 acre lot on which three Kennedy houses are clustered stands on a small point separating the Sound from Hyannis Port's small harbor. It is an area rich in memories for the Kennedy family, and, in season, with Kennedy children. In the summer no less than

*Inaugural Address, 1961

Lights burned late at John F. Kennedy's Hyannis Port house on Election eve, 1960. The house, built about 1910, now has eleven rooms, five baths and a patio. (© Jacques Lowe.)

nineteen of Ambassador Kennedy's grandchildren, divided into two battalions of below and above five-year-olds for group play activities, are likely to be scampering over the sun-dried lawns and tennis court. The summer week-end refuge for the President is his own two-story white-shingled house, built in the early 1900s and added onto until now it has eleven rooms, five baths. Inside it is decorated, as the President's wife puts it, "so that wet bathing suits and children's sandy feet can't hurt it." The walls are painted white, to set off the early American antiques (many purchased locally), but most of the chairs are big and comfortable; the atmosphere is clearly meant for relaxing.

A favorite spot is the brick-paved patio, out of sight, and, as nearly as possible in an area that often looks like a children's summer camp, out of earshot. Here in the old wicker lounge chairs with their scarlet coverings slightly faded by the sun the President likes to sit. A young apple tree is barely tall enough to cast a shade, but an old red umbrella stands over the white garden table; flowers ring the patio; a carved wooden seagull is propped up on its feet and in one corner dozes his daughter Caroline's giant-sized stuffed dog.

But even in an atmosphere of livability and comfort, where khaki shorts and old shirts are the proper uniform, touches of elegance are present. For as Jacqueline Kennedy has dramatically proved, she is a First Lady of taste and refinement. Nor is her touch lacking even in the casual furnishings at the Hyannis Port house. One of Jacqueline's favorite colors is yellow, and at Hyannis Port it provides the color accent, with a yellow linen sofa and yellow linen wing chair. The large reading table is stacked high with magazines, journals of opinion, and

The three-story house at 83 Beals Street, Brookline, Massachusetts, is President Kennedy's birthplace. In marked contrast to most early Presidents, who, were rooted in their ancestral acres, John F. Kennedy has remained restlessly on the move. At Harvard College, Kennedy lived in Winthrop House, a structure that, while it was built in the 1930s, is a fine example of Georgian architecture.

newsmagazines for the President, French news and fashion magazines for the First Lady. On the walls are the bright, *naif* paintings that Jacqueline paints as a hobby, and among them one muscular oil depicting the Riviera port of Villefranche, a solo effort executed by the President himself.

Already Hyannis Port has taken its place in presidential history. Here were waged the early fist-fights of Joe, Jr., and Jack Kennedy, boys as pugnacious as Dwight Eisenhower and his brothers. But woe betide the outsider, for to attack one Kennedy is to attack them all. No matter whom the Kennedys used to play in their youthful Labor Day softball games (the referee on one occasion was Boston's Cardinal Cushing) the opponents were invariably called contemptuously "The Pansies." Here at Hyannis Port the Kennedys plotted their sailing races, and here, on Election Eve of 1960, they waited through the night in the Ambassador's house until well on toward noon to claim the victory, one earned by the narrowest of percentages in the history of presidential campaigns.

"You hear a lot today about togetherness," Joe Kennedy, Sr., once remarked. "Long before it became a slogan, I guess we had it." Supreme Court Justice William O. Douglas has added, "Most youngsters, as they grow up, seek their main stimulation and interest outside the home but the Kennedys found these in their own family circle. After all, it was an exciting home, a good place to be, full of fun and games and plenty of fascinating talk about world affairs and world leaders. It was hard for them to find anything as attractive outside. This is why they are so attached to each other, and so secure."

Another strong cohesive force was the fact that in Yankee New England the Kennedys were, if not "lace-curtain Irish," at least what Mayor James Curley once called "cut-glass Irish." Both the President's grandfathers had been hurrahing political bosses, who would snort that Beacon Hill was paved with the skulls of Irishmen. As Joe Kennedy, Sr., drove, hard-fisted with no partners and no holds barred, into banking, shipbuilding, real estate, the imported liquor business, Hollywood, and the stock market, he saw his fortune mount until by the mid-1950s it was estimated as high as $250,000,000; there were Kennedy apartments in Bronxville, in Manhattan (in fact, whole apartment houses), a rented villa on the Riviera, a white-stucco-and-red-tile-roof six-bedroom winter home at 1095 Ocean Drive in Palm Beach. For his children, Joe, Sr., set up three million-dollar trust funds: "I put them in a position where each one of them could spit in my eye and tell me where to go," he explained. "There was nothing to prevent them from becoming rich, idle bums if they wanted to. Luckily, they didn't turn out that way."

Backed by his father's wealth, Jack Kennedy thus emerged as the first of the Irish Brahmins. He went to the right schools (Canterbury and Choate), tried Princeton (but fell behind, and then left, when he came down with jaundice), then switched to Harvard, the alma mater of his father ('07) and of four United States Presidents (the two Adamses and the two Roosevelts). The most bookish of the Kennedys, Jack in 1939 was able, as the son of the then-Ambassador to the Court of St. James's, to make a tour of Europe as it tottered on the brink of World War II. Leaving Berlin, Jack was given a verbal message by United States Chargé d'Affaires Alex Kirk to bring his father: there would be war within one week. There was. Back in Cambridge for his senior year, Kennedy turned his observations

During his junior year, Kennedy made a tour of Europe, staying with his father, United States Ambassador to the Court of St. James's, at 14 Princess Gate, London.

President Kennedy occasionally uses the tile-roofed, six-bedroom vacation house belonging to his father in Palm Beach. When in New York, he stays in his thirty-fifth-floor duplex suite at Madison Avenue's Hotel Carlyle.

into a *magna cum laude* thesis, later published it as the best-selling *Why England Slept.* He donated the foreign profits to the bombed-out town of Plymouth, England; with the American royalties he bought himself a new Buick.

It was as a war hero, the skipper of PT-109 which had been sliced in half by a Japanese destroyer in the Solomons, that skinny, boyish, shy Jack Kennedy in 1946 doggedly campaigned for his first political office, United States Representative from the 11th Congressional District, an area that included both Harvard and the Irish and Italian slums of Boston. On the eve of his first primary victory, his eighty-three-old grandfather, John F. "Honey Fitz" Fitzgerald climbed up on the table of the Kennedy headquarters in Boston's Bellevue Hotel and to celebrate the occasion gave a triumphant tenor rendition of his old campaign special, "Sweet Adeline."

It was, indeed, a tremendous victory for a young veteran whose natural inclinations ran more toward writing, teaching, or journalism. Jack's destiny had been determined since the death of the family's white political hope, Joe, Jr., in a hazardous bombing mission during World War II. "Just as I went into politics because Joe died," Jack said later, "if anything happened to me tomorrow, my brother Bobby would run for my seat in the Senate. And if Bobby died, Teddy would take over for him." In 1952, it was all Kennedys together to bring home a victory over Henry Cabot Lodge, a victory that bucked the current of the Eisenhower sweep and settled an old feud: in 1916 Henry Cabot Lodge, Sr., had edged out "Honey Fitz" for the U.S. Senate by a thin margin of 30,000 votes.

It is a reflex of John F. Kennedy to turn to writing following an ordeal of extreme stress; after the death of his older brother, he had edited the privately printed *As We Remember Joe.* He suffered for years from an injured spinal vertebra, resulting from college football and aggravated later when his PT boat was rammed. Twice, surgery for the ailment brought him near death. Kennedy filled his pain-racked nights by researching and writing his Pulitzer-prize-winning *Profiles in Courage,* a study of congressional fortitude in placing national over regional loyalties, first inspired by Jack's admiration for the support John Quincy Adams gave to his father's enemy, Thomas Jefferson. While he was in the hospital under sedation, he wrote a speech censuring rabble-rousing Senator Joe McCarthy, on the narrowest of grounds; unfortunately, it was never read into the Senate record and his liberal friends quipped, "The Senator needs less profile and more courage."

Whatever courage his observers felt to be lacking was more than adequately in evidence during his 1960 campaign. He met the issue of his faith head-on by flying for a face-to-face meeting with the Protestant ministers of Dallas, firmly and eloquently expounded his belief that the Constitution calls for the separation of church and state. But his long months in the hospital, his close—but fortunately unsuccessful bid for the vice-presidential nomination with Adlai Stevenson in the 1956 Democratic Convention—and his wife's miscarriage all ended up to years of incredible stress. Jacqueline wryly commented on these years by drawing "How the Kennedys Spent Wedding Anniversaries," a series of tableaux in which either one or the other of them is shown flat out on a hospital bed.

When the John F. Kennedys moved into the White House on January 20, 1961, one of Mrs. Kennedy's strongest resolves was that

President-elect John F. Kennedy strolled with his daughter along the Georgetown streets familiar to two other Massachusetts Presidents, John and John Quincy Adams.

she and her husband would have "another home," one to which they could retreat and where their children, Caroline and John, Jr., could escape, briefly at least, from the publicity inevitably focused on the First Family.

The house picked by Jacqueline Kennedy was the 400-acre estate on Glen Ora, forty-one miles from the White House and a mile and a half south of Middleburg, in Fauquier County, Virginia—only seven miles from President James Monroe's Oak Hill. Glen Ora is situated in Virginia's finest fox-hunting country; three hunts (the Middleburg, Piedmont, and Orange County) ride over Glen Ora's split-rail and stone fences, and, as hunt masters put it, "hounds are seldom cast without drawing a covert." For an enthusiastic rider, as Mrs. Kennedy has been since her early childhood, this was a pleasing prospect. As a residence, however, Glen Ora falls into the somewhat musty status of most Virginia estates. Buried deep in its tall groves of trees, Glen Ora is ringed round with stables, a greenhouse, smokehouse, springhouse, tennis courts, and an unfiltered pool at the bottom of which, so locals claim, a lost buggy was once found only after

As Senator, Kennedy lived in a Federalist house on Georgetown's N Street. At left, he is seen saying goodbye to his wife and daughter beneath the fan-shaped transom of the front entryway. (© Jacques Lowe.)

the water was drained in the fall.

The house, owned by Mrs. Raymond F. Tartiere, has been built and rebuilt until it defies style description (French Provincial is the usual compromise). Its oldest section is an 1810 rectangular building, now plastered over with yellow stucco, to which have been added two large wings and further dependencies, while the present front door has been cut where a window originally was. But with the help of a Manhattan decorator, Mrs. John Parrish, the interior has been almost entirely refurbished; the drawing room is now a soft green, with the sofa covered in a flowered chintz against eggshell white. For the dining room, which has a Duncan Phyfe table and Heppelwhite chairs, Mrs. Kennedy has added her distinctive touch of yellow in the curtains and painted the walls green-gray. The only room not extensively changed was the pine-paneled library, with its rows of leather-bound French first editions.

When the President first flew down from the White House in February 1961, landing on the newly made helicopter pad near the house, he found most of the Kennedys' Georgetown-house furniture

Glen Ora, the estate rented by the Kennedys in Virginia, is only seven miles from President Monroe's Oak Hill. Dating back to 1810, Glen Ora has been changed over the years to a rambling, French Provincial mansion. (Below) Caroline practices riding, helped by her mother.

installed. In his own Glen Ora bedroom (one of six in the house) were his three-quarters mahogany sleigh bed, with a lyre design on both head and foot, his mahogany chest of drawers and leather-topped kneehole desk, and lounge chair covered to match the bedspread's brick-red and white toile. Adjacent is the First Lady's bedroom, papered in a mixed flower print, primarily pink; the single headboard of her bed is covered in chintz to match the wallpaper. Nearby is the new pink-and-white nursery for Caroline and John, Jr.

This all adds up to an impeccable background for living, a well-servanted atmosphere capable of bracing itself to the whirlwind pace of the Kennedys. In its emphasis on broad work spaces, with chairs arranged in clusters of conversational groups, and the love of what is time-hallowed in taste, Glen Ora establishes an aura of wealth and comfort. Touches of French eighteenth-century elegance combine naturally with handy pantry kitchens for late snacks and well-stocked bar trays. The flavor of the Kennedy personality is to be found more, however, in the distinctive personal touches, the delicacy of French paintings and the love of souvenir knicknacks, family pictures (Mrs. Kennedy), and volumes of new books fresh off the press (the President).

It is perhaps an irony of politics that the Presidents of this century, while personifying the great popular trends of their time, have been aloof from the parallel movements in art and architecture. Instead they have increasingly grouped around the canons of neoclassic taste. The gadgets, from telephones and radios to television and electric clocks, are modern, but of the artistic upheavals of the twentieth century, there is barely a trace to be found. President Kennedy's taste in paintings, for instance, is for old naval scenes, as was F.D.R.'s. The taste of the present First Lady in official White House decor shows a reverence for the high canons exemplified by President Monroe in an era of severe and refined classicism. It was to this same period that Theodore Roosevelt returned in renovating the White House, and this, too, was the goal of both Lou Hoover and Grace Coolidge.

It is significant that after the President and First Lady had strolled together in the historic gardens of Versailles on their first official visit to France, they should on returning find something of the same sense of tradition in Washington's Mount Vernon. One of Kennedy's most brilliant official fêtes was the one given for the visiting President of Pakistan in the candle-lit rooms of Mt. Vernon. In taste, the Founding Fathers have found their true descendent in the thirty-fifth President. It was with this in mind that the poet laureate, Robert Frost, in his poem to John F. Kennedy on January 20, 1961, spoke of:

> The glory of the next Augustan age
> Of power leading from its strength and pride,
> Of young ambition eager to be tried. . . .
> A golden age of poetry and power
> Of which this noonday's the beginning hour.*

*Robert Frost, *In the Clearing* (New York: Holt, Rinehart and Winston, 1962).

At a state dinner for President Mohammed Ayub Khan of Pakistan and his daughter, John F. Kennedy, the Thirty-fifth President of the United States, returned to Mount Vernon, home of the first President, discovered that the historic mansion made as delightful a background for official entertainment in the twentieth century as it had nearly two centuries before.

About the Authors

CRANSTON JONES was born in Albany, New York, on March 12, 1918, and grew up in Greenwich, New York (the boyhood home of Chester A. Arthur). He graduated from Phillips Academy, Andover, in 1936, and from Harvard College in the now famous Class of 1940, having majored in American History and Literature. While at Harvard he captained the fencing team and was president of the Harvard *Monthly*. After graduation he was briefly with *Time* magazine before joining the U.S. Naval Reserve. During World War II he served in the Caribbean and Central Pacific aboard subchasers and destroyer escorts, and at the war's end was commanding officer of the USS *Crouter,* DE-11. He returned to *Time* as a correspondent, reporting from San Francisco, London, Paris, and Rio de Janeiro, where he was *Time-Life* Bureau Chief. Upon returning to the United States, he became Art Editor of *Time* for five years, winning three awards for excellence in architectural criticism from the American Institute of Architects. He is now a senior editor of *Time.* He is the author of *Architecture Today and Tomorrow; Marcel Breuer, Work and Projects 1921–1961;* and *Homes of the American Presidents.* He has also written on art and architecture for *Life, Fortune, Architectural Forum, Sports Illustrated, Horizon, L'Oeil,* and *Preuves.* In 1949 he married the former Jean Campbell (Radcliffe, Class of 1944); they now have two children, Abigail Ainsworth and Baird Campbell.

WILLIAM H. SCHLEISNER was born in New York City and became a professional architectural photographer in 1935. He is a graduate of New York University and studied at the Clarence H. White School of Photography. He has been associated with Mr. Samuel H. Gottscho from the beginning of his photographic career. Mr. Schleisner is a member of the New-York Historical Society and The Museum of the City of New York, where there is a Gottscho-Schleisner collection of pictures.

The historic sites in and around New York have intrigued Mr. Schleisner since his earliest years, and his interest in history, and particularly the history of the United States, has always been keen. Over the years he has often found opportunities to unite this interest with his profession, photographing many historic houses and shrines for newspaper and book illustrations and for such magazines as *Life, Better Homes and Gardens, House Beautiful, Architectural Forum,* and *Progressive Architecture.* In the process, he has traveled all over the country, and has been able to learn at first hand a great deal about the background of American culture. Mr. Schleisner is also a garden enthusiast, and has had the pleasure of photographing some of the most beautiful gardens in the country.

Mr. Schleisner is married to the former Doris Gottscho, a graduate of Barnard College. The Schleisners, with their young son Jon, make their home in Jamaica, Long Island.

224

Acknowledgments

Without the interest and friendly assistance of many persons, the compilation of these photographs would not have been possible. Below we list those people and organizations that have our deep appreciation and gratitude:

The publisher of Time, *The Weekly Newsmagazine, for permission to use photographs I took for an article that appeared in* Time, *January 18, 1960. Photographs not otherwise credited are my own.*

Mount Vernon Ladies Association for the Union, Mr. Charles A. Wall, Director

Adams National Historic Site, Mrs. Wilhelmina S. Harris, Superintendent

The United States Department of the Interior, National Park Service

Massachusetts Historical Society, Mr. Stephan Riley

The Metropolitan Museum of Art

Thomas Jefferson Memorial Foundation, Mr. James A. Bear, Jr., Curator

The New York Public Library, Old Print Room

The Valentine Museum

The Virginia Historical Society, Mr. William Rachal

James Monroe Law Office Museum, Mr. Laurence Gouverneur Hoes, President

Alderman Library of the University of Virginia, Miss Anne Freudenberg and Mr. William H. Gaines, Jr.

The Ladies Hermitage Association, Mrs. John Reid Woodward

The University of the State of New York, Gladys Ladue

Albany Institute of History and Art, Mr. Norman S. Rice, Curator

Francis Vigo Chapter, D.A.R., Mrs. H. T. Watts, Curator

James K. Polk Memorial Association, Mrs. Knud Baagoe

The Courier Journal, The Louisville Times

The Library of Columbia University

Buffalo and Erie County Historical Society, Mr. Ivan E. Whitney

James Buchanan Society for the Preservation of Wheatland, John Rengier, President

The Mercersburg Academy, Mr. Robert R. Black, Alumni Secretary

State of Illinois, Division of Parks and Memorials, Mr. Richard Hagan

The Lincoln National Life Foundation, Mr. R. Gerald McMurtry, Director

Andrew Johnson National Monument, Hugh A. Lawing, Acting Superintendent

Greenville Chamber of Commerce, Inc., Mr. Charles E. Earnest, Manager

The Rutherford B. Hayes Library, Mr. Watt P. Marchman, Director

State of Vermont, Supervisor of Historic Sites, Mr. Frederick N. Cook

State of New Jersey, Department of Conservation and Economic Development

Recreational Division of the New Hampshire Forestry and Recreational Commission, Miss Susan Pierce

The Stark County Historical Society, Mr. E. T. Heald, Historian

The Ohio Historical Society, Mrs. Elizabeth Martin

The Canton Repository, Mr. John G. Green, Editor

Theodore Roosevelt Association, Mrs. Harold Kraft and Miss Helen MacLachlan

William Howard Taft Memorial Association, Mrs. Samuel Beall

Woodrow Wilson Birthplace Foundation

Woodrow Wilson Foundation, Mrs. Paul Herzog

National Trust for Historic Preservation, Mrs. Helen Duprey Bullock

The Harding Memorial Association, Dr. Carl W. Sawyer

National Archives and Record Service, Harry S Truman Library, Mr. Philip C. Brooks

National Archives and Record Service, Franklin D. Roosevelt Library, Miss Elizabeth Drewery

The Eisenhower Foundation, Mr. J. Earl Endacott

The Library of Congress, Miss Virginia Daiker

Frick Art Reference Library

The New-York Historical Society, Mr. A. B. Carlson

The National Gallery of Art, Mr. William P. Campbell

The Corcoran Gallery of Art, Mrs. Mary Hoffman Forbes

Hon. David K. E. Bruce, Ambassador to Great Britain

Hon. John D. Hickerson, Ambassador to the Philippines

Mr. Robert Taft, Jr.

President of the Philippines, Mr. Antonio P. Garcia

Yale University Library, Jane W. Hill

Samuel H. Gottscho

William Herrmann

J. Ch. Daney

William P. Kilroy

Hirschl and Adler Galleries

General and Mrs. Dwight D. Eisenhower

Miss Ishbell Ross

Mr. Cornelius W. Heine

Mr. and Mrs. Jay Johns

Mr. and Mrs. John B. Gravelle

Mr. and Mrs. J. Alfred Tyler

Mr. and Mrs. Malcolm Jamieson

Mr. P. S. Potter

Mr. Michael J. Phillips

Mrs. Robert Homans

Mellon Collection

Mrs. Gouverneur Hoes

I. N. Phelps Stokes

Edward S. Hawes

Alice Mary Hawes

Marion Augusta Hawes

Picture Credits

American Embassy: 219 Upper
Acme: 207 Upper, 211
Adams National Historic Site: 40
Benjamin Harrison Home: 148 Upper, 149, 150, 151, 152, 153
Bettmann Archive: 92, 113 Right, 116, 131, 133, 140 Upper, 141 Lower
Brady: 67
Brown Bros.: 53, 127 Lower, 129, 130 Upper, 131 Lower left, 139 Lower left, 178 Lower, 180, 192
Buffalo & Erie Historical Society: 95 Lower, 96, 97
Chicago Historical Society: 128
Colonial Studio: 77
From the collection of The Corcoran Gallery of Art: 69 Left, 81 Upper, 86, 90, 121 Left, 139 Upper
Berton Crandall: 194
Culver: 113 Lower left, 114, 115 Upper left, 131 Upper left, 132, 147, 154, 172 Lower, 178 Upper
G. M. Cushing: 36 Lower
H. H. Davis: 91, 92 Lower
Francis Vigo Chapter, D.A.R.: 78, 79
Franklin Delano Roosevelt Library: 200 Upper, 201, 202
Frank Leslie's Illustrated Newspaper: 108, 109, 110, 118 Lower
Frick Art Reference: 56
Harper's Magazine: 93
Harper's Weekly: 143
Harvard University: 218 Lower
Herbert Hoover Birthplace: 193
James Monroe Law Office Museum: 57, 58, 59
John Scott Harrison 4th: 72, 78, 79 Lower
Kansas Industrial Development Commission: 212
Ladies Hermitage Association: 61, 65, 66
Library of Congress: 42, 43, 54, 60, 63, 64, 68, 70, 71, 76, 80, 84 Upper, 94 Lower, 130 Upper, 138, 140 Upper, 149 Upper & Middle, 177, 179 Left
Lincoln Life Insurance Company: 115 Lower

Jacques Lowe: 216, 221 Left
Mercersburg Academy: 106
Missouri Historical Society: 126
Mount Vernon Ladies Association of the Union: 28, 29, 30, 33
Museum of Natural History: 166
National Gallery of Art: 37, 39 Upper, 52, 55, 107
National Trust for Historic Preservations: 179 Upper & lower left
New-York Historical Society: 39 Lower left, 44 Upper, 49, 52, 69 Right, 81 Lower, 95 Upper left & right, 105, 121, 131 Lower right, 139 Lower
New York Public Library: 48, 71 Upper, 148 Lower
Pach Bros.: 198 Lower
Republic of the Philippines: 171
Rutherford B. Hayes Library: 134, 135, 136, 137
Edward Serjan: 203 Lower
Shores Studies: 79 Right
Bradley Smith: 207 Lower
Southworth-Hawes: 41
Stark County Historical Society: 155, 157, 158, 159
Theodore Roosevelt Association: 160, 161, 162, 164, 167
Thomas Jefferson Memorial Foundation: 34 Left, 42, 43, 47
Twentieth Century–Fox Film Corp.: 174, 175 Upper & middle, 176, 177
United Press International: 145 Lower, 146, 169, 181 Upper & middle, 191, 195, 196, 198 Upper, 200 Upper, 202 Lower, 206 Upper, 208, 210, 211, 215, 217, 218 Upper, 219 Middle & lower, 220, 221 Right, 222, 223
University of Virginia, 55 Upper
Valentine Museum: 50
Vermont Development Commission: 142
Wide World: 94 Upper, 127 Upper, 156 Middle, 172 Upper, 175 Top, 206 Lower, 210
Wiles-Hood: 61 Right
William Howard Taft: Memorial Association: 168, 169, 170, 171
Woodrow Wilson Birthplace: 175 Lower & Upper
Mrs. J. Taylor Woodward: 145 Upper
Yale University: 173

GUIDE

* Indicates open to public

†Indicates a Registered National Historic Landmark, also open to the public

1 GEORGE WASHINGTON

* Washington's Birthplace, National Monument, Westmoreland County, Virginia. A reconstruction of the original house, off State Route 204. Maintained by the National Park Service. Open to the public, 8:00 A.M. to 5:00 P.M. Admission $.25.

† Mount Vernon, home of George Washington, Mount Vernon, Virginia, off Mount Vernon Memorial Highway (State Highway 235). Maintained by The Mount Vernon Ladies' Association of the Union. Open every day at 9 A.M., closes 5 P.M. March 1–October 1, 4 P.M. October 1–March 1. Admission $.75. Organized school groups, 7th through 12th grades: $.40. Fee waived for children under 12, members of armed forces, and organized youth groups through the 6th grade.

2 & 6 THE ADAMSES

† Birthplace of John Adams, 133 Franklin Street, Quincy, Massachusetts. Maintained by the City of Quincy. Open daily except Monday, from 10 A.M.–5 P.M., April 19–October 31. Admission $.50, children $.30. Special rates for organized youth groups.

† Birthplace of John Quincy Adams, 141 Franklin Street, Quincy, Massachusetts. Open same times as John Adams Birthplace (*above*). Fifty-cents admission fee includes both houses.

* Adams National Historic Site, "Peacefield," home of the Adams family for four generations (1787–1927), 135 Adams Street (State Route 135), Quincy, Massachusetts. Maintained by the National Park Service. Open daily 9 A.M.–5 P.M., April 19–November 10. Admission $.25.

3 THOMAS JEFFERSON

* Birthplace, "Shadwell," Charlottesburg, Virginia. A reconstruction of Jefferson's birthplace, which burned in 1770. Tradition has it that Jefferson planted the two aged sycamore trees on his twenty-first birthday. Open to the public.

† "Monticello," the home of Thomas Jefferson, Highway No. 20 and 53 from Charlottesville, Virginia. Maintained by the Thomas Jefferson Memorial Foundation, Inc. Open daily at 8 A.M., closes 5 P.M. March 1–October 31, at 4:30 P.M. November 1–February 28. Admission $1.00, under 12 free. Group rates.

"Poplar Forest," near Lynchburg, Virginia. An octagonal brick house designed by Jefferson as a summer retreat and where he fled to escape the hordes of admirers and curious. Fire gutted the house in 1845 and much of the restoration was inferior. Privately owned. Not open to visitors.

4 JAMES MADISON

† Octagon House, 1735 New York Avenue, N.W., Washington, D.C. Madison's residence following the burning of the Executive Mansion in the war of 1812. Now the national headquarters of the American Institute of Architects.

† "Montpelier," Madison's home, Orange County, Virginia. Privately owned. Not open to public.

5 JAMES MONROE

Birthplace, Westmoreland Co., Virginia, off State Route 205, between Oak Grove and Colonial Beach.

* James Monroe Law Office Museum, Charles Street, Fredericksburg, Virginia. Contains furnishings used by President Monroe while in the White House. Maintained by the James Monroe Memorial Foundation. Open daily 9 A.M.–6 P.M. Admission $.25.

* "Ash Lawn," Charlottesville, Virginia, two miles from Jefferson's "Monticello" and President Monroe's home from 1798–1820. Privately owned by Mr. and Mrs. Jay Johns. Open daily 7 A.M.–7 P.M. Admission $.75.

† "Oak Hill," Loudon Co., Virginia, on U.S. Route 15, between Aldie and Leesburg. President Monroe's home 1820–1830. Privately owned.

7 ANDREW JACKSON

† "The Hermitage," home of Andrew Jackson, 13 miles north of Nashville, Tennessee, on Route 70 N (Lebanon Pike). Owned by the State of Tennessee and maintained by The Ladies Hermitage Association. Open every day except Christmas from 8 A.M.–4 P.M. (C.S.T.), October–April, and 8 A.M.–5 P.M., April–October. Admission $.75, children under twelve, $.10.

8 MARTIN VAN BUREN

† "Lindenwald," Kinderhook, New York, one and a half miles south of the village of Kinderhook, on Route 9 H. Van Buren's home after the White House. Now privately owned by Mr. and Mrs. Kenneth F. Campbell. Open to the public. Admission $1.00 to house and grounds, $.50 for grounds only. Children under twelve, half price.

9 WILLIAM HENRY HARRISON

* Birthplace, "Berkeley Plantation," Charles City, Virginia, located on Route 5, midway between Williamsburg and Richmond, Virginia. A Georgian mansion, historic seat of the Harrison family and birthplace of the Nation's Ninth President. "Taps" was composed here during the Civil War. Restored by its present owners, Mr. and Mrs. Malcom Jamieson. Grounds, basement, and main floor open to visitors daily. Admission $1.25.

† "Grouseland," a Registered National Historic Landmark, Vincennes, Indiana, adjacent to the campus of Vincennes University. House built by General Harrison and his residence while Governor of the Indiana Territory, 1804–1812, when it was known as "The White House of the West." Open weekdays 9 A.M.–5 P.M., Sundays 12:30 P.M.–5 P.M. Admission $.35, children under 12, $.15.

10 JOHN TYLER

† "Sherwood Forest," plantation and home of President Tyler, designated a National Historic Landmark, Charles City, Virginia, on Route 5 (John Tyler Memorial Highway), 30 miles east of Richmond and 20 miles west of Williamsburg, Virginia. Still the residence of the Tyler family. Main floor and grounds open to visitors each weekday, 9 A.M.–5 P.M. Admission $1.00.

11 JAMES K. POLK

† James Knox Polk Ancestral Home, Columbia, Tennessee, on U.S. Route 31 to Nashville, Tennessee. Maintained by the Polk Memorial Auxiliary, contains original furnishings used by President Polk in the White House. Open weekdays 9 A.M.–5 P.M., Sunday 1 P.M.–5 P.M. Admission $.50.

12 ZACHARY TAYLOR

Taylor Boyhood Home, 5808 Apache Road, Louisville, Kentucky. Privately owned by Mr. and Mrs. W. Carleton Simmons. Not open to the public.

13 MILLARD FILLMORE

No house survives.

14 FRANKLIN PIERCE

† Pierce Homestead, Franklin Pierce's home from infancy until his marriage in 1834, Hillsboro, New Hampshire, on State Route 31. Maintained by the New Hampshire State Recreation Division. Open 9:30 A.M.–5 P.M., June 9–October 12. Admission $.35.

* Franklin Pierce House, 52 South Main Street, Concord, New Hampshire. Residence of the ex-President until his death. Privately owned by Mr. and Mrs. John Gravelle. Open on occasion April 1–December 25 by application to the Colonial Inn. No charge for admission.

15 JAMES BUCHANAN

Birthplace, Mercersburg Academy, Mercersburg, Pennsylvania. Log cabin, formerly at Stony Batter, now stands on the Academy's campus. Open on occasion.

† "Wheatland," a Registered National Historic Landmark, home of President Buchanan, 1120 Marietta Avenue, Lancaster, Pennsylvania. Maintained by The James Buchanan Foundation for the Preservation of Wheatland assisted by the Junior League of Lancaster. Open daily 9 A.M.–5 P.M., Sunday 10 A.M.–5 P.M. Admission $.75, children under 12, free.

16 ABRAHAM LINCOLN

* Abraham Lincoln Birthplace, a National Historic Site, three miles south of Hodgenville, Laure County, Kentucky, on U.S. 31 E–State Route 61. The traditional birthplace cabin is enclosed in a marble memorial building. Maintained by The National Park Service. Open 8:00 A.M. to 5:00 P.M. (7:00 P.M. in summer). Admission free.

* Lincoln Boyhood Memorial, one mile south of Lincoln City, Spencer County, Indiana. Includes the 200-acre Thomas Lincoln farm and grave of Lincoln's mother. Maintained by the National Park Service.

* New Salem State Park, New Salem, Illinois, off State Route 97 to Petersburg. Reconstruction of village Lincoln lived in 1831–1837, including thirteen cabins, Rutledge Tavern, mills, and stores. Maintained by State of Illinois Department of Conservation, Division of Parks and Memorials. Cabins open daily, except Thanksgiving, Christmas, and New Year's, 8:30 A.M.–5 P.M.

* Abraham Lincoln's Home, Eighth and Jackson Streets, Springfield, Illinois. This is the only house Lincoln owned and the one from which he left for the White House. Contains many pieces of Lincoln's original furniture. Maintained by the State of Illinois Department of Conservation, Division of Parks and Memorials. Open to public daily, 9 A.M.–5 P.M., Sunday, 12 M.–5 P.M. Admission free.

* William Petersen House, where Lincoln died, 516 Tenth Street, Washington, D.C., across the street from the Lincoln Museum (Ford's Theatre). Administered by the National Park Service. Open to the public 9:00 A.M. to 5:30 P.M., Admission $.25.

17 ANDREW JOHNSON

* Birthplace, in Pullen Park, Raleigh, North Carolina, originally on Fayetteville Street, Raleigh, North Carolina. Present location: east of North Carolina State College and south of Hillsboro Street.

* Andrew Johnson National Monument, a National Historic Site, Greeneville, Tennessee. Administered by the National Park Service. Includes: * Johnson's Tailor Shop, Dept and College Streets.
　　* Cemetery and monument at end of Monument Avenue.
　　* Homestead, on South Main Street, one block south of Summer Street.
Admission free. National Monument open year round; cemetery and tailor shop, 8 A.M. to 5 P.M.; and Johnson home 9 A.M. to 5 P.M. Tuesday through Sunday.

N.B. Johnson's first home, now known as the Kerbaugh House, is on College Street, across from the Tailor Shop. Privately owned.

18 ULYSSES S. GRANT

* Birthplace, Grant Memorial State Park, Point Pleasant, Ohio. The restored weatherboard cabin contains Grant mementos (cradle, Bible, West Point records). A state memorial, administered by The Ohio Historical Society. Open every day except Monday, 9:30 A.M.–12 M., 1 P.M.–5 P.M. Admission $.15, children under 12, $.10.

Boyhood Home, 219 Grant Avenue, Georgetown, Brown Co., Ohio. The house was built in 1823 by Jesse Grant, father of the President; veranda and concrete wall were added in 1909. Private.

* Grant Schoolhouse, South Water Street, Georgetown, Ohio. Contains a collection of Grant memorabilia (flag carried at Missionary Ridge, sketch signed U. H. Grant). Maintained by the Grant Memorial Association. Open to the public.

† Grant Home State Memorial, Bouthillier Street, Galena, Illinois. House, built in 1859, given to General Ulysses S. Grant by grateful townspeople at the end of the Civil War and used by Grant 1865–1881. Contains many original Grant pieces, souvenirs, and Grant's White House china. Maintained by the State of Illinois Department of Conservation, Division of Parks and Memorials. Open to the public daily 9 A.M.–5 P.M. Admission free.

N.B. Also in Galena, the old Grant Leather Store, 120 Main Street, in which Grant clerked before the Civil War. Also Grant's first Galena house at 121 High Street, now privately owned.

* Drexel Cottage, Mount McGregor, New York. Cottage where Grant died. On exhibit is Grant's cherrywood bed and clock (stopped at moment of his death).

19 RUTHERFORD B. HAYES

"Spiegel Grove," a State Park at the junction of Hayes Avenue and Buckland Avenue, Fremont, Ohio. The house, surrounded by a 25-acre park, was built in 1859 and was the residence of President Hayes from 1873 to 1893. The house is still occupied by the Hayes family, descendants of the President, and is not open to the public.

NB* The Rutherford B. Hayes Library, at Memorial Gateway to "Spiegel Grove," 1337 Hayes Avenue, Fremont, Ohio, contains a museum with memorabilia of President Hayes and his family, as well as an extensive reference library. Open to the public daily 9 A.M.–5 P.M., Sundays and holidays 1:30–5 P.M. Closed Thanksgiving, Christmas, and New Year's Day.

20 JAMES A. GARFIELD

* "Lawnfield," James A. Garfield's home, a Victorian house at 1059 Mentor Avenue, Mentor, Ohio. Open to the public daily 9 A.M.–5:30 P.M. Admission $.25.

21 CHESTER A. ARTHUR

* Birthplace, North Fairfield, Vermont, 3½ miles east of Fairfield Station on State Route 108. The replica is owned by the State of Vermont and operated by the Vermont Board of Historic Sites. Open to public from late May to Labor Day and on week ends to September 30, daily except Sunday 10 A.M.–5 P.M. Admission $.25.

Boyhood home, Woodlawn Avenue, Greenwich, Washington Co., New York. The Baptist parsonage in which Arthur lived aged nine to fourteen. The house was formerly on Church Street in the lot adjacent to the Bottskill Baptist Church. Privately owned by Mr. and Mrs. Meldrem Weaver. Not open to the public.

23 BENJAMIN HARRISON

Birthplace, destroyed by fire, stood at SW corner of Symmes and Washington Avenues, North Bend, Ohio.

Boyhood Home, "The Point," John Scott Harrison Homestead, North Bend, Ohio.

* Benjamin Harrison Home, 1230 North Delaware Street, Indianapolis, Indiana. Maintained by the Arthur Jordan Foundation. Open to public Monday through Saturday, 10 A.M.–4 P.M., Sunday 12:30–4 P.M. Admission $.30, children under 12, $.10.

22 & 24 GROVER CLEVELAND

* Birthplace, 207 Bloomfield Avenue, Caldwell, Essex Co., New Jersey. Formerly the manse of the First Presbyterian Church of Caldwell, where Cleveland's father was minister and Cleveland lived until he was four. Contains furnishings and memorabilia of Cleveland's time there. Administered by the State of New Jersey Department of Conservation and Economic Development. Open weekdays 10 A.M.–12 M., 1–5 P.M., except Monday; open Sunday 2–5 P.M. Admission, $.25, children under 12, $.10. Special rates for youth groups.

Washington, D.C. Summer Home, "Woodley," a 1793 mansion on Cathedral Avenue, Cleveland Park, N.W. Also used by Presidents Van Buren, Tyler, and Buchanan. Privately owned.

"Westland," Princeton, New Jersey, home of President Cleveland 1896–1908. Privately owned.

25 WILLIAM MCKINLEY

* Birthplace, Niles, Ohio, commemorated by the McKinley Memorial in Georgian marble. Second floor contains McKinley memorabilia. Open 10 A.M.–12 M., 1–4 P.M. Admission free.

Canton, Ohio, house has been destroyed.

* N.B. In McKinley's home town of Canton there is a McKinley Room at the Hotel Onesto, which contains murals of McKinley's life.

*The First Methodist Church at S.E. corner of West Tuscarawas Street and Cleveland Avenue, has the McKinley pew marked. *The McKinley Monument, 7th Street, N.W., adjacent to the Westlawn Cemetery, contains the tomb of the President and Mrs. McKinley, open 8:30 A.M.–4 P.M. *The Stark County Historical Society's McKinley Memorial Room, McKinley Monument Park, containing murals and memorabilia, will open July 1, 1963. Admission free.

26 THEODORE ROOSEVELT

* Theodore Roosevelt Birthplace and Museum, 28 East 20th Street, New York 3, New York. Reconstructed Victorian town house of Theodore Roosevelt, Sr., with museum in adjacent town house. Administered by the Theodore Roosevelt Association. Open to visitors weekdays, except Monday, 10 A.M.–5 P.M. Admission $.50.

* "Sagamore Hill," Cove Neck Road, Oyster Bay, Long Island, New York. Built by Theodore Roosevelt in 1884–85 and the "Summer White House" 1901–1909. Administered by the Theodore Roosevelt Association. Open to visitors daily, except Tuesday, 10 A.M.–5 P.M. Admission $1.00, children under 12 accompanied by parent, free.

27 WILLIAM HOWARD TAFT

Birthplace, 2038 Auburn Avenue, Cincinnati, Ohio, and Taft's home for his first twenty-five years. Privately owned.

1763 East McMillan Street, Cincinatti, Ohio. House to which Taft brought his bride and where first son, Robert, was born. Privately owned.

Washington, D.C., residences: 5 Dupont Circle (1890–92), 1603 K Street, N.W. (1904–08), 2215 Wyoming Ave., N.W. (1921–30)

New Haven, Connecticut, residences: 367 Prospect Street, 113 Whitney Avenue.

Summer home, Murray Bay, Province of Quebec, Canada (burned).

Summer home while President: Beverly, Massachusetts.

28 WOODROW WILSON

* Woodrow Wilson Birthplace, 24 North Coalter Street, Staunton, Virginia, an 1846 brick Greek-Revival house and the former Presbyterian manse, in which Woodrow Wilson was born. Contains Wilson's childhood playroom, bed used while President of Princeton. Open daily 9 A.M.–5 P.M. Admission $.75, children $.35 (under 10, free).

"Library Place," Cleveland Lane, Princeton, New Jersey. House owned and designed by Wilson while a professor at Princeton. Privately owned. Not open to the public.

* Woodrow Wilson House, 2340 S Street, N.W., Washington, D.C. Large Georgian brick structure designed by Waddy B. Wood, in which Wilson lived after leaving the White House until his death on February 3, 1924. Includes his furniture, many of his books, as well as mementos from the White House. Deeded to the National Trust for Historic Preservation. Preparations are in progress to open it to the public.

29 WARREN G. HARDING

* Harding Home & Museum, 380 Mt. Vernon Avenue, Marion, Ohio. Maintained by the Harding Memorial Association. Open weekdays 10 A.M.–5 P.M., Sundays 1–7 P.M. Admission charged.

* N.B. The Harding Memorial is one mile away. The old *Star* Building, in which Warren G. Harding edited his newspaper, is three blocks away, at 195 East Center Street.

30 CALVIN COOLIDGE

* Coolidge Homestead, Plymouth Notch, Vermont, off State Route 100-A. Owned by the State of Vermont and operated by the Vermont Board of Historic Sites. Childhood home and later the President's summer retreat 1923–29. Oath-of-office room, scene of unique swearing-in ceremony following death of President Harding. Open to public from late May to mid-October, 9 A.M.–5 P.M. daily, including Sunday. Admission, $.25.

* N.B. Old Coolidge General Store in which President was born is across the road. Privately owned by Mr. and Mrs. Herman Pelkey. Open to public. Admission charged.

* Family church is also across from the Homestead, open to public from late May to mid-October, 9 A.M.–5 P.M., daily and Sundays.

31 HERBERT HOOVER

* Herbert Hoover Birthplace, Downey Street, West Branch, Cedar Co., Iowa. Renovated small Quaker cottage near Hoover's father's blacksmith shop. Also the Herbert Hoover Memorial Library, administered by the National Archives and Records Service, General Services Administration. Open to the public. Admission free.

Hoover Home, 623 Miranda Street, Palo Alto, California, now the Lou Henry Hoover House, official residence of the President of Stanford University. Property of the University. Closed to the public.

* "Rapidan," Hoover's Summer Home while in the White House, now part of Shenandoah National Park. Administered by the National Park Service.

32 FRANKLIN D. ROOSEVELT

* Birthplace and home of Franklin Delano Roosevelt, a National Historic Site, Hyde Park, New York, on U.S. Route 9, two miles south of the town of Hyde Park. Roosevelt's ancestral home and the Summer White House during his terms as President, maintained as it was at the time of President Roosevelt's death. Administered by the National Park Service. Open to the public daily (except Monday; open Monday, June 15 through Labor Day) and on week ends 9 A.M.–5 P.M. Admission $.25.

* N.B. Adjacent to the Roosevelt Home at Hyde Park is the Franklin D. Roosevelt Library, containing documentation and manuscripts pertaining to the New Deal years, as well as Roosevelt's extensive ship-model and marine-print collection. Administered by the National Archives and Records Service, General Services Administration. Open to the public. Admission $.25.

* "The Little White House," Warm Springs, Georgia, house built by F.D.R., in which he died April 12, 1945. Rooms have been preserved as the President left them, including his Ford convertible in the garage. Maintained by the Franklin D. Roosevelt Warm Springs Memorial Foundation. Open 9 A.M.–6 P.M. (5 P.M. in winter). Admission free.

33 HARRY S TRUMAN

* Birthplace, a five-room white frame house, Lamar, Missouri, administered by the Missouri State Park Board. Open to the public free of charge.

Harry S Truman Residence, 219 North Delaware Street, Independence, Missouri. Private home of former President Harry S Truman and Mrs. Truman. Not open to the public.

Truman Farm, Blue Ridge Extension, Grandview, outside Kansas City, Missouri. Farm belonging to Harry S Truman's mother, on which Truman worked before the first World War. Privately owned.

* Harry S Truman Library, Independence, Missouri, housing papers of Harry S Truman including books, audiovisual collection, and museum as well as reproduction of the President's White House office. Administered by the National Archives and Records Service, General Services Administration. Museum open to public, weekdays 9 A.M.–4:30 P.M., Sunday 10 A.M.–5 P.M. (2–5 P.M., Sept. 16–May 15). Admission $.50, free to students and researchers.

34 DWIGHT D. EISENHOWER

* Eisenhower Birthplace, Birthplace State Park, corner of Lamar and Day Streets, Denison, Texas. Administered by the Texas State Park Board. Open to public daily except Monday, September through May, 10 A.M.–12 M., 1–5 P.M.; from June 1 to Labor Day, 8 A.M.–7 P.M. Admission $.25, children under 12, $.10.

* The Eisenhower Boyhood Home, 201 South Fourth Street, Abilene, Kansas. Open to public 9 A.M.–5 P.M. Admission by registration card obtained free of charge at office.

* The Eisenhower Museum, adjacent to the Eisenhower Home (*above*), and open the same hours. A $3,000,000 collection of gifts, personal history, and mementos covering President Eisenhower's life. Managed by The Eisenhower Foundation. Admission $.50, under 18, $.25.

* The Eisenhower Library, across the street south of the Museum. Contains papers, photos, films, and books relating to Eisenhower's years in the White House. Administered by the National Archives and Records Service of the General Services Administration. Open same hours as Eisenhower Boyhood Home (*above*). Admission free.

Residence of General and Mrs. Dwight D. Eisenhower, 3 miles south of Gettysburg, Pennsylvania, adjacent to the Gettysburg Battlefield. Not open to the public.

35 JOHN F. KENNEDY

Birthplace, 83 Beals Street, Brookline, Massachusetts. Privately owned by Mrs. Louise Pollack. Not open to public.

Summer residence, Irving Avenue, Hyannisport, Cape Cod, Massachusetts. Owned by President Kennedy. Not open to the public.

* Official residence: The White House, 1600 Pennsylvania Avenue, N.W., Washington, D.C. Open to the public, Tuesday through Saturday, 10 A.M.–12 M. Admission free.

Selected Bibliography

Adams, Henry, *The Education of Henry Adams,* Houghton Mifflin Company, Boston, 1918.

Adams, James Truslow, *The Adams Family,* Little, Brown and Company, Boston, 1930.

Adams, John, *The Adams Papers, Diary and Autobiography of John Adams,* L. H. Butterfield, ed., vols. I–IV, Belknap Press of Harvard University Press, Cambridge, Mass., 1961.

Adams, Samuel Hopkins, *Incredible Era, The Life and Times of Warren Gamaliel Harding,* Houghton Mifflin Company, Boston, 1939.

Andrews, Wayne, *Architecture, Ambition and Americans,* Harper & Brothers, New York, 1955.

Anthony, Katharine, *Dolly Madison, Her Life and Times,* Doubleday & Company, Inc., New York, 1949.

Barnard, Harry, *Rutherford B. Hayes and His America,* The Bobbs-Merrill Company, Inc., Indianapolis and New York, 1954.

Bowers, Claude G., *The Young Jefferson,* Houghton Mifflin Company, Boston, 1945.

Bowers, Claude G., *Jefferson in Power,* Houghton Mifflin Company, Boston, 1947.

Brant, Irving, *James Madison,* 6 vols. The Bobbs-Merrill Company, Inc., Indianapolis and New York, 1942–1962.

Burns, John MacGregor, *John Kennedy, A Political Profile,* Harcourt, Brace & Company, New York, 1960.

Butler, Joseph Thomas, *"Wheatland, 1848–1868, The Home of James Buchanan,"* unpublished Master of Arts thesis, Faculty of the University of Delaware, 1957.

Cleaves, Freeman, *Old Tippecanoe: William Henry Harrison and His Time,* Charles Scribner's Sons, New York, 1939.

Connally, Ernest Allen, *The Andrew Johnson Homestead at Greeneville, Tennessee,* East Tennessee Historical Publications No. 29, 1957, distributed by the Greeneville Chamber of Commerce, Greeneville, Tenn.

Coolidge, Calvin, *The Autobiography of Calvin Coolidge,* Cosmopolitan Book Corporation, New York, 1929.

Cranston, Ruth, *The Story of Woodrow Wilson,* Simon and Schuster, New York, 1945.

Curtis, George Tichnor, *The Life of James Buchanan,* 2 vols., New York, 1883.

Daniels, Jonathan, *The Man of Independence,* J. B. Lippincott Company, Philadelphia, 1950.

DeVoto, Bernard, *The Year of Decision, 1846,* Little, Brown and Company, Boston, 1953.

Douglas, Lee, "The Ancestral Home of James Knox Polk," pp. 5–10, published by the James K. Polk Memorial Association of Nashville and the James K. Polk Auxiliary of Columbia, Columbia, Tenn.

Dows, Olin, *Franklin Roosevelt at Hyde Park,* American Artists Group, Inc., New York, 1949.

Eisenhower, Dwight D., *Crusade in Europe,* Doubleday & Company, Inc., New York, 1948.

Frary, I. T., *Thomas Jefferson, Architect and Builder,* 3rd ed., introduction by Fiske Kimball, Garrett and Massie, Richmond, Va., 1950.

Freeman, Douglas Southall, *George Washington,* 6 vols., Charles Scribner's Sons, New York, 1948–1952; Vol. 7 edited posthumously by Carroll, J. A., and Ashworth, M. W.

Grant, U. S., *Personal Memoirs of U. S. Grant,* 2 vols., Charles L. Webster & Company, New York, 1885.

Hagedorn, Hermann, *A Guide to Sagamore Hill,* Theodore Roosevelt Association, 28 East 20th St., New York, 1953.

Hagedorn, Hermann, *The Roosevelt Family of Sagamore Hill,* The Macmillan Company, New York, 1954.

Hamilton, Holman, *Zachary Taylor,* The Bobbs-Merrill Company, Inc., Indianapolis, 1951.

Harbaugh, William Henry, *Power and Responsibility: The Life and Times of Theodore Roosevelt,* Farrar, Straus and Cudahy, New York, 1962.

Harnsberger, Caroline Thomas, *A Man of Courage: Robert A. Taft,* Wilcox and Follett Company, New York, 1952.

Hatch, Alden, *Edith Bolling Wilson, First Lady Extraordinary,* Dodd, Mead & Company, New York, 1961.

Hatch, Alden, *General Ike,* Henry Holt & Company, Inc., New York, 1952.

Hicks, Frederick, C., *William Howard Taft, Yale Professor of Law & New Haven Citizen,* Yale University Press, New Haven, Conn., 1945.

Hoover, Herbert, *The Memoirs of Herbert Hoover,* 3 vols., The Macmillan Company, New York, 1951–1952.

Horn, Stanley F., *The Hermitage, Home of Old Hickory,* Garrett & Massie, Richmond, 1938.

Howe, George Frederick, *Chester A. Arthur, a Quarter Century of Machine Politics,* Dodd, Mead & Company, New York, 1934.

Irwin, Will, *Herbert Hoover, a Reminiscent Biography,* The Century Co., New York, 1928.

Fuess, Claude M., *Calvin Coolidge, The Man From Vermont,* Little, Brown and Company, Boston, 1940.

Gunther, John, *Eisenhower, the Man and the Symbol,* Harper & Brothers, New York, 1951, 1952.

Jensen, Amy La Follette, *The White House and Its Thirty-two Families,* McGraw-Hill Book Company, Inc., New York, 1958.

Johnson, Gerald W., *Andrew Jackson, An Epic in Homespun,* Minton, Balch & Company, New York, 1927.

Johnston, William Davison, *TR, Champion of the Strenuous Life, A Photographic Biography of Theodore Roosevelt,* Farrar, Straus and Cudahy, New York, 1958.

Klein, Frederic S., "Wheatland," *American Heritage,* V, Spring, 1954, pp. 44–49.

Kornitzer, Bela, *The Great American Heritage, The Story of the Five Eisenhower Brothers,* Farrar, Straus and Cudahy, New York, 1955.

Lathem, Edward Connery, ed., *Meet Calvin Coolidge, The Man Behind the Myth,* The Stephen Greene Press, Brattleboro, Vt., 1960.

Lomask, Milton, *Andrew Johnson: President on Trial,* Farrar, Straus and Cudahy, New York, 1960.

Lorant, Stefan, *Lincoln: His Life in Photographs,* Duell, Sloan and Pearce, New York, 1941.

Lunch, D. T., *An Epoch and a Man: Martin Van Buren and His Times,* Liveright, 1929.

McAdoo, Eleanor Wilson, *The Woodrow Wilsons,* The Macmillan Company, New York, 1937.

McCarthy, Joe, *The Remarkable Kennedys,* The Dial Press, New York, 1960.

McGee, Dorothy Horton, *Herbert Hoover, Engineer, Humanitarian, Statesman,* Dodd, Mead & Company, New York, 1959.

McKinley, Silas Bent, and Bent, Silas, *Old Rough & Ready,* The Vanguard Press, New York, 1956.

McNaughton, Frank, and Hehmeyer, Walter, *Harry Truman, President,* Whittlesey House, McGraw-Hill Book Company, Inc., New York, 1956.

Marchman, Watt P., *The Hayes Memorial,* The Ohio State Archaeological and Historical Society, Columbus, Ohio, 1950.

Martin, Asa E., *After the White House,* Penns Valley Publishers, Inc., State College, Pennsylvania, 1951.

Marx, Rudolph, M.D., *The Health of the Presidents,* G. P. Putnam's Sons, New York, 1960.

Merriam, George Ernest, ed., *More Precious than Fine Gold, Washington Commonplace Book,* G. P. Putnam's Sons, New York, 1931.

Myers, William Starr, ed., *Woodrow Wilson, Some Princeton Memories,* Princeton University Press, 1946.

Nevins, Allan, *Grover Cleveland, A Study in Courage,* Dodd, Mead & Company, New York, 1932.

Nichols, Roy Franklin, *Franklin Pierce, Young Hickory of the Granite Hills,* Oxford Press, 1931.

Orton, Vrest, *Calvin Coolidge's Unique Vermont Inauguration,* The Tuttle Publishing Co., Rutland, Vt., 1960.

Rayback, Robert J., *Millard Fillmore,* Buffalo Historical Society, Buffalo, N. Y., 1959.

Ross, Ishbel, *Grace Coolidge and Her Era,* Dodd, Mead & Company, New York, 1962.

Ross, Ishbel, *The General's Wife, The Life of Mrs. Ulysses S. Grant,* Dodd, Mead & Company, New York, 1959.

Roosevelt, Eleanor, *The Autobiography of Eleanor Roosevelt,* Harper & Brothers, New York, 1961.

Roosevelt, Theodore, *The Works of Theodore Roosevelt,* ed. Hermann Hagedorn, 20 vols., Charles Scribner's Sons, New York, 1926.

Roosevelt, Theodore, *The Autobiography of Theodore Roosevelt,* Charles Scribner's Sons, New York, 1913.

Sandburg, Carl, *The Prairie Years and The War Years,* 1 vol., Harcourt, Brace and Company, New York, 1954.

Scully, Vincent J., Jr., *The Shingle Style, Architectural Theory and Design from Richardson to the Origins of Wright,* Yale University Press, New Haven, 1955.

Sherwood, Robert, E., *Roosevelt and Hopkins, an Intimate History,* Harper & Brothers, New York, 1948.

Sievers, Harry J., S. J., *Benjamin Harrison, Hoosier Warrior. 1833-1865,* Henry Regnery Company, Chicago, 1952.

Sievers, Harry J., S. J., *Benjamin Harrison: Hoosier Statesman. From the Civil War to the White House 1865-1888,* University Publishers Incorporated, New York, 1959.

Sipe, C. H., *Mount Vernon, a Handbook,* The Mount Vernon Ladies' Association of the Union, Mount Vernon, Va.

Steeholm, Clara and Hardy, *The House at Hyde Park, together with Sara Delano Roosevelt's Household Book,* Viking Press, New York, 1950.

Steinberg, Alfred, *The Man from Missouri, the Life and Times of Harry S Truman,* G. P. Putnam's Sons, New York, 1962.

Styron, Arthur, *The Last of the Cocked Hats, James Monroe and the Virginia Dynasty,* University of Oklahoma Press, Norman, Okla., 1945.

Truman, Harry S, *Mr. Citizen,* Bernard Geis Associates, New York, 1960, Popular Library, New York, 1961.

White, Theodore, Jr., *The Making of the President, 1960,* Atheneum Publishers, New York, 1961.

White, William Allen, *A Puritan in Babylon,* The Macmillan Company, New York, 1938.

Index

DATE DUE

GAYLORD			PRINTED IN U.S.A.